Education Matters

TITLES IN THE
LONGMAN TOPICS READER SERIES

Education Matters
Exploring Issues in Education

MORGAN GRESHAM
University of South Florida St. Petersburg

CRYSTAL McCAGE
Husson College

PEARSON
Longman

New York   San Francisco   Boston
London   Toronto   Sydney   Tokyo   Singapore   Madrid
Mexico City   Munich   Paris   Cape Town   Hong Kong

Executive Editor: Lynn M. Huddon
Senior Sponsoring Editor: Virginia L. Blanford
Executive Marketing Manager: Megan Galvin-Fak
Production Manager: Bob Ginsberg
Project Coordination, Text Design, and Electronic Page Makeup:
    Pre-Press PMG
Cover Design Manager: Wendy Ann Fredericks
Cover Photo: Riser/Getty Images, Inc.
Senior Manufacturing Buyer: Roy L. Pickering, Jr.
Printer and Binder: RR Donnelley & Sons Company/ Harrisonburg
Cover Printer: Coral Graphic Services, Inc.

For permission to use copyrighted material, grateful acknowledgment
is made to the copyright holders on pp. 00–00, which are hereby made
part of this copyright page.

Library of Congress Cataloging-in-Publication Data

Education matters : exploring issues in education / [edited by]
Morgan Gresham, Crystal McCage.
        p. cm. — (A Longman topics reader)
    Includes bibliographical references and index.
    ISBN 0-321-33899-5 (alk. paper)
    1. Education—United States. I. Gresham, Morgan. II. McCage, Crystal.
    LA209.2.E237 2008
    370.973—dc22

                                2007034169

Copyright © 2008 by Pearson Education, Inc.

Visit us at www.ablongman.com

ISBN-13: 978-0-321-33899-5
ISBN-10:   0-321-33899-0

2345678910—DOH—10 09

"At the highest educational level, where the instructors are the most credentialed and the students the most capable, teaching is the most biased."

CHAPTER FOUR Progressive Education?
Race and Education
in America   137

fostered a 'drill and kill' approach to teaching, mistakenly labeled successful schools as failing, driven teachers and middle-class students out of public schools and harmed special education students and English-language learners through inappropriate assessments and efforts to push out low-scoring students in order to boost scores."

"I believe we've done a better job of selling students on the dream of a college degree than on ensuring they have the skills to attain it. This is especially true—and hurtful—when it comes to aspiring first-generation college graduates."

"I see the vast majority of American colleges as cross-eyed creatures. One eye is focused on the financial status of the college, the other on the desires of the student. This dual focus has caused harm and requires a correction in course."

WHY EDUCATION MATTERS

Most of us retain powerful memories of our educational experiences—positive, negative, or both, for our education helps shape us, helps us become the people we are. Educational experiences are important to us as individuals. Teachers especially played important roles in our lives. Crystal remembers how her second-grade teacher inspired her love of reading by reading stories aloud to the class every day, as well as how her junior-level college English professor inspired her to go to graduate school and become a college professor. But she also remembers writing very little in high school and struggling every day in college in her first semester of freshman composition. Morgan remembers learning to read in first grade; she still treasures her third-grade teacher's gifts to her—two mice pins—and remembers writing weekly timed essays for her high school English teacher. Despite all of her writing experiences in high school, Morgan too struggled with her first-year college writing course because the expectations for compositions were so different—no longer three-point essays, but ones that engaged readers on multiple levels. Morgan also remembers her first visit to the college writing center, which made such a difference not only in her writing but also in her career path, and the teachers who guided and befriended her along the way.

So many of us have inspiring stories as well as not-so-inspiring stories to share, draw from, and learn from. But education is more than individual stories; it is a collective representation of a culture. Literacy rates affect a society's quality of life, and access to affordable education is a key issue in the economic success of a culture. And perhaps now more than ever before, education is on our minds.

MAKING OUR EDUCATIONAL SYSTEM BETTER

Budget cuts in the last several years have had negative effects on K–12 public schools as well as an colleges and universities. Schools must cut instructional days and programs to save money, to become more "efficient," while research tells us that quality education and efficiency do not necessarily go hand-in-hand.

Recently, Congress approved a federal budget that would keep federal Pell Grants at the same level they have been for the last three years, while the cost of tuition continues to increase at staggering rates. Although we live in a country where we are fortunate to have public schools and colleges, we must ask ourselves if we can make things better. The authors of this text think we can, and many of the readings and writing assignments in this text ask you to think about this very topic.

ABOUT THIS BOOK

The reading selections in this text were chosen to prompt students to think about a variety of issues in education: teachers, class, gender, race, and reform. Each chapter includes a brief introduction, and each reading is preceded by information about the author and followed by questions relating to content and rhetorical intention. The first four chapters ask students to think about successes and struggles in several areas of the U.S. educational system, while the last chapter asks students to think about what we can do to make that system— and thus the nation as well— better and stronger. Making improvements is no easy task, complicated even more so when we consider such issues as teacher pay, gender equality, racial equality, and so many others, but we cannot move forward without considering these issues thoughtfully. Therefore, we have chosen an eclectic mix of readings—from mass media reports to scholarly articles—on these issues to give a variety of perspectives. The shorter readings are meant to whet appetites and get thoughts flowing as we consider some of the important issues in education. The longer readings are meant to provoke a greater intensity and number of reactions to the issues while also preparing students for the more complex readings they will encounter in other classes and disciplines.

Whereas the readings are meant to help students think about issues in education from many perspectives, writing assignments are meant to give both students and teachers choices. End-of-chapter writing assignments are organized into four types of writing assignments: personal response essays; essays that require seeing the issue through someone else's eyes; essays that require some kind of call for social action, encouraging students to take their ideas to different types of audiences; and research opportunity essays. Our goal with these assignments is to provide students with choices so that they are more likely to find a prompt that interests them. These writing assignments also provide teachers with some variety so that they have the basis of several good prompts that fit within the requirements of their writing programs. The semester- or quarter-long writing assignments are designed to encourage deep thought and research and help students thoroughly investigate some of the issues discussed in this book.

We came to this book after teaching writing classes focused on issues in education for many years and at several institutions. We found that our students consistently respond well to writing about education, as they all have stories to share and opinions that matter. Whether it is the first-year student who is eager to share her stories from high school or the single dad who is worried about the condition of his children's schools, students have something to say about education in this country, and first-year composition is a particularly good time and place for them to say it. This book is inspired by all of our students who have shared their educational narratives and problems and successes with us so willingly.

ACKNOWLEDGMENTS

We wish to thank our generous reviewers for their insightful comments: Sharon E. Andrews, Augustana College; Todd Finley, East Carolina University; Patrice K. Gray, Fitchburg State College; Bonnie K. Sonnek, Western Illinois University; and Eleanor Vernon Wilson, University of Virginia. We thank our colleagues and friends at other institutions who helped us along the way, particularly Hugh Burns and Peggy O'Neill for getting-started conversations about education. We are especially grateful for our editors at Longman, Lynn Huddon and Ginny Blanford, without whom *Education Matters* wouldn't exist. We want to thank the students who inspired us to move forward with this project and Frank Dyess who assisted during the permissions phase of the project. Last but not least, we want to thank our families (Michael, Kahler, and Marisa, and Wesley and Joseph) for their encouragement and support.

Morgan Gresham
Crystal McCage

Education Through the Eyes of a Teacher

Teachers have historically played a very important role in our culture as the educators of our citizens and future leaders. But as America's economy changes and the education of individuals becomes even more important for success in our culture, teachers play an even more critical role in our society. Yet, nationally, teacher pay remains low compared to other degreed professionals, and school budget cuts across the country have negatively affected working conditions for many teachers. Jacques Barzun, a French-American writer, educator, and historian said, "Teaching is not a lost art, but the regard for it is a lost tradition."

In this chapter, "Education Through the Eyes of a Teacher," we ask you to consider some important issues about the people who influence so many of us—teachers. Why does teacher pay remain low compared to other degreed professionals? Is there, as Barzun asserted, a lack of respect for the field of teaching? What makes people want to become teachers? What stereotypes exist about teachers and teacher pay? What makes a good teacher? What struggles do teachers face in their lives and in their professions?

The first reading in this chapter is a blog posting from Kenneth J. Bernstein, a social studies teacher at Eleanor Roosevelt High School in Greenbelt, Maryland. In this reading Bernstein tackles the question, what does it mean to be a teacher? The second reading, by Katherine C. Boles and Vivian Troen, "America's New Teachers: How Good, and for How Long?" explores the problems inherent to the profession of teaching that make it difficult to be a good teacher right now. Anna Quindlen adds her own ideas to this issue, focusing specifically on teacher pay in the third reading of this chapter, "The Wages of Teaching." As an outsider looking in on the profession, Quindlen argues for better pay for the very important job of teaching. This chapter concludes with an excerpt from *Teachers Have It Easy,* a recent book on the everyday lives of teachers. "Look Dad, My Biology Teacher Is Selling Stereos at Circuit City" offers narratives from teachers who must take second jobs in order to support their families. These readings are meant to make you ask some tough questions about the nature of the field of teaching and how the working conditions for teachers can impact all of us.

Using your own experiences and considering the perspectives offered in this chapter, we ask you at the end of this chapter to think about teachers on a personal, local, and national level. Your mind may be changed about the teaching profession, or the readings and questions in this chapter may reaffirm what you already know. But you will certainly finish this chapter with a greater understanding of teachers, the ones who make education possible.

What Does It Mean to Be a Teacher?
KENNETH J. BERNSTEIN

Kenneth J. Bernstein is a National Board Certified Teacher of social studies at Eleanor Roosevelt High School in Greenbelt, Maryland. He is a frequent online writer (blogger) about education and other subjects on Daily Kos (see his writings at http://teacherken.dailykos.com). The following blog posting tackles the multiple questions that follow when asked, what does it mean to be a teacher?

◆

WHAT DOES IT MEAN TO BE A TEACHER?

by teacherken
Sun Mar 20, 2005 at 10:34:11 AM PDT

What does it mean to be a teacher? I am often asked why I became a teacher, which question is far easier to answer. I can give the history, which I will not here recapitulate. I can, as I often do, say that I wanted my life to make a difference, which I think it has. But that does not answer the far more difficult question with which I began this essay: what does it mean to be a teacher?

This will not be an intellectual exploration. I could offer that, but there are others far more capable and far more experienced than am I. It will instead be a personal reflection, drawn from my experience in this time and place, inspired in part by the self-examination I am undergoing as part of preparing to submit my portfolio for certification by the National Board for Professional Teaching Standards. It will also be influenced by the active role I have taken in writing about educational issues here at dailykos. Consider yourself forewarned. Should you choose to continue reading, below the break, you now have some idea what you will encounter.

TEACHERKEN'S DIARY :: ::

It is now a Sunday afternoon. Soon I will have to do lesson plans for this upcoming week in detail. This will be a short week, as the students enter Spring break at the close of school Wednesday. I have been thinking since Friday afternoon, off and on, how I can keep them involved with what is happening in the class, move forward through the material, while they are counting the hours—and soon the minutes—until they have 11 days off.

Even were it a normal weekend, my mind would rarely be far from similar tasks. What is there in the paper, or on television, which can serve as a means to connect their interest to what we are actually studying? For Social Issues, where we currently explore the death penalty, this is not hard to do, although there I must find a way to push them beyond their immediate gut reactions, to explore the complexities and subtleties of various positions. My 9th graders in US History are finishing their study of the Vietnam period. There are points of connection, but there are also serious differences, with what they can perceive about our involvement in Iraq. This week they will encounter aspects of shame—My Lai, our hurried departure, the fall of Saigon and the triumph of the Khmer Rouge in Cambodia. While these events are crystal clear in my memory, I have students with parents who were at best infants when these things happened. Others are recent immigrants to this nation, so this history has not been part of the fabric of their families.

Why am I explaining all of this? Perhaps because for me the task of being a teacher is certainly not one of peeling back students' scalps and pouring in the knowledge. It is rather an ongoing struggle to help them make sense of material. It requires me to approach it from many different ways, to try to find ways in which it will connect with their lives. And this is a process that never stops. If I read something of interest in the paper or on-line, the first thought that runs through my mind is "how can I use this for my students?" When I encounter someone well known or of distinction, I become brash, approach them, try to say something nice, then ask if they would be willing to come and talk to students. The answer is almost always yes. That enables me to extend the world of my classroom to a larger world, one that I can bring into the building. It has at times led to internships and other relationships for some students, and for all it has meant a learning experience beyond what I can personally provide them.

During the school year I rarely have "down time." No matter how well planned a lesson may be, I have to be prepared to abandon it instantaneously if it is not working. As a wise central administrator I know once told a group of us,

> if the horse you are riding is dead, beating it won't make it go any faster.

It could be that there is something else of importance on the minds of the students, about which they need to talk. If that is not addressed, they will still not learn the material I planned for them. Or perhaps partway through the lesson it touches on something that raises issues for which I had not planned, but which are relevant to this particular group of students. Or maybe it is just one student, but s/he is someone who can if personal needs are not addressed totally disrupt the class. I could exert the force of my will to suppress such disruptive behavior but that could lead to resentment and sullenness on the part of other students.

Teaching is exhausting. If there are 30 students in the room at that moment, the number of interactions going on are in the hundreds. There are separate interactions between me and each of the students, there are interactions between each of their minds and different pieces of the material, and there are so many interactions among the students. All of this is part of the foundation upon which I am trying to build a meaningful educational experience. No, I do not claim that I can even notice more than a fraction of these interactions. I have to select to which of these I will pay due attention, and that becomes a real high wire act with true potential for disaster!

Then there are all the things about individual students. One has to be aware of any changes in patterns. A normally solid student suddenly does not come prepared. Why? Should I pull that student aside and ask immediately, because there may be a real family crisis about which appropriate people should be informed? Or is this a student who needs a little room to self-correct, and if I ask directly I may cause that student to erect a barrier between us? What if when I ask a student shares information with me that I am legally required to report, such as physical, sexual or emotional abuse (and this has happened more often than you might imagine)? How can I persuade that student that I am not violating her confidence by reporting it to the guidance department, where since each counselor has more than 400 students and right now the counselors are in the midst of doing registration for next year they have little time to breathe?

I can hear the thoughts in some of your minds. What does this   10 have to do with teaching? My answer is that it may be more important than anything else I do. I am able to push my students outside their comfort zones, to have them challenge themselves, only insofar as they are willing to trust me. It does not matter that an older sibling or a friend has raved about me. Each student presents me with a *de novo* situation. I must prove to each one that I am worthy of their trust. I may get some benefit of the doubt from what they have heard, but that will not sustain me beyond the first week. Students do not always have to understand why I do what I do, but if I make some attempt to explain they are far more willing to take steps down a road that might be very unknown to them.

Each student who comes into my room is entitled to be known as the individual he is, absolutely unique, and entitled to respect for that uniqueness. I consider this fairness, but it is a different kind of teacher behavior than some have come to expect. I do NOT treat all students exactly the same, because their needs are different. Sometimes I therefore make mistakes in what I do, because I cannot hide behind the excuse that I am simply enforcing the rules. I will apologize, to students, to a class, to parents, when appropriate. I must model for my students what I expect of them, which is taking responsibility for one's actions, even if the hurt we cause is unintentional, even if our purpose in such actions was meant to be a positive.

But that is an impossible task. I cannot really know all 170 students currently in my care. I try to see them in their various activities at least once, so that they will know that I value their lives outside my classroom. But that too is impossible—too many activities overlap, and even though I am a Gemini I cannot physically split myself that way. So part of every school day has to include the time to reflect—where did I make mistakes, what did I miss, with whom did the lesson, or I, not connect? What can I do to fix these problems, while still trying to move each class forward? How can I keep each class lively enough that I don't cause kids to zone out? And how can I do this while maintaining some space for myself, my family? Again it is a high wire balancing act. If I try to do too much, then I exhaust myself and am not sharp enough to notice problems in the classroom.

And when I am teaching I must be constantly monitoring far too many things. Which students are getting it? Which are not? Did I cover what they need to know? If some are not getting it and others are, do I move on, do I stop for those not getting it? I may have a half second to make up my mind and make adjustments. Oh, there's a fire drill, so I've lost 5 or more minutes of instructional time, in this class, plus the additional time to settle them down after they come back. How do I adjust for this class without slowing down the lesson for other classes for which there is no such disruption?

And while I am teaching probably 3 different levels of American History (because one talented and gifted class is far less able than the other two) as well as Social Issues, I have to be thinking about next year, when I will be teaching Government, including for the first time AP Government, and also Comparative Religion.

Because I teach high school, I am also involved with writing   15
recommendations (fortunately complete for the current cycle), and helping students explore postgraduate opportunities, which for most but not all will mean college at some level. At which colleges should they look? Why? If I have built relationships with my students such that they will exert themselves for me in my work, then they are likely to turn to me for counsel on issues like these, and it would be unfair of me not to respond.

I have not talked about all the e-mails with parents and students, about phone calls, about parent conferences. I have not talked about non-classroom responsibilities such as faculty and departmental meetings, ordering books, helping schedule guest speakers and field trips for other teachers, mentoring student teachers and new teachers, attempting to do joint planning with others in the department.

Nor have I mentioned the biggest current burden, the preparation of my portfolio for NBPTS, due in Ewing NJ by March 31, and I will be pushing the deadline. I have given more than enough detail about my responsibilities without attempting to list all of them. My school day—including commuting time when I am thinking actively about my teaching and the work I do at home—usually runs about 12 hours a day, not including time spent in coaching or in attending events in which my students participate. And yet I have not really addressed my original question. Since I have forced you to read this much, perhaps I should now focus more closely on the main topic—you have enough foundation.

What does it mean to be a teacher? The answer I will assay at this point is mine alone, but one I expect would find strong agreement from many other teachers. To be a teacher means to be consumed—with the care of one's students, with a passion for one's subject, with not wanting to ever miss a chance to make a difference. It is to go out on a wire without a net, because one never knows what actions one takes or words one says will make a difference, and whether that difference will be positive or negative. Sometimes it can mean pouring oneself out without being as fortunate as I have often been to get feedback from parents and students that encourages me to go on, even when I am exhausted and worrying about my failure in reaching some students. It means that one's family will have to accept the limitations—in time and money—the choice of being a teacher will impose on them. It means recognizing that one's own learning—of students, of material, of how to help the students connect with the material—is a never-ending process. It means one has to constantly operate on several levels simultaneously, observing things—about oneself, about the students and the class—about which one can do nothing at the moment but which will have to be processed and addressed at some point.

For me being a teacher also means having to take stands for what I believe is correct. It requires me to challenge those who would impose on our schools, teachers, and students requirements that would be counterproductive to the real learning to which all of our students should be entitled. It means I have to find ways to enable my students to succeed on examinations imposed from the outside which I find either meaningless or destructive of real learning while at the same time trying to maintain and live by my best lights of what I think SHOULD be occurring in my classroom, with these particular students, at this time and in this place. It means that I cannot "teach" as if their lives outside my classroom did not exist, but must find ways to include their lives as a coequal part of the learning I wish them to experience in my classroom.

And it means using whatever gifts I may have on behalf of my students. I had ceased being very active politically, until

I realized that my political activity is also part of what makes me the teacher I am, for good or not others will decide. Financial irresponsibility on the part of government restricts the ability of our schools to serve our students. Those who would impose one way of thinking on issues deprive our students of the chance to explore and come to their own conclusions. Misperceptions about what test scores mean and what they measure can lead to further distortions of the educational experience available to our students. Lack of understanding of the real educational issues can allow ideologues to impose on our schools things that are destructive of real learning, of the excitement with which most students originally enter school. Thus even my blogging and my writing on listservs and even the occasional op-ed pieces and Letters to the Editor are part of what it means for me to be a teacher.

For anyone who has read this far, I have now burdened you enough. Through my earphones as I write I listen to Bach's Art of the Fugue, played by a string quartet. The music is appropriate to this topic—it is complex, but its complexity is built from many details themselves of relatively simplicity. And I am reminded of the words at the end of T. S. Eliot's poem "Little Gidding," that I think accurately portray what it means, to me, to be a teacher:

> Quick now, here, now, always—
> A condition of complete simplicity
> (Costing not less than everything)
> And all shall be well and
> All manner of thing shall be well
> When the tongues of flame are in-folded
> Into the crowned knot of fire
> And the fire and the rose are one.

Thinking About Content

1. How many tasks does Bernstein list in what it means to be a teacher? Which of those tasks would you expect teachers to consider part of their jobs? What were the unexpected tasks Bernstein names?
2. Bernstein addresses the outside lives of the students in his classroom and suggests that his own outside life remains politically active. What are some of the reasons for including the outside lives of students and teachers in the classroom? How do those lives affect the lives inside the classroom?

Thinking About Strategy

1. Bernstein's text comes from a blog posting. What different conventions apply to blog posts than would apply to a more traditional essay?
2. Included at the end of Bernstein's post are eight lines from a T. S. Eliot poem that Bernstein says accurately portrays his understanding of what it means to be a teacher. How do conventions of poetry differ? How does the poetry work? What do you see in a poem that you don't see in the blog posting itself?

America's New Teachers: How Good, and for How Long?

KATHERINE C. BOLES AND VIVIAN TROEN

Katherine C. Boles and Vivian Troen are both veteran classroom teachers. Katherine C. Boles teaches at Harrard University Graduate School of Education, and Vivian Troen teaches at Brandeis University. They are the authors of the 2003 book from Yale University Press Who's Teaching Your Children?: Why the Teacher Crisis Is Worse Than You Think and What Can Be Done About It. *The book explores the shortage of qualified teachers in the United States and offers proposals for reform. The following essay appeared in the teacher's journal* Education Week *in 2000.*

———————— ✦ ————————

There is a story we tell at conferences about an educational reformer who holds a seance in order to call up the ghost of John Dewey. Frustrated with the pace of reform, this person asks the great philosopher of progressive education how to bring about real change in American schools.

"Do you want the realistic way, or the miraculous way?" Dewey asks.

"Well, the realistic way, of course," says the reformer.

"A million angels would come down from heaven and visit every classroom in America, wave their hands, and education reform would immediately become established," Dewey replies.

"Then what would be the miraculous way?" asks the puzzled   5
reformer.

"Educators would do it themselves," explains Dewey.

The story always gets a laugh, because no one knows better than educators themselves how fiendishly difficult it is to institute lasting school reform. Earlier in this Congress, federal lawmakers haggled over how to spend some $2 billion on teacher recruitment and training. We have to ask ourselves why, despite the billions already spent, the problems of public education remain intractable.

We believe the answer lies in the nature of schools and the job of the teacher, both legacies of their 19th-century industrial-style origins, with principals viewed as bosses and teachers as replaceable workers on an assembly line. This history has bred a school culture of isolation and egalitarianism that effectively stymies all attempts at reform.

But don't blame the teachers. Blame their job. Teaching is a flat career that offers no promotions and pay raises based almost exclusively on years of service or earned academic degrees (which can be in any unrelated or irrelevant subject). There are few external incentives or rewards for acquiring knowledge, sharpening skills, or improving performance. Too often, teaching is a dead-end job with low status, uncompetitive salaries, and poor working conditions.

Creative and highly motivated teachers need career options   10 and professional growth in order to stay interested in classroom teaching. But teachers find little support in attempts to improve their practice. In the rigid school culture, star performance is discouraged by the egalitarian notion that each teacher is the "equal" of every other teacher. This is a system which rewards only seniority and not merit, or knowledge, or expertise, or contributions to the profession. If all teachers are equal, then none is outstanding, and there are no failures.

Obviously, common sense alone discredits the doctrine of equality among teachers, since all students and parents, and teachers as well, understand that there are exceptional teachers who deserve the highest rewards, and incompetent teachers who should not be allowed inside a classroom. That neither happens is symptomatic of other factors hindering professional growth: no mentoring, poor supervision, and practically no accountability.

It's no wonder teaching is a job that discourages longevity. Currently, according to some estimates, the best and brightest stay in teaching an average of five years before moving into other fields. That should be of serious concern to those who would spend billions aggressively recruiting and training people who are likely to leave the field when they find out what the job is really like.

If excellent teachers are to be induced to stay in teaching as a lifelong career, then the job itself must undergo fundamental change.

Already, the movement toward what educators call "professional-development schools" (collaborations between K–12 schools and colleges for teacher training) is gaining momentum and shows promise of bringing significant change to the landscape of American education. Professional development schools aspire to a model similar to teaching hospitals, with students taking graduate-level courses in the art and science of teaching and working daily with a mentor teacher, much as an intern works with a veteran doctor. Teachers, much like doctors in teaching hospitals, teach some of the graduate-level courses, and teaching interns observe master-teachers practice their craft. Professional-development schools are achieving a certain success because they have the potential to alter the school culture that has prevented past reforms from taking hold.

We helped pioneer this movement 12 years ago, when, as two   15 classroom teachers, we founded the Learning/Teaching Collaborative of Boston and Brookline, Mass., a professional-development school that continues to create new career opportunities for classroom teachers. The collaborative gives neophyte teachers the benefits of close supervision as practitioners in working classrooms. Just as important, it provides opportunities for veteran teachers to be mentors, time to engage in meaningful professional-development activities like research and curriculum development, and a forum for sharing ideas and solutions in a team approach to teaching both children and graduate students.

Moreover, these teachers get extra pay for extra work. Many of them tell us that, were it not for the Learning/Teaching Collaborative, they would have left teaching years ago. Graduates from the collaborative are highly sought after and land jobs in the best schools (or the worst schools—their choice) in America.

Other professional-development schools are in place all over the country, from San Jose State University in California, to Teachers College at Columbia University in New York City, to Baylor University in Texas, and hundreds of other schools in between. There is a growing realization that this model could lead the way toward the next generation of school reform. Professional-development schools are successful because they take the first positive steps toward altering the culture that has prevented past reforms from taking hold. What is needed next is to change the job of the teacher even further—instituting career ladders that offer opportunities for real promotions, pay raises based on achievement and performance, and a consequent strengthening of public awareness that teaching is a profession worthy of status and respect.

Yes, we need more teachers, and we need better teachers. But we have to give good teachers a job that shows promise for the future as well as fulfillment for today.

Our society can no longer afford to perpetuate an education system that, by its very nature, expels the best of its practitioners so early in their careers.

Thinking About Content

1. What problem do Boles and Troen feel needs to be remedied? Explain.
2. The authors write, "Don't blame the teachers. Blame their job." Do you agree or disagree with their assertion?

Thinking About Strategy

1. The authors begin this short essay with a joke about teachers and education reform. What purpose does such an opening serve?
2. Boles and Troen clearly state their thesis at the end of this essay. Did you find this strategy effective? How does saving the thesis until the end of the essay change the reading of the essay? How can you use this strategy in your own writing?

The Wages of Teaching
ANNA QUINDLEN

Anna Quindlen is a best-selling novelist, Pulitzer Prize-winning columnist, and social critic. She has published nonfiction and two children's books and also writes a column for Newsweek *magazine. The following essay on teachers and teachers' salaries appeared in her* Newsweek *column in November 2005.*

———————◆———————

A couple of years ago I spent the day at an elementary school in New Jersey. It was a nice, average school, a square and solid building with that patented classroom aroma of disinfectant and chalk, chock-frill of reasonably well-behaved kids from middle-class families. I handled three classes, and by the time I staggered out the door, I wanted to lie down for the rest of the day.

Teaching's the toughest job there is. In his new memoir, *Teacher Man*, Frank McCourt recalls telling his students, "teaching is harder than working on docks and warehouses." Not to mention writing a column. I can stare off into the middle distance with my chin in my hand any time. But you go mentally south for five minutes in front of a class of fifth-graders, and you are sunk.

The average new teacher today makes just under $30,000 a year, which may not look too bad for a twenty-something with no mortgage and no kids. But soon enough the newbies realize that they can make more money and not work anywhere near as hard elsewhere. After a lifetime of hearing the old legends about cushy hours and summer vacations, they figure out that early mornings are for students who need extra help, evenings are for test corrections and lesson plans, and weekends and summers are for second and even third jobs to try to pay the bills.

According to the Department of Education, one in every five teachers leaves after the first year, and almost twice as many leave within three. If any business had that rate of turnover, someone would do something smart and strategic to fix it. This isn't any business. It's the most important business around, the gardeners of the landscape of the human race.

Unfortunately, the current fashionable fixes for education   5
take a page directly from the business playbook, and it's a terrible fit. Instead of simply acknowledging that starting salaries are woefully low and committing to increasing them and finding the money for reasonable, recurring raises, pols have wasted decades obsessing about something called merit pay. It's a concept that works fine if you're making widgets, but kids aren't widgets, and good teaching isn't an assembly line.

McCourt's book is instructive. Early in his 30-year career, he's teaching at a vocational high school and realizes that his English students are never more inspired than when forging excuse notes from their parents. So McCourt assigns the class to write excuse notes, the results ranging "from a family epidemic of diarrhea to a sixteen-wheeler truck crashing into the house." Pens fly with extravagant lies. You can almost feel the imaginations kick in.

The point about tying teaching salaries to widget standards is that it's hard to figure out a useful way to measure the merit of what a really good teacher does. You can imagine the principal who would see McCourt's gambit as the work of a gifted teacher, and just as easily imagine the one who would find it unseemly. Tying raises to pass rates is a flagrant invitation to inflate student achievement. Tying them to standardized tests makes rote regurgitation the centerpiece of schools. Both are blind to the merit of teachers who shoulder the challenging work of educating those less able, more troubled, from homes where there are no pencils, no books, even no parents. A teacher whose Advanced Placement class sends everyone on to top-tier colleges; a teacher whose remedial-reading class finally gets through to some, but not all, of a student group that is failing. There is merit in both.

The National Education Association has been pushing for a minimum starting salary of $40,000 for all teachers. Why not? If these people can teach six-year-olds to add and get adolescents to attend to algebra, surely we can do the math to get them a decent wage. Since the Corporate world is the greatest, and richest, beneficiary of well-educated workers, maybe a national brain trust might be set up that would turn a tax on corporate profits into an endowment to raise teacher salaries. Maybe states and communities could also pass regulations with this simple proviso: no school administrator should ever receive a percentage raise greater than the raise teachers get. Neither should state legislators.

In recent years, teacher salaries have grown, if they've grown at all, at a far slower rate than those of other professionals, often lagging behind inflation. Yet teachers should have the most powerful group of advocates in the nation: not their union, but we the people, their former students. I am a writer because of the encouragement of teachers. Surely most Americans must feel the same, that there were women and men who helped them levitate just a little above the commonplace expectations they had for themselves.

At the end of his book, McCourt, who is preparing to leave   10
teaching with the idea of living off his pension and maybe writing—and whose maiden effort, *Angela's Ashes*, will win the Pulitzer—is giving advice to a young substitute. "You'll never know what you've done to, or for, the hundreds coming and going," he says. Yeah, but the hundreds know, the hundreds who are millions who are us. They made us. We owe them.

Thinking About Content

1. What is the average salary for a new teacher? According to Anna Quindlen, when does this salary become problematic for teachers? Why?
2. Quinden cites the Department of Education statistic that one in every five teachers quits after the first year. Quindlen proposes higher salaries to help

with this problem. What are some other strategies you can think of that might help with this situation?

Thinking About Strategy

1. How does Quindlen's position as someone outside the field of teaching affect the persuasiveness of her argument?
2. In the last sentence of this essay, Quindlen says "we owe them." Why is this a powerful ending? Is it effective for you? Why or why not?

Look Dad, My Biology Teacher Is Selling Stereos at Circuit City
DANIEL MOULTHROP, NÍNIVE CLEMENTS CALEGARI, AND DAVE EGGERS

Dave Eggers is an acclaimed author, Pulitzer Prize finalist, cofounder of 826 Valencia (a nonprofit tutoring and writing center), and the son and brother of teachers. Nínive Clements Calegari is a teacher and founding executive director of 826 Valencia. Daniel Moulthrop is a journalist and former teacher. These three writers who have strong connections with education joined together in 2005 to write Teachers Have It Easy: The Big Sacrifices and Small Salaries of America's Teachers, *a book exploring how low pay affects teachers' abilities to support themselves and their families as well as to focus on their jobs. The following essay is a chapter from* Teachers Have It Easy.

———————————— ✦ ————————————

At least 20 percent of public school teachers report having second jobs outside of the field of education. Their reasons vary. Some younger teachers are supplementing their income to help pay off their student loans. More experienced teachers with families often need the extra income to pay for necessities as their families grow. Many teachers live paycheck to paycheck, the extra job providing them with cash they can actually save.

Resorting to second jobs during the summer is a popularly accepted custom for America's teachers. It has long been common for a student to see her English teacher working at a local restaurant, or her history instructor painting houses. No one, neither teachers nor parents, makes much of a fuss about it—though whether or not such moonlighting enhances or diminishes public respect for the teaching profession is up for debate. And as wages stagnate, the problem seems to be getting worse.

A 2004 survey conducted by Sam Houston State University in Texas found that 35 percent of the teachers who responded had extra jobs, compared to 22 percent in 1980. Teachers worked an average of 9.9 hours per week outside of school during the school year. Seventy-six percent of those who held extra jobs felt it was detrimental to their performance. In addition to their hours in the classroom, these Texas teachers worked as counselors, farmers, antique shop clerks, office administrators, cabinet makers, church choir directors, newspaper delivery persons, service managers, ministers, waitresses, and cake designers.

On the following pages, we will hear from a range of teachers, mostly men, who work at least two jobs. The strain these extra work hours put on their teaching and on their families is obvious. That teachers would have to take on these sorts of jobs is a troubling by-product of their poor pay, underscoring America's complex and somewhat incongruous attitude toward educators. There is no comparable occupation whose importance is acknowledged by society but which is not quite considered an actual, fulltime job.

ERIK BENNER, 32, HISTORY—CROSS TIMBERS MIDDLE SCHOOL, GRAPEVINE, TEXAS

I've been teaching history for eight years now, and the whole   5
time, I've been working nights and weekends at the local Circuit City. It pays decently, and it helps me make ends meet. We've got three-year-old twins and an eleven-year-old. Without the second job, it would be extremely difficult. The irony is that the extra job, which helps buy my kids nice things, takes me away from them on the weekends. I work at the store every weekend, and some weeknights. If I have a day off and I'm not at school or I'm not at the store, I go pick up the kids from day care. I'll have them home and have dinner ready for Mom when she gets home. I guess we make the best of what we do have. You have to.

I coach, too. Football season is pure chaos because I have games two or three nights a week, and then I work at Circuit City. During football, I can work as much as eighty to one hundred hours at both jobs combined. And then, right after football ends, because it's retail and Circuit City does well in December, I've got to get ready for the Christmas season. When I'm on vacation, I try to work a full-time pay period. My last paycheck will be for seventy hours. That covers Christmas break—I pulled fifty hours in one week.

I get to school at 6–6:30 in the morning, open the gym and locker room up for morning football practice, and then I go through my normal teaching day. We have practice until 4:30 or 5 in the afternoon. If there are games, I won't be home until 9:30 at night. Every Friday night we have to go scout other teams and film games and stuff like that. It's Texas. Football's big. It's a twelve-hour day if there are no games. And if there are no games, then I can work four and a half or five hours at the store. I also work Saturday and Sunday. Normally, right now, I'd be at work, but I've got a cushy schedule this weekend. I'm working the nights both days.

I have a buddy who started at Circuit City the same time I did. He's actually a store manager now—he has his own store. I think he just has an associate's degree, but he's making the same as I do working two jobs. Here I am with a degree. It's a little disheartening. I know if I went that route, I could be a manager at Circuit City, but I wouldn't enjoy it.

Working my second job, I'm making more money than somebody with a master's and twenty-plus years of experience, which is sad. But I wonder: Will I ever be able to stop working two jobs? I guess if you want nice things, you've got to work extra.

It doesn't bother me. It bothers my wife more than it bothers 10 me, because I've done it for ten years. I'm used to it. But, being newlyweds, she'd like me to have weekends off. She doesn't like having to go to church by herself.

DANIEL BEUTNER, 38, FIFTH GRADE—KYRENE DEL SUREÑO MIDDLE SCHOOL, CHANDLER, ARIZONA

In college, I remember thinking teachers don't get paid very much, but that's okay. My first teaching contract was in 1988 and I made $19,500. As a college student, that's a lot of money when you're used to making $4,000 a year. I thought, I could do that; I could make it work because I'm not materialistic. As time went on, I got married, had two kids, and realized, wow, bills add up. We were having all kinds of problems, because my wife was a teacher, too. So I started taking on part-time jobs.

When I was twenty-one years old and working as a teacher, summer came around and I thought, What am I gonna do? A parent approached me and gave me a job with his landscaping company. I was one of the guys, making five bucks an hour pushing a lawnmower. They had contracts with local strip malls, and they were making a lot of money.

The next school year, I figured that rather than working for five bucks an hour, I could start my own business. So I started doing it on my own, cutting residential lawns. Every weekend for ten years, I would go out, cut people's grass and install sprinklers, that kind of thing. I reached the point where I realized I could do this and make more money as a landscaper than I could as a teacher. I didn't want to do that; I wanted to teach. So I started my own little business: DB's Lawn Service.

When I cut lawns, the kids would come out and say, "Mr. Beutner's here!" It was a big exciting thing. And I just said, "Hey! How's it going?" I figured I was showing them a good work ethic. I was never embarrassed about it. More often than not, I would cut grass for other teachers, female teachers whose husbands made money. That didn't bother me. I think it was just the lack of free time. I wanted to make it work but I wasn't home much. That didn't make me real happy. At a certain point I figured if I ever was going to make money, it was going to have to be outside the profession of teaching.

At one point I was working three jobs. I was a teacher, I had my own landscaping company, and I delivered newspapers early in the morning. I did that for a solid year. I would get up at three in the morning, get in my car and go down to the local high school where the newspaper truck would be. I'd pick up 250 papers or so, bag them in the middle of the night, and deliver them. Then I would get home, take a shower, go to school, and teach all day. After I'd done my planning for the next day, I'd go home, make dinner, spend a little time with the family, and go to bed.

In the morning, if the truck with the newspapers was late, I would sit there in the parking lot. It would be about four in the morning and I'd just keep my car running and grade papers while I waited for the newspaper truck to come.

MATTHEW CHEESEMAN, 38, SCIENCE—EAST NICOLAUS HIGH SCHOOL, NICOLAUS, CALIFORNIA

When I first started teaching, I'd look in the newspaper and see if someone needed a mover for the day. I'd show up and just be part of a team that would move furniture and stuff. I think I got $20 an hour. I'd take anything where I could just grab some extra cash to pay off a bill, that kind of thing.

It was really hard for me this past year because I couldn't find a summer job. At East Nicolaus High, with only 280 students, we don't have a summer school. We don't have any K through 8 schools in our district—just the high school. So, technically, I'm the only science teacher in the district. I applied to several places to teach summer school, and for whatever reason, I wasn't even interviewed. Washington Unified openly told me at the door, when I turned in the application, that they were going to offer summer school positions to all of their own district people—especially anybody they had laid off. So I applied to Home Depot and Lowe's for a part-time summer job, but was declined because I could only work four weeks.

This second-job survival strategy is not always sustainable for teachers who want to raise a family. It's one thing to be young and running from your classroom to the restaurant where you bar-tend, but it's a different scenario altogether to be missing time with your family in order to pay for basic expenses. These situations are familiar to many lower-middle-class families, but it's hard to blame professionals with master's degrees for expecting a single paycheck that might suffice. After all, how many of their similarly educated peers who work in other professions also spend their nights bussing tables or cleaning other people's homes?

RACHEL CROSS, 30, HISTORY AND ALGEBRA—ONEIDA MIDDLE SCHOOL, ONEIDA, TENNESSEE

I'm a single mom, and I did everything at school I could do, as far as tutoring and summer school. But it's gotten so bad that for almost a year, I cleaned houses. I'd just take my son with me and go clean houses. It's not that I think I'm too good for that. It didn't bother me to sweep, and it didn't bother me to mop. But every time I would scrub a toilet, I would think, "I went to school for four years and did very well, and I'm doing this."   20

I was doing it two to three times a week at night and on Saturdays, probably four to five hours, and making about $30 to $40—about $100 a week total. I would get off work and go clean houses and then get home at ten.

I have cried several times, and it's like, you're on your knees in front of this toilet, and you're almost praying, praying that it'll get better, that you won't have to do this forever. But at the same time, you've got to be thankful, because this'll be thirty extra dollars. It's a tank of gas, or it may be part of your co-pay if your child gets sick.

There's always something. That's the nature of having a child. One afternoon, he was riding home with my mother and she gave him a couple of dollars because we were going to go to the movies or something, and he said, "I'm going to give this to my mommy, because even though she doesn't tell me, I know she doesn't have a lot of money." That just broke my heart. He was probably four at the time.

SKIP LOVELADY, 42, SCIENCE—REDWOOD HIGH SCHOOL, LARKSPUR, CALIFORNIA

Outside of school, I'm a waiter at Plumpjack Café in San Francisco. I've been there since the restaurant opened. I also do a fair amount of independent computer support work for some small companies and individuals, doctors and so on. I do graphics and digital work and digital video editing, but I also do troubleshooting and help with hardware and software and things like that. I've taught summer school here for eight summers in a row now, which is fairly grueling—it's another five weeks of teaching.

I've been married twenty-three years. I'm trying to stay married, but my wife and I never go out on Saturday nights. I never take a day off at Plumpjack. I work every Saturday night, all year long. I'll be off this Saturday because of the science fair—and I've had to save a bunch of money to compensate for that. But yeah, it's just tough. We had made a commitment not to leave our son anywhere except with his parents. No day care, none of that. So I started taking on extra jobs—tutoring, and the restaurant—and everything else I could get my hands on.

I tutor one to three nights a week. One hour per kid, which turns out to be an hour and a half, two hours by the time I drive there and drive back. I miss storytelling time for my kid, bedtime, you know, stuff like that. I'm out of the house two or more evenings per week.

Ultimately, I do all of those things for the money. All those jobs, except for the restaurant work, have an academic component to them, which I love. I'm glad I could find extra work in that field. I support my family with that. If it really was just about the money, then I could find other work that pays more, outside of school. But the truth is, if I didn't need the money I really wouldn't take on all those evening jobs, even if they were academically related. On average, teachers nationwide earn an additional $3,250 a year from moonlighting. The bitter irony is that a good deal of the teachers earning extra money end up putting it right back into the classroom. In 2001, the National Education Association asked teachers to calculate how much of their own money they had spent during the past school year to meet the needs of their students. The average was $443, a 9 percent increase over the 1994–1995 average of $408.

STEVEN HERRAIZ, 40, KINDERGARTEN—JOHN MUIR ELEMENTARY SCHOOL, SAN FRANCISCO, CALIFORNIA

Now, nine months out of the year, I work sixteen hours a week at a bar. I spend about fifty hours a week teaching. On the weekends, on Friday nights and Sunday mornings, I work at the bar. Fridays I come home after teaching and take a nap. And then I go to work at nine on Friday night and come home at four in the morning. By the time I come home on Saturday morning, it's this huge marathon of work and I'm exhausted, so I sleep most of Saturday. Then on Sunday morning, I go back to the bar from seven in the morning until two in the afternoon.

What's really tragic is that when I first started teaching, I was making the same amount of money bartending two days a week 30 as I was teaching five days a week.

I spent $3,900 of my own money last year on my classroom. That's a lot of money. And it's not anything extravagant. It's stuff like paper clips and art supplies and paint and the things you would assume that the district provides and they don't. It's horribly demeaning and I try not to focus on it. I was active in union work a couple of years ago, but I didn't get anywhere with it. I didn't feel like we were being heard. There are so many obstacles to being a good teacher that I just said, What can I control myself? I can have a second job and not have to worry about supplies.

I kept thinking that the second job was going to give me the extra money I need to be an effective teacher. In other words, I can buy snacks for my kids. For the last eight years, I've been buying the food that gets them through the morning. A typical day has me stopping at the market because the school doesn't provide any sort of nutritious snack for the kids. And the kindergartners need to eat every few hours to get through the day.

Many teachers are surprisingly good-natured about this job juggling, especially when they can look back on it after their earnings allow them to concentrate on teaching full-time. But it's apparent that these years of strain take a permanent toll on one's psyche.

RICHARD ADELMAN, 52, ENGLISH—JOHN BARTRAM HIGH SCHOOL, PHILADELPHIA, PENNSYLVANIA

There was a time in my life when I worked four jobs. I worked as a teacher, and then in the summer I worked all kinds of jobs—as a restaurant manager in Atlantic City, in an auction house, as a photographer, and as an SAT tutor.

I generally worked the summer until I was about thirty-five   35
years old. For a while I worked on the boardwalk in Atlantic City during the summer. They were always glad to have me because before casinos, there wasn't much doing before the summer started. Once the season started, they needed a lot of people, but they were anxious also to get rid of people once the summer ended. So a teacher is perfect. That summer job was murder. Some of those jobs I had as restaurant manager were fourteen, sixteen hours a day.

On the weekends, according to the season, I would do two, three, even four photography jobs. If I did four weddings in a weekend, that would be basically from 8:30 in the morning on Saturday until late on Saturday night, 12 o'clock. And then on Sunday morning, maybe from twelve to ten at night. If I had one wedding job, it was an easy weekend, just a Saturday night. It depended on the season. There are a lot of bar mitzvahs and weddings in the autumn and the spring. I did children's portraits. I would teach at school, and then I would have, let's say, a children's portrait at 4:30, in New Jersey. So I'd have to run out of school and run over and photograph a kid.

I was trying to make ends meet. I don't think I ever really shirked my fatherly responsibilities. I don't remember ever feeling guilty about that. What I didn't have a lot of time for, as I recall, was fun. I lost all my friends, because when you work on the weekends and you can't keep track of your friends, when you have a lot of responsibilities and a lot of work to do, your friends end up being the people you know at work. I had friends I had made at college but I lost them. That part of my life is the one I . . . regret losing touch with all the friends I had throughout the course of my life.

It's almost as though I was traumatized by all the work I did—a kind of post-traumatic stress syndrome.

The effects of teacher moonlighting are obvious and varied. Teachers who run themselves ragged working two jobs—while juggling their family lives besides—are unlikely to be functioning at the highest levels. Thus, low teacher pay makes the most ambitious teachers—those who want to teach so badly that they're willing to sell stereos on the weekends—less effective educators. The teachers most inclined toward excellence are the first to be spun out of the teaching profession, because they realize that they cannot succeed at a level that's acceptable to their sense of achievement. The strain of the two-job lifestyle prevents them from teaching at a satisfactorily high level, and prevents them from being adequately present for their families. Their students suffer, their families suffer, and so these teachers are much more likely to burn out. And even working two or more jobs, most teachers cannot afford to live in the communities in which they teach.

Thinking About Content

1. Describe, in your own words, one or two of the narratives you found most compelling. What did you learn from these narratives?
2. What are the broader implications for the extra work teachers often have to take on to make ends meet? Have you or someone you know dealt with these implications?

Thinking About Strategy

1. Describe the effectiveness of a title like the one the authors use for this piece. How does it get the reader interested in and prepared for the essay that follows?
2. The authors make their argument by providing a series of personal narratives from teachers describing their financial struggles. How are these individual stories effective? How do these stories appeal to the emotions of the audience?

Prompts for Extended Writing Assignments

Personal Response
Write a letter to a former teacher that links what you learned from that teacher to where you are now. In your letter, mention some of the things you learned about teachers from the readings in this chapter. Be prepared to mail your letter to your teacher and share any response with the class.

From Another's Perspective
Interview a teacher. Write an essay in which you explore why this teacher chose the profession, what motivates him or her, and what you learned from the interview experience. In your essay, connect this teacher's experiences with the readings from this chapter.

Call for Social Action
Go online and research to compare starting salaries for teaching with the fields you are considering for a career. You may use www. publicagenda.org as a good starting point. Write an essay making an argument for or against raising teachers' salaries nationally. Be sure to support your argument with specific evidence, drawing from the readings in this chapter.

Research Opportunity
Research retention rates for beginning teachers. Explore some of the motivations behind staying and leaving teaching. What conclusions can you draw from the retention trends in teaching? Be sure to connect with the readings in this chapter.

Changing Classes?
The Promises and
Pitfalls of Education

For members of the lower classes in the United States, education is the way to move up the social ladder. With the rise of open admissions in colleges in the United States during the mid-twentieth century came the idea that education could help make citizens of the nation more equal. But our country continues to struggle with class issues in education. Studies show direct correlations between socioeconomic status and success on the SAT exam used in admissions in most universities across the country. Research also indicates that socioeconomic status plays an important role in students' successes once they enter college. As tuition costs rise and federal funding to schools decreases, critics of America's educational system argue that we are adding to the widening gap between the rich and the poor in this country.

As you read this chapter on education and class, we want you to think about what role class plays in our educational system, what obstacles exist for members of the lower classes in the different levels of our educational system, and what we can do to eliminate some of these obstacles.

Indian Education
SHERMAN ALEXIE

Sherman Alexie is a poet, fiction author, and filmmaker who grew up on the Spokane Indian Reservation in Wellpinit, Washington. In "Indian Education," Alexie, a Spokane/Coeur d'Alene Indian, writes about his educational experiences in both the tribal school on the reservation and in an all-white school. While Alexie's narrative gives the reader insight into his cultural heritage, it is important to note the socioeconomic issues at work on most Native American reservations. Reservations have some of the highest rates of poverty in the United States.

——————————— ✦ ———————————

FIRST GRADE

My hair was too short and my U.S. Government glasses were horn-rimmed, ugly, and all that first winter in school, the other Indian boys chased me from one corner of the playground to the other. They pushed me down, buried me in the snow until I couldn't breathe, thought I'd never breathe again.

They stole my glasses and threw them over my head, around my outstretched hands, just beyond my reach, until someone tripped me and sent me falling again, facedown in the snow.

I was always falling down; my Indian name was Junior Falls Down. Sometimes it was Bloody Nose or Steal-His-Lunch. Once, it was Cries-Like-a-White-Boy, even though none of us had seen a white boy cry.

Then it was a Friday morning recess and Frenchy SiJohn threw snowballs at me while the rest of the Indian boys tortured some other *top-yogh-yaught* kid, another weakling. But Frenchy was confident enough to torment me all by himself, and most days I would have let him.

But the little warrior in me roared to life that day and   5
knocked Frenchy to the ground, held his head against the snow, and punched him so hard that my knuckles and the snow made symmetrical bruises on his face. He almost looked like he was wearing war paint.

But he wasn't the warrior. I was. And I chanted *It's a good day to die, it's a good day to die*, all the way down to the principal's office.

SECOND GRADE

Betty Towle, missionary teacher, redheaded and so ugly that no one ever had a puppy crush on her, made me stay in for recess fourteen days straight.

"Tell me you're sorry," she said.

"Sorry for what?" I asked.

"Everything," she said and made me stand straight for fifteen   10
minutes, eagle-armed with books in each hand. One was a math
book; the other was English. But all I learned was that gravity can
be painful.

For Halloween I drew a picture of her riding a broom with
a scrawny cat on the back. She said that her God would never
forgive me for that.

Once, she gave the class a spelling test but set me aside and
gave me a test designed for junior high students. When I spelled all
the words right, she crumpled up the paper and made me eat it.

"You'll learn respect," she said.

She sent a letter home with me that told my parents to
either cut my braids or keep me home from class. My parents
came in the next day and dragged their braids across Betty
Towle's desk.

"Indians, indians, indians." She said it without capitalization.
She called me "indian, indian, indian."

And I said, *Yes, I am. I am Indian. Indian, I am.*   15

THIRD GRADE

My traditional Native American art career began and ended with
my very first portrait: *Stick Indian Taking a Piss in My Backyard.*

As I circulated the original print around the classroom,
Mrs. Schluter intercepted and confiscated my art.

Censorship, I might cry now. *Freedom of expression*, I would
write in editorials to the tribal newspaper.

In third grade, though, I stood alone in the corner, faced the
wall, and waited for the punishment to end.

I'm still waiting.   20

FOURTH GRADE

"You should be a doctor when you grow up," Mr. Schluter told
me, even though his wife, the third grade teacher, thought I was
crazy beyond my years. My eyes always looked like I had just hit-
and-run someone.

"Guilty," she said. "You always look guilty."

"Why should I be a doctor?" I asked Mr. Schluter.

"So you can come back and help the tribe. So you can heal people."

That was the year my father drank a gallon of vodka a day   25
and the same year that my mother started two hundred different quilts but never finished any. They sat in separate, dark places in our HUD house and wept savagely.

I ran home after school, heard their Indian tears, and looked in the mirror. *Doctor Victor*, I called myself, invented an education, talked to my reflection. *Doctor Victor to the emergency room.*

FIFTH GRADE

I picked up a basketball for the first time and made my first shot. No. I missed my first shot, missed the basket completely, and the ball landed in the dirt and sawdust, sat there just like I had sat there only minutes before.

But it felt good, that ball in my hands, all those possibilities and angles. It was mathematics, geometry. It was beautiful.

At that same moment, my cousin Steven Ford sniffed rubber cement from a paper bag and leaned back on the merry-go-round. His ears rang, his mouth was dry, and everyone seemed so far away.

But it felt good, that buzz in his head, all those colors and   30
noises. It was chemistry, biology. It was beautiful.

Oh, do you remember those sweet, almost innocent choices that the Indian boys were forced to make?

SIXTH GRADE

Randy, the new Indian kid from the white town of Springdale, got into a fight an hour after he first walked into the reservation school.

Stevie Flett called him out, called him a squawman, called him a pussy, and called him a punk.

Randy and Stevie, and the rest of the Indian boys, walked out into the playground.

"Throw the first punch," Stevie said as they squared off.   35
"No," Randy said.
"Throw the first punch," Stevie said again.
"No," Randy said again.

"Throw the first punch!" Stevie said for the third time, and Randy reared back and pitched a knuckle fastball that broke Stevie's nose.

We all stood there in silence, in awe. 40

That was Randy, my soon-to-be first and best friend, who taught me the most valuable lesson about living in the white world: *Always throw the first punch.*

SEVENTH GRADE

I leaned through the basement window of the HUD house and kissed the white girl who would later be raped by her foster-parent father, who was also white. They both lived on the reservation, though, and when the headlines and stories filled the papers later, not one word was made of their color.

Just Indians being Indians, someone must have said somewhere and they were wrong.

But on the day I leaned through the basement window of the HUD house and kissed the white girl, I felt the good-byes I was saying to my entire tribe. I held my lips tight against her lips, a dry, clumsy, and ultimately stupid kiss.

But I was saying good-bye to my tribe, to all the Indian girls 45 and women I might have loved, to all the Indian men who might have called me cousin, even brother.

I kissed that white girl and when I opened my eyes, she was gone from the reservation, and when I opened my eyes, I was gone from the reservation, living in a farm town where a beautiful white girl asked my name.

"Junior Polatkin," I said, and she laughed.

After that, no one spoke to me for another five hundred years.

EIGHTH GRADE

At the farm town junior high, in the boys' bathroom, I could hear voices from the girls' bathroom, nervous whispers of anorexia and bulimia. I could hear the white girls' forced vomiting, a sound so familiar and natural to me after years of listening to my father's hangovers.

"Give me your lunch if you're just going to throw it up," I said 50 to one of those girls once.

I sat back and watched them grow skinny from self-pity.

Back on the reservation, my mother stood in line to get us commodities. We carried them home, happy to have food, and opened the canned beef that even the dogs wouldn't eat.

But we ate it day after day and grew skinny from self-pity.

There is more than one way to starve.

NINTH GRADE

At the farm town high school dance, after a basketball game in an   55
overheated gym where I had scored twenty-seven points and pulled down thirteen rebounds, I passed out during a slow song.

As my white friends revived me and prepared to take me to the emergency room where doctors would later diagnose my diabetes, the Chicano teacher ran up to us.

"Hey," he said. "What's that boy been drinking? I know all about these Indian kids. They start drinking real young."

Sharing dark skin doesn't necessarily make two men brothers.

TENTH GRADE

I passed the written test easily and nearly flunked the driving, but still received my Washington State driver's license on the same day that Wally Jim killed himself by driving his car into a pine tree.

No traces of alcohol in his blood, good job, wife and two kids.   60
"Why'd he do it?" asked a white Washington State trooper.

All the Indians shrugged their shoulders, looked down at the ground.

"Don't know," we all said, but when we look in the mirror, see the history of our tribe in our eyes, taste failure in the tap water, and shake with old tears, we understand completely.

Believe me, everything looks like a noose if you stare at it long enough.

ELEVENTH GRADE

Last night I missed two free throws which would have won the game against the best team in the state. The farm town high school I play for is nicknamed the "Indians," and I'm probably the only actual Indian ever to play for a team with such a mascot.

This morning I pick up the sports page and read the headline: INDIANS LOSE AGAIN.

Go ahead and tell me none of this is supposed to hurt me 65 very much.

TWELFTH GRADE

I walk down the aisle, valedictorian of this farm town high school, and my cap doesn't fit because I've grown my hair longer than it's ever been. Later, I stand as the school board chairman recites my awards, accomplishments, and scholarships.

I try to remain stoic for the photographers as I look toward the future.

Back home on the reservation, my former classmates graduate: a few can't read, one or two are just given attendance diplomas, most look forward to the parties. The bright students are shaken, frightened, because they don't know what comes next.

They smile for the photographer as they look back toward tradition.

The tribal newspaper runs my photograph and the photograph of 70 my former classmates side by side.

POSTSCRIPT: CLASS REUNION

Victor said, "Why should we organize a reservation high school reunion? My graduating class has a reunion every weekend at the Powwow Tavern."

Thinking About Content

1. What are some of the struggles Alexie experiences in the tribal school? What struggles does he have when he attends the all-white school?
2. According to Alexie, how do his former classmates from the reservation feel when they graduate? Are any of them ready for college? Why or why not?

Thinking About Strategy

1. How would you describe Alexie's style in this piece? Do you think it is an effective way to talk about a difficult subject? Why or why not?

2. Alexie ends most sections with a one-sentence comment that seems to sum up the lesson of that section. For example, at the end of "Eighth Grade," he writes, "There is more than one way to starve." Look for other examples of this strategy, and write about why you think Alexie would choose to do this.

Do No Harm: Stopping the Damage to American Schools

PETER SACKS

The following essay is taken from Peter Sacks's 2001 book, Standardized Minds: The High Price of America's Testing Culture and What We Can Do to Change It, *in which Sacks discusses the problems with standardized testing and the consequences of our culture's obsession with such testing. Sacks has also published essays on education in* The American Enterprise *and* The New York Times *.*

——————————— ✦ ———————————

Our inauspicious era of educational crimes and punishments shows no signs of waning. Young people like Kelly Santos, whom we met earlier, aren't isolated examples of the fallout from the national crusade for more "accountable" schools. Texas is among some nineteen states that require high school "exit" tests, and more are in the offing. Dozens of states hold schools, students, teachers, and principals "accountable" on the basis of standardized test scores. "We have been, frankly, inundated with calls from states that are looking at their accountability laws and want to strengthen them," says one official at the Education Commission of the States.

Indeed, states are engaged in an elaborate round of musical acronyms, replacing one testing system for another one, more often than not with one that has significantly higher stakes for all people involved. Some states have abandoned their efforts to try alternatives to standardized tests, such as performance assessments, which strive to permit children to think and perform in deeper and more creative terms than allowed by multiple-choice sound bites, worksheets, and test drills. But such new approaches—promising as they might be to refocus attention on learning instead of scoring—aren't easily fitted into the politically driven objective of school accountability. That objective? Apparently to compare test scores of individual children across the state or the nation and show the public that policymakers are tough on academic standards by punishing those who don't measure up. Some examples:

- In a Hawthornesque variant to the scarlet A, Louisiana's accountability law requires school districts to identify and publish the names of all schools scoring in the bottom fifth on the state's standardized test. All Louisiana school districts but New Orleans comply with the 1997 law, pending the outcome of a lawsuit. One of the plaintiffs, a local state representative, ridicules the mandate as tantamount to requiring a public declaration of "Here are the dummy schools."

- In a case of school achievement levels determined simply by which test one chooses to use, school officials in Idaho wring their hands over reading scores of fourth-graders when one exam finds that 60 percent of the children can't read at grade level, while another test indicates just 18 percent cannot. A battle of name-calling, disavowals, and insults ensues over which test was right.

- Illustrative of the newfound lack of concern among some school officials over the educationally dubious practice of "teaching the test," Milwaukee public schools in Wisconsin agree to pay an Arizona consulting firm almost $400,000 for a program called TargetTeach. The firm specializes in getting test scores up in schools "with a problem." The firm, Evans-Newton Inc., promises a 20 to 200 percent surge in test scores in just a year.

- In Chicago, 1 in 10 of Chicago schools' 424,000 students are sent to summer school on the basis of standardized test scores. Thousands of others are forced to repeat a grade even after summer school because of poor showings on a retest. Under the hammer, students at Amundson High School in Chicago spend six weeks of class time on intensive test preparation and coaching for the upcoming test.

- In California, funding for a performance-based assessment system known as CLAS, which had been in place to assess learning without reliance on standardized testing, is vetoed by Governor Pete Wilson. In its place, the state legislature invents STAR, the Standardized Testing and Reporting program, which requires all children in the second through eleventh grades to take a commercial multiple-choice test. A group of several school superintendents from major California cities condemn the plan as educationally regressive, one that "wastes taxpayer dollars and will impede, rather than support, our statewide push toward higher performance."

ADDING THE DAMAGE

Without a doubt, crackdowns such as these on public schools, as well as tales of amazing turnarounds in test results in such locales as Tacoma, Washington, and Northampton Country, North Carolina, reflect the good news of American schools for many elected officials, corporate executives, parents, newspaper editorial writers, and others working under the mantle of school reform.

Tales of higher academic standards and achievement test scores beyond expectations sustain popular belief in the reform crusade's holy trinity: standards, accountability, and testing. For many, such stories show that the accountability movement is indeed having the reformers' desired effects: reinforcing high academic standards, forcing teachers and principals to do their jobs, and providing meaningful incentives for students to achieve.

The evidence from the previous three chapters shows just   5
how empty those beliefs are. In fact, while the rhetoric is highly effective, remarkably little good evidence exists that there's *any* educational substance behind the accountability and testing movement. In fact, when one adds up the real costs of the uniquely American model of school accountability and compares them to the minimal or nonexistent benefits, the inescapable conclusion is that the nation's fifteen-year experiment has been an unmitigated failure. Let's sum up the damage:

One: Educational considerations have been subordinate to the political and ideological motivations of politicians, educational bureaucrats, and business leaders. These interests have wielded political power over schools in order to assert their control and to demonstrate preconceived failures of the school system as the means to sustain that power. This was as true at the beginning of the American testing movement in Horace Mann's Massachusetts as it was in Johnson County, North Carolina, in the 1990s.

Two: Blatant and harmful misappropriations of standardized tests for fallacious uses have been a constant of America's historical experience with standardized testing in schools. Zealots, for instance, have taken tests intended to broadly assess achievement at the school, district, or state level, to instead rank and sort individual children. The opposite has also been true: tests intended to evaluate individual achievement have been used to base unfounded conclusions of the educational quality of entire school systems.

Three: In the ongoing struggle between educational equity among social classes and an efficiently managed school system, public policy toward schools has historically tended to side with the latter. Public schools have borrowed the management, surveillance, measurement, and control techniques of American business in order to achieve this efficiency.

Four: The notion of "accountability" itself has been defined in terms analogous to the corporate model, such as profits and returns to shareholders. In practice and in public belief, the educational product of schools has come to be judged almost exclusively by test scores. Borrowing, too, the market-driven ideology of the corporate world, policymakers have created pseudo-market systems of rewards and punishments to schools. Test scores are the currency of these incentives.

Five: The modern accountability movement became "federalized," in some decidedly tangible and pervasive ways. The federal government's markings on the accountability movement occurred, not insignificantly, as a result of the federal Title 1 law that has meted out many billions of dollars in federal funding to schools using test scores as a key part of the calculus. Further, prominent national leaders, including three recent American presidents, have ratcheted up the stakes for public schools to that of a national crusade for educational reform, with accountability testing as its linchpin.

Six: The underlying belief in the school reform crusade of the past few decades is that the American way of life was at grave risk because of lax standards and poorly educated schoolchildren. Evidence has proven this belief to be politically convenient mythology, wrong on at least three counts: First, academic achievement was never as horrible as the crusaders made it out to be; next, in the aftermath of an alleged deterioration of American schools, the U.S. economy continued to remain the most productive in the world; and finally, contrary to the implicit assumption that more testing and greater accountability will produce higher academic achievement, states with the most testing and the highest consequences of testing have fared worse on independent measures of achievement than states with no or low stakes to their testing programs.

10

Seven: Focused on test scores and the means to effect higher scores, the accountability movement has been curiously oblivious to the unintended damage to the learning environment. The movement has ignored the distortions to teaching and learning resulting from teachers, students, and others in the system acting in their own perceived best interest.

Schools and teachers, under intense pressure to boost achievement scores, have discovered the educationally dubious practice of teaching to tests. That, in turn, has narrowed what's taught to material that closely matches items on multiple-choice, standardized tests. Too, teaching to tests has had a dumbing effect on teaching and learning, as worksheets, drills, practice tests, and similar rote practices consume greater amounts of teaching time.

The greater the consequences attached to the test, the more severe these distortions are on teaching and learning. Indeed, a widely discussed international study of math and science performance of twelfth-graders suggests American students' relatively poor performance can be traced to the superficiality of their classroom experiences, which in turn can be linked to the rise of accountability testing.

Eight: Schools have also discovered they can boost test scores   15
by drilling students on practice test items, but gains won in this fashion prove to be ephemeral in the long run. In the short run, schools can jack up scores on one standardized test, only to see scores go back down when a new test comes along. Similarly, achievement that is apparently high on the test for which schools have prepared and drilled turns mediocre with a different test for which there was little or no specific preparation.

Nine: An important element of the calculus of school reform, as defined by the modern accountability movement, has been a heavy emphasis on state regulation of schools, similar to other regulatory agencies. State utility regulators, for instance, have historically monitored electric companies to ensure that rates are kept to a reasonable level. Similarly, the new school regulators have tried to ensure the academic integrity of schools through rules on educational "infractions" and punishments to schools and schoolchildren. "Violators," in this sense, have been the children, schools, teachers, and others that perform poorly on standardized achievement tests. Punishments for these "violators" have been severe.

But that seemingly attractive analogy collapses in the end. Whereas determining reasonable rates of profit for electric companies is a relatively straightforward exercise in measurement, assessing educational quality is exceedingly problematic. Is educational quality measured by results on standardized tests? Is it measured by how well students perform on tasks that require them to integrate skills and knowledge from several subjects, such as writing an essay or creating a multimedia presentation? Or does educational quality boil down to the success of graduates in college or in jobs after they leave the school system? Educational quality may be all these. Even a modicum of justice to this complex, ephemeral concept—and especially for the sake of people whose lives are affected by decisions about what constitutes educational quality—would undoubtedly require an equally complex measurement system. Such a system would have to assess educational quality from a variety of perspectives to be fair, complete, and accurate. But, again, choosing efficiency over equity, Americans through their elected officials have largely chosen to assess quality of schools in exceedingly narrow and often inaccurate terms.

Beyond these social and economic costs of current notions of school accountability, however, is one costly and pernicious piece of damage that framers of the accountability movement have virtually ignored over the past twenty-five years. Obsessed with test results and holding schools accountable for those results, the entire accountability enterprise has studiously avoided confronting the real problems of American schools. I've alluded to the powerful correlations between socioeconomic factors and test scores, taking note, for instance, of the huge economic gaps between communities like Tacoma and Mercer Island, or Northampton County and Chapel Hill. Quite simply, one can't write a book about standardized testing in American schools without confronting the effects of poverty, race, and class on test scores.

From *A Nation at Risk* to Bill Clinton's Goals 2000, the 20 accountability crusaders have given no more than lip service to the uncomfortable schism in the American school system between rich and poor, one that in recent years has increasingly resembled the economic and social stratification in the larger society. The accountability movement has sustained, and been sustained by, a big but comfortable lie: that schools themselves are the agent for social and economic change, rather than a reflection and reinforcer of existing social and economic divisions. In practice, this illusion has implied that "fixing" schools— via gains in achievement test scores—will also fix unemployment, crime, and poverty as well as racial and economic inequality. The entire accountability project in the United States over the past two decades has been based on a refusal to even acknowledge the far more difficult prospect that the causal relationships between schools and the larger society might in fact work largely in exactly the opposite direction to that wishful thinking.

As a result of this denial, the accountability machine's damage to children from families that aren't economically comfortable and highly educated or who are African American or Mexican American, has been inestimable, as we saw specifically in Texas, North Carolina, and in Tacoma. In those places and in hundreds more like them across the country, poor and minority schoolchildren have borne the brunt of the accountability machine's punishments.

Indeed, if social engineers had set out to invent a virtually perfect inequality machine, designed to perpetuate class and race divisions, and that appeared to abide by all requisite state and federal laws and regulations, those engineers could do no better than the present-day accountability systems already put to use in American schools.

Inequality in the larger society bleeds through the education system. Rich schools and poor schools match the income levels and occupational status of parents. Compared to rich schools, poor schools, whose children come from homes with incomes of less than $20,000 a year, are more likely to have relatively poorly paid teachers who are also teaching out of their fields of expertise and have less access to special learning tools like the Internet. Quite simply, compared to a rich school district, such as Mercer Island, a relatively poor one like Tacoma is likely to spend significantly less money on each of its students. In one recent year, for example, the nation's richest school districts spent almost 60 percent more per student than the country's poorest schools.

CLASS IS PARAMOUNT

To be sure, inequality may not be on the minds of a lot of parents, except to steer as far away from it as possible when choosing a school. Many parents in Boise, Idaho, were known to choose schools for their children based on test scores and child poverty rates; the higher the scores and the lower the poverty, the better the school in the eyes of many parents. Those parents might have been behaving quite rationally—but only up to a point. As it turns out, the economic class of individual children and their parents bears decisively on a child's chances of success in the school system, regardless of a particular school's test scores.

Let's digress momentarily to Chuck Lavaroni, the former   25
teacher and school superintendent in Marin County, California, a community of high-achieving, well-paid professionals and schools boasting exceedingly high test scores. At the end of our two-session conversation, Lavaroni somewhat reluctantly confided his hypothesis concerning his Marin County students, which he'd arrived at after years of rumination about his experiences.

"You could take kids (in Marin County) who have grown up in that environment and not send them to school at all and they'd still pass the (standardized) test," Lavaroni told me. "If one of those schools drops below the ninety eighth percentile, they worry."

That was Lavaroni's highly educated guess, after years of experience in education. But he may in fact be close to the sober reality about the powerful relationship of class background and a child's success in test-driven school systems. We can go back to a sweeping 1972 study for some enlightening discoveries along these lines that should still give parents and educators on the edge of the millennium reason to pause. That study suggests Lavaroni's guess is hardly a novel idea nor an unproven supposition. Titled *Inequality: A Reassessment of the Effect of Family and Schooling in America*, the three-year project was led by the sociologist Christopher Jencks and several other coauthors at the Center for Educational Policy Research at Harvard. The researchers examined how educational "attainment"—whether one obtains, for instance, a high school diploma or a medical degree—is related to such factors as class background, IQ scores, and average test scores of schools attended. As we've already seen, educational attainment is perhaps the most powerful of all indicators of educational quality, because attainment bears most directly on one's economic prospects and well-being.

Contrary to popular belief in the power of a school's average test scores as an indicator of a child's future academic success, the study found that "school quality" measured by scores has in fact a small effect on how much schooling a given child who attends that school will eventually obtain. "We can be almost certain," Jencks wrote, "that a child's going to a grade school with top-drawer test scores will add less than a year to his or her total years of schooling—and probably far less than even that."

Absent any significant effects of schools' average achievement scores on one's years of educational attainment, that leaves such individual characteristics as cognitive abilities, behavioral traits, and the class background a child is born into as possible explanations.

As it turns out, the class background of a child's parents, com-   30 bined with the behavioral traits about school which that class background imparts to children, appear to explain most of the variation in how much schooling someone eventually obtains. According to the Jencks study, a child's social and economic origins, measured by her father's occupational status and income, alone accounts for some 55 percent of her eventual educational attainment. Put another way, upper-middle-class children will obtain a total of four more years of schooling than lower-class kids, simply by virtue of the families they were born into. Further, so-called cognitive abilities, measured by IQ scores, account for less than 10 percent of the variation in the child's educational attainment.

On the other hand, the far more subtle behavioral traits often found in high-achieving households that "nurture the cognitive skills that schools value" have a far more substantial effect— something on the order of 25 percent—than IQ scores in explaining a child's educational achievement. Even then, the authors say, it's not clear that academic aptitude is that important to how much schooling one gets. Rather, attainment could be more related to "coming from the right family." Comparing, for instance, people with significantly different aptitude test scores raised in the same household, the study found that people who were more capable on the tests only attained less than a year of additional schooling. Again, class rules.

"Overall, the data lead us to three general conclusions," Jencks writes. "First, economic origins have a substantial influence on the amount of schooling people get. Second, the differences between rich and poor children is partly a matter of academic aptitude and partly a matter of money. Third, cultural attitudes, values, and taste for schooling play an even larger role than aptitude and money."

INCOME AND POVERTY

Thus, the effects of social and economic class on how much schooling people get are immense, as most parents of schoolchildren implicitly know and understand. Where many parents often get it wrong is in believing that by associating their children with other high-scoring children in top schools, parents can do sort of an end-run around the powerful effects of *family* socioeconomic background. Tragically, this belief in the power of test scores by association sustains the beliefs that schools can either make or break a middle-class child's academic prospects in school or fix the horrendous problems of underachievement in the nation's poor and minority communities. The belief fuels the nation's unhealthy obsession with test scores, while we avoid the underlying problems and inequities.

The uncomfortable truth, however, is that the accountability movement that many states have embraced for their schools has, in fact, accomplished nothing to address the real problems with American schools. Instead of alleviating the problems of schools, which are clearly associated with the vast differences in wealth and privilege, the accountability machine's hard-core system of crimes and punishments has merely stiffened barriers to academic success for many.

Indeed, states have erected these barriers with virtually no 35 firmly grounded evidence that they work to anyone's benefit except to those politicians, educators, and policy elites who professionally benefit from the bombardment of bad news about schools and from the engineering of high test numbers.

Besides the high correlation of class background to levels of attainment in the American school system, the relationship between poverty and achievement test scores has been firmly established in various field studies. Consider the Cleveland City School District, where fully 80 percent of schoolchildren are poor, as measured by their eligibility for school lunch programs. In 1990, the Ohio legislature told schools to administer a standardized test to ninth-graders to determine whether students might receive a full-fledged diploma or a downgraded "certificate" at their high school graduation. Students would have to pass all four parts of the test to receive a diploma, and they'd get two chances. James Lanese, of the Cleveland school district, looked into the question that had been troubling some skeptics: Would the state's testing program further punish schoolchildren in places like Cleveland, whose schools and families were already damaged by poverty?

Examining thirty-one school districts of various socioeconomic classes in Cuyahoga County, including Cleveland, Lanese applied the techniques of statistical correlation analysis to find out. Indeed, correlations between poverty levels of a district and success on the statewide tests were considerable. Lanese later told his peers at a meeting of the American Educational Research

Association in San Francisco, "The comparison of district level performance on the Ohio Proficiency Test as a function of each district's poverty rates indicates a strong positive relationship exists between the economic status of the district's pupils and their performance on the test."

Perhaps it comes as no surprise, then, that in the initial stages of the new testing program, just one-third of Cleveland students had passed the proficiency test by their junior year in high school. That's compared to three out of four students who had passed statewide. A year after the Lanese report, Michael Gallagher, also of the Cleveland school district, confirmed Lanese's results with slightly greater precision, accounting for more variables that might explain differences in pass rates. Specifically, Gallagher controlled for the confounding effects that occur between school districts, such as curriculum, racial makeup, and per-pupil spending. He looked at both income and poverty rates of the neighborhoods that surround individual schools within the Cleveland school district.

Even then, Gallagher found both household income and   40
poverty were significantly correlated with the chances of passing the Ohio proficiency test. In fact, for every 10 percent drop in the number of pupils eligible for free lunches, a school would produce a 4 percent gain in its passing rate on the standardized test. He also discovered that, as a school approached having almost no pupils eligible for free lunches, the closer to the state average in the rate at which its students passed the test.

Hold it a minute, some readers might interject: "But most studies have shown that differences in the *actual funding* of schools don't come close to explaining the yawning gaps of achievement between rich schools and poor ones." Indeed, there have been at least 100 such studies, and few have demonstrated any significant relationship between school funding levels— unequal as they are—and test scores.

And all of those studies may be seriously flawed, taken as a whole. In fact, virtually none have been based on nationwide samples of schools. In perhaps the first study to remedy this shortcoming and investigate the effects on achievement of school funding *on a national basis*, a team led by Bruce Biddle at the University of Missouri compared test scores on three national and/or international studies against the variables of poverty and school funding. Even when controlling for such variables as race and curriculum, the team found the combined effect of poverty and school funding was "mammoth," accounting for the lion's share of differences among average achievement scores in states.

Further, the Biddle team came to a startling conclusion when applying their analysis to the entire pool of nations participating in a recent international comparison of mathematics achievement, on which the American students generally fared poorly. When accounting for economics, the Biddle team estimated that math scores in "advantaged" American schools (those with high funding and low poverty rates) would beat *all* European counterparts and come in second only to Japan. On the other hand, scores for typically disadvantaged American schools would be below all European nations and approach those of many developing countries.

Evidence like this is why the accountability crusade's push for more and more testing persists in going off into left field while the real action is at home plate. Summing up his research team's remarkable findings in *Phi Delta Kappan*, the highly regarded magazine about education, Biddle says:

> The effects I report here help us understand why setting higher standards will have so little impact on achievement. If many, many schools in America are poorly funded and must contend with high levels of child poverty, then their problems stem not from confusion or lack of will on the part of educators but rather from lack of badly needed resources. In fact, setting higher standards for those disadvantaged schools can even make things worse. If they are told that they now must meet higher standards, or—worse—if they are chastised because they cannot do so, then they will have been punished for events beyond their control.

Adding fuel to the flames that hurt rather than help children from poorer backgrounds, schools in poor neighborhoods bear the greatest brunt of public and official pressure to raise test scores. At these schools, teachers are most pressured to turn teaching and learning into a rote exercise of practice and drill for the next standardized test. We saw evidence of this disparate burden placed on the poor in Tacoma, Washington, in Northampton County, North Carolina, and in San Antonio, Texas. But further quantitative evidence on a wider scale underscores the observations from those case studies.

For example, investigators Joan Herman and Shari Golan 45 examined eleven medium and large school districts in nine states to quantify the effects of big-stakes testing programs. Most noteworthy, the authors said, were the disproportionate effects of such testing on schools with lots of poor children and high numbers of minorities. The poorer the children attending the schools, the more pressure schools place on teachers to raise test scores, and the greater chance that the teachers will focus on the tests in their instruction rather than on deeper understanding.

And to what benefit? In the Herman study, teachers were asked whether the testing programs helped their schools to improve. On a scale of one to five (one corresponding to definite agreement, three to a neutral opinion, and five to definite disagreement), teachers in both wealthy and poor areas were inclined to rate standardized testing as more harmful than helpful for school improvement. Teachers in the poorer areas were least sanguine. "In the minds of teachers," the researchers conclude, "test results are of uncertain meaning and of uncertain value in school improvement."

A PROPOSAL

Judging by the evidence compiled in the previous three chapters, there's abundant reason to believe that the clearest route to raising the achievement levels of schoolchildren, in a real and lasting sense, may be—quite contrary to popular belief—to diminish reliance on standardized testing and high-stakes accountability systems. Instead of helping minority children and children of low and moderate incomes get past already stiff barriers to academic success, the accountability machine has given us bad teaching and perpetuated rather than dampened a powerful structure of economically segregated and unequal schools.

To be sure, that's not the sort of message that flies well in these times, when efforts to attack the problems of schools at the fountainheads of poverty and wealth are frowned on as failed strategies of a bygone era of liberal ideology. Above all, the accountability movement has been incredibly successful at framing the debate about school reform and improvement in the United States, persuading a largely uninformed public that more testing, more standards, and greater accountability for schools and teachers are the panaceas for whatever ails schools. Indeed, a 1997 public opinion poll conducted for Phi Delta Kappa International, the educational organization, showed that two in three Americans highly favored a national standardized test; that well more than half favored Bill Clinton's proposal for a national exam; and that most Americans are content to believe that the massive quantities of standardized testing in their schools is "about right."

Perhaps the public is right in believing that government programs cannot rectify the social and economic inequalities that reproduce more inequality in public schools. But Americans fail to engage a genuine debate over the real problems with their schools at their collective peril. To continue to avoid that debate, to remain out of touch to the hard problems of American schools, means taxpayers will keep throwing good money after bad. They will continue to erroneously believe that more testing and higher consequences for poor test results, enforced by the power of the state, will fix what is wrong with American schools. The public will also be led down a particularly troublesome slippery slope: The nation remains at risk because the standards, testing, and accountability movement never went far enough. Repeating the age-old pattern that the fix for American schools lies in some new technological solution, Americans are likely to be told by the next generation of crusaders about the imperative for *national* standards and a *national* test to measure student performance against those world class standards.

Indeed, the next generation was already coming on the scene 50 as I was writing this. About the time of the fifteenth anniversary of the 1983 *A Nation at Risk* report, a prominent group of school reformers and Washington policy elites, led by Ronald Reagan's former education secretary, William J. Bennett, had come out with just that message, in what might be called *Risk II*. Not surprisingly, they dubbed the sequel, *A Nation Still at Risk: An Education Manifesto*.

To be sure, *Risk* was in dire need of an update. Unfortunately for the movement's followers, it had been eclipsed by reality. The American economy's performance relative to all its international competitors was outright defying crusaders' gloomy predictions. Educational attainment was improving, as was student performance on the National Assessment of Educational Progress.

Addressing those difficulties for its message, *Risk II* pleaded that Americans had lapsed into a state of complacency about their schools, and it labeled critiques of the schools-in-crisis mentality as mere "fantasy." Recent poor international showing of American high schoolers on math and science was a key piece of new cannon fodder for the movement. Also, *Risk II* trotted out the tried-and-true straw men, including my favorite, supposedly held by "many educators" that "some boys and girls—especially those from 'the other side of the tracks'—just can't be expected to learn much." Demonstrating such concern for America's down-trodden provided much needed modernization for the crusaders' message.

Still, the take-home message of *Risk II* was the same as always: The nation's in peril because American schools are in a state of crisis. And the way to fix the problem was also essentially the same, but with some updated wrinkles. Yes, more standards, testing, and accountability—but make them national ones. Additionally, give parents and students more school "choice," permitting "public dollars to . . . follow individual children to the schools they select."

All such solutions, in my view, will do little to address the root causes of the achievement gaps between rich and poor. In fact, these solutions constitute highly flammable rocket fuel that will make the underlying problems all the more severe, wasteful, and tragic.

STOPPING THE DAMAGE

The lesson for parents, taxpayers, and policymakers seems clear.   55 Addressing the real problems with American schools means coming to grips with the relationships between academic success and the pervasive influences of class, poverty, and race. I don't mean to be glib, but perhaps the very best way a parent can ensure their children's success in the school system, in terms of achievement and attainment, would be to obtain as much education for oneself as possible. But to do so, parents need the help of policymakers. If politicians are really interested in promoting equality, improving schools, and helping the American economy, they would, at a minimum, tear down false barriers to educational attainment that have been erected in the era of school accountability, barriers that have no proven benefit.

Indeed, if government can't feasibly "buy" equality in the schools owing to the political infeasibility of doing so in these neo-conservative times, policymakers could try an alternatively novel approach, one of a genuinely conservative bent. How about just *get out* of the nation's classrooms? I'd like to stipulate for policymakers a maxim from the medical profession: First and foremost, *DO NO HARM*. In other words, if policymakers' endless tinkering, controlling, measuring, punishing, and manipulating of schools has failed children, the best thing they could do would be to stop hurting them.

To do that, state legislatures must go back to basics about the role of schools in a democratic society. In a larger society that tends to produce great inequalities between socioeconomic classes and ethnic groups, public schools have little place being a regulatory or credentialing agency that places the Good Housekeeping Seal of Approval on a school system's graduates. Schools should not be handmaidens to American business interests, which demand cheap and easy—and publicly subsidized—certification of alleged competency through achievement scores. *Public schools ought to have one overarching purpose in a free society: Provide citizens an opportunity to learn and ensure that those opportunities are equal across the lines of class and race.* American citizens ought to begin to question any public policy that does harm to that simple purpose. The public should apply their well-honed skepticism of modern institutions to hold accountable the accountability machine itself.

But a few affirmative, practical steps are in order as well. I would not go so far as to suggest that standardized tests have no legitimate purpose in American schools. In fact, they do; and that purpose is to periodically take the pulse of achievement but do so in a way that doesn't interfere with what should be the real business of schools: teaching and learning for understanding and long-term, sustainable achievement.

That means policymakers need to defang standardized testing programs, exorcizing the punishing consequences of poor test scores for students, teachers, and schools. Schools should compile and report testing data only for broad educational jurisdictions, and do so in terms of running averages over several years. That alone would discourage public and media obsession with meaningless, short-term changes in test results. States should reduce the economic drain of testing programs by rotating schools through the assessment system on a sampling basis. Doing this would also ensure that the test is broad in content, so results are sufficiently reliable and are an adequate indication of broad levels of student achievement. In short, such a test would be guided by the maxim that educational policymakers, first and foremost, *Do no harm.*

Alas, it might surprise some readers to learn that such a "test" already exists. In fact, it's been functioning remarkably well as America's educational barometer for some thirty years, and it's called the National Assessment of Educational Progress. Indeed, the NAEP isn't even really a test, in the sense standardized tests have come to mean in the accountability era. In a very real sense, NAEP, known as America's "report card," is simply a regularly

60

conducted national survey of educational achievement in reading, writing, math, science, geography, and U.S. history, of Americans in grade school, middle school, and high school.

A report by the U.S. Office of Technology Assessment reminds us of the beauty of NAEP. "The designers of the NAEP project took extreme care and built in many safeguards to ensure that a national assessment would not, in the worst fears of its critics, become any of the following: a stepping stone to a national individual testing program, a tool for Federal control of curriculum, a weapon to 'blast' the schools, a deterrent to curricular change, or a vehicle for student selection or funds allocation decisions."

Between the politically sensitive lines of that OTA report is a grave and prescient concern over any attempt to tinker with the NAEP that transforms it into a national standardized test along the lines of the Clinton and Bush administrations' proposals, a national test complete with individual scores and the horse-race mentality that invariably accompanies such an approach. Commenting on the safeguards built into the NAEP that recent national testing proposals had threatened to undermine, the University of North Carolina's Lyle Jones, one of the original technical advisers on NAEP's development, says, "Were these features not to have been maintained, I believe that NAEP would have become so controversial that it would not have survived to be the useful indicator of educational progress that it is today."

The NAEP should be left alone, and it should remain the nation's report card. It's the only report card America really needs.

As anybody who's gone to school knows, there's certain beauty in a report card, that periodic summary boys and girls have taken home to moms and dads since the beginnings of formal public education in the United States. Whether they're compiled in terms of As, Bs, or Cs, in the precise terms of decimal points, or even in narrative form in a teachers' handwriting, a report card is a meaningful thing.

A report card is a simple summation of a teacher's intimate   65
and expert knowledge of a child's progress in school to that point. It is a simple answer to simple questions: *How am I doing? How's my child doing?*

And we all know this truth: A teacher knows. Teachers, working day in and day out with a child, who sees, hears, and reads the real work that child has actually accomplished at school, know. When parents really want to know the answer to the question, *How is my child doing?* they also know this: They go to the teacher, and they ask.

Teachers write down what they know about schoolwork of boys and girls in the report card. Parents have always put good report cards on the refrigerator door, and they have always known what a good report card meant. It meant keep up the good work. And they have always known what a bad report card meant. It meant there was room for improvement. It meant "work harder," "study more." Teachers and moms and dads did not need a standardized test or an accountability system to tell them what they already knew. They did not need to put the standardized test scores on the refrigerator door.

Thinking About Content

1. Sacks asserts that "class is paramount" when it comes to students' success in school. How does he support this claim?
2. How does Sacks propose we stop the damage being done in America's schools?

Thinking About Strategy

1. Sacks begins his essay on class and education by summarizing some of the many problems with the recent movement in America toward high-stakes standardized testing. What are the effects of such an opening?
2. What is the purpose of including secondary research in a piece of writing? How does Sacks's knowledge of educational research add to his credibility on his topic?

The Role of Higher Education in Social Mobility

ROBERT HAVEMAN AND TIMOTHY SMEEDING

Robert Haveman is John Bascom Professor Emeritus of Economics and Public Affairs at the University of Wisconsin–Madison. Timothy Smeeding is Maxwell Professor of Public Policy at the Maxwell School of Syracuse University. The following article was published in the fall of 2006 in The Future of Children, *a publication of the Woodrow Wilson School of Public Policy and International Affairs at Princeton University and the Brookings Institution, a private, nonprofit research organization that focuses on independent research and public policy solutions.*

───────────── ✦ ─────────────

Median income in 2000 for Americans with a bachelor's degree or higher was more than double that for high school graduates.[1] By 2010, 42 percent of all new U.S. jobs are expected to require a postsecondary degree.[2] Tomorrow, even more than today, postsecondary education will be among the most important determinants of labor market success, and therefore one of the nation's most crucial means of reducing persistent economic inequalities. President George W. Bush, among others, considers education a primary force for economic and social mobility in the United States. Indeed, during the second 2004 presidential debate, he cited it as the single most important means of improving mobility and leveling social and economic differences.

Traditionally, the nation's higher education system, especially its public component, has had two primary goals: economic efficiency and social equity. As to the first, without collective intervention in support of higher education, individuals by themselves are unlikely to invest sufficiently in postsecondary schooling, because they fail to take into account the social benefits that accrue to their added spending. Hence, a strictly market-based approach to postsecondary schooling would provide the nation's labor force with insufficient advanced skills and training. Society thus subsidizes postsecondary schooling in a variety of ways—through preferential loans, public provision, and below-cost tuition.

In addition to promoting economic efficiency, collective measures to support higher education have a second goal—to contribute to an "even start" for the nation's youth. The case for public provision of higher education and for public financial support to reduce the private costs of higher education (indeed, the case for public education in general) has long rested on the desire to reduce the connection between parents' social class and their children's economic position as adults.

However, despite past U.S. efforts to promote postsecondary schooling for youth from lower-income backgrounds, evidence is mounting that income-related gaps both in access to higher education and in college graduation rates are large and growing. About 85 percent of eighth-grade students in the United States aspire to a college degree.[3] But in 2001, only 44 percent of high school graduates from the bottom quintile of the income distribution were enrolled in college in the October after they graduated from high school, as against almost 80 percent of those in the upper quintile.[4] Thomas Kane reports that even among students with similar test scores and class ranks and from identical schools, students from higher-income families are significantly more likely than those from lower-income families to attend college, particularly four-year colleges.[5] Indeed, since the 1970s students from lower-income families have increasingly become clustered in public two-year postsecondary institutions, which often turn out to be the end of their formal education.[6]

These disparities in college access lead to widening gaps in   5
the share of students remaining in college until graduation. Of eighth graders surveyed in the National Education Longitudinal Study (NELS) of 1988 conducted by the Department of Education, 51 percent from the highest socioeconomic quartile reported having a bachelor's degree twelve years later, as against only 7 percent of those from the lowest quartile.[7] Melanie Corrigan reports that 59 percent of low-income students who began postsecondary education in 1998 had a degree or were still in school three years later, as against 75 percent of higher-income students.[8] Students from low-income families are less likely than students from high-income families to estimate accurately the cost of college, more likely to take remedial courses in college, and less likely to understand the college application process, in part because their parents did not attend college themselves and in part because their high schools, which send few students on to four-year baccalaureate degrees, lack useful and timely advice on college preparation.[9]

HIGHER EDUCATION, INEQUALITY, AND SOCIAL MOBILITY

The traditional role of colleges and universities in promoting social mobility has attracted the attention of both policymakers and social science researchers. In his discussion of what he calls "education-based meritocracy," John Goldthorpe explains that a merit-based higher education system can offset the role of social class in determining economic outcomes. In a merit-based system, he notes, postsecondary schooling is a filter that keeps parents' economic position from simply passing straight through to their children, thus simultaneously promoting economic efficiency, social justice, and social mobility.[10]

Goldthorpe posits three requirements for moving toward a less class-based society. First, the link between individuals' social origins and their schooling must increasingly reflect *only* their ability. Second, the link between their schooling and their eventual employment must be *strengthened* by qualifications acquired through education. And third, the link between schooling and employment must become *constant* for individuals of differing social origins.[11]

Goldthorpe notes that Michael Young, in his important 1958 book on *The Rise of Meritocracy*, feared that in Britain the effect of higher education on social equality was being undermined by the interaction of public policies, the selectivity of colleges and universities, and evolving labor-hiring practices. He notes that Young was concerned about the way that "the purposes of the Education Act of 1944 were being interpreted by post-war governments. The Act established 'secondary education for all,' and was intended to give all children the fullest possible opportunity to develop their abilities, whatever form or level they might take."[12] In Young's view, the 1944 law was being used increasingly as a means of social selection—in the name of "merit"—for different grades of employment with differing levels of reward in terms both of money and of status.

Young's fear, in mid-twentieth-century Britain, was that the employment process was undermining the goal of social equality. Today, however, the selection processes within higher education itself also appear to be a problem. The high concentration in the nation's colleges and universities of youth from the top echelons of parental income and social class is disturbing and appears to be increasing. It exists at all levels of postsecondary schooling but is especially evident at the nation's best (most selective) colleges and universities.

Two forces, operating in different directions, appear to have caused these growing inequalities. First, increasingly affluent higher-income parents with one or two children invest time, money, and influence to ensure their children's academic success from preschool through graduate school. And second, children of less well-educated and less well-to-do parents begin the "college education game" later, with fewer choices and fewer resources. For example, in 2000 parents at the ninetieth percentile of the income distribution had available an average of $50,000 to support each child, including his or her schooling, as against $9,000 per child for families in the tenth percentile.[13]

Although resilience, luck, and persistence pay off for a minority of low-income children, the odds are increasingly stacked against their success.[14] Therefore, policies designed to address these inequalities should focus not simply on the point at which students move from secondary to postsecondary education, but on the long-term path from kindergarten through college graduation.

Contrary to its stated goals and repeated claims, the U.S. higher education system fails to equalize opportunities among students from high- and low-income families. Rather, the current process of admission to, enrollment in, and graduation from colleges and universities contributes to economic inequality as measured by income and wealth. The system thus seems to intensify and reinforce differences in economic status. Though college attendance rates are rising, college graduation rates for U.S. students are growing slowly, if at all, and changes in the composition of the college-eligible and college-graduating populations appear to perpetuate existing class differences. If so, the current system of higher education will contribute to growing income and wealth inequality, which in turn will exacerbate these inequalities across future generations.

Does this mean that higher education retards social mobility? Not necessarily. But it seems clear that higher education does not promote social equality as effectively as it often claims to do and as it is popularly perceived to do.[15] We therefore suggest some policies that would increase and equalize access to higher education and hence improve social mobility.

In this article, we explore the broad issues facing educators and policymakers seeking to eliminate income- and wealth-related disparities in college attendance and graduation. We first summarize some research findings and present some new measures of inequality in college access and enrollment. We then explore how elementary and secondary education contribute to inequality in postsecondary education, as well as how differences in the kind of information available to youth of different backgrounds affect how they apply to college, how they navigate the admission process, and once they are admitted, how long they continue in college and whether they graduate. We also consider the implications for college success of the different varieties of higher education, including the community college system and remediation programs designed to ease inequalities among enrolled students. Each is important for assessing the overall effect of higher education on both economic inequality and mobility. Finally, we suggest policies that would enable higher education to enhance social mobility and advance the life chances of disadvantaged children.[16] We concentrate on the most recent trends in college-going, but refer to the work of others who present evidence on longer trends in earlier periods.[17]

ON HIGHER EDUCATION AND SOCIAL MOBILITY: WHAT DO WE KNOW?

One of the stated objectives of the nation's colleges and universities   15
is to be a meritocratic filter between the economic position of the families in which children grow up and those children's economic position as adults. Higher education is expected to promote the goal of social mobility and to make it possible for anyone with ability and motivation to succeed. To be effective in this role, colleges and universities must seek out ability, motivation, and preparedness wherever it lies and then provide high-quality educational services to their students. The labor market will do the rest, rewarding those who acquire the skills that the nation's postsecondary system has to offer.[18]

How well are college and university admission, training, and completion fostering this meritocratic goal? If true "merit" could be measured, answering that question would be easy. One could simply assess the extent to which the most meritorious youth were being sought out, admitted, and trained. Indeed, if merit—ability, motivation, and preparedness—were equally distributed among youth regardless of family income or economic position, an effective higher education sector would offer an equal chance of admission and graduation to all—high-income and low-income youth alike. But ability, motivation, and preparedness are all linked to the economic position of the children's families. Children from well-to-do families tend, on average, to have more of all three traits; children from disadvantaged families, to have less. Genetics plays a role in the allocation of ability and motivation, as do the choices made by and the environment created by families of differing incomes. As for preparedness, the nation's primary and secondary school systems train youth from various economic backgrounds for postsecondary schooling. Other articles in this volume address these precollege patterns.[19]

The absence of a reliable merit marker makes it more difficult to assess how well higher education promotes social mobility. One would be surprised if rates of college admission, matriculation, and graduation were equal regardless of families' varying economic circumstances, and as we will show, they are not. The question, then, becomes whether the inequality in the provision of higher education services is consistent with a pattern of training being offered to those with the most merit. Even more relevant, perhaps, is whether the inequality in higher educational attainment is increasing or decreasing.

Levels and Trends in Economic Inequality in Higher Education

Table 2.1 presents an overview of some of the findings of David Ellwood and Thomas Kane in their review of early research on the relationship between schooling and economic background over time. The type of schooling described in the table, college-going, says little about total years of completed schooling or college graduation. For students who graduated from high school during 1980–82, the overall rate of college-going is 80 percent for youth from the top income quartile of families, as against 57 percent for youth from the bottom quartile. Youth from the poorest families

Table 2.1 Proportion of Students Who Enroll in Colleges and Universities within 20 Months of Graduating from High School

Percent

Cohort	Total	Vocational/ technical school	2-year college	4-year college
High school class of 1980–82				
Bottom quartile	57	12	16	29
Top quartile	80	6	19	55
Total	68	10	19	39
High school class of 1992				
Bottom quartile	60	10	22	28
Top quartile	90	5	19	66
Total	75	7	23	45

Source: David Ellwood and Thomas J. Kane, "Who is Getting a College Education: Family Background and the Growing Gaps in Enrollment," in *Securing the Future: Investing in Children from Birth to College*, edited by Sheldon Danziger and Jane Waldfogel (New York: Russell Sage Foundation, 2000). Data are taken from the High School and Beyond study.

were concentrated in vocational and technical institutions, while those from the richest families tended to enroll in four-year colleges.[20]

Between 1980–82 and 1992, the overall college enrollment rate rose 7 percentage points. But the rate for the highest-income youth increased 10 points, while the rate for the lowest-income youth increased only 3 points. In terms of attendance at four-year colleges, the gap between the highest- and lowest-income youth widened far more during this period. While the share of most disadvantaged youth enrolled in four-year colleges *fell* slightly (from 29 to 28 percent), that for the most well-to-do youth *rose* substantially (from 55 to 66 percent). The gap between the two groups widened from 26 percentage points to 38 percentage points.[21]

Inequality and the Quality of Colleges and Universities

The patterns revealed by Ellwood and Kane are consistent with tabulations of Anthony Carnevale and Stephen Rose, who analyzed detailed data from the High School and Beyond study and from the NELS of 1988.[22] They divided all four-year colleges and universities into four tiers by quality, based on the Barron index of college selectivity, putting community colleges into a separate category; and divided all families into four socioeconomic status categories, based on their income and parental education and occupation.[23] Their findings are summarized in table 2.2.

Table 2.2 Socioeconomic Status of Entering Classes, by College Selectivity

Percent		
	Socioeconomic status quartile[a]	
Colleges grouped by selectivity	**Bottom**	**Top**
Tier 1	3	74
Tier 2	7	46
Tier 3	10	35
Tier 4	16	35
Community colleges	21	22

Source: Anthony P. Carnevale and Stephen J. Rose, "Socioeconomic Status, Race/Ethnicity, and Selective College Admission," in *America's Untapped Resource: Low-Income Students in Higher Education,* edited by Richard D. Kahlenberg (New York: Century Foundation Press, 2004), pp. 101–56. Data are from the National Education Longitudinal Study of 1988.

a. Compared to 25 percent of all youth in each quartile.

In the 146 top-tier colleges and universities (accounting for about 10 percent of all college students), 74 percent of the entering class is from the highest socioeconomic quartile and only 3 percent from the lowest quartile. In the 253 colleges in the second tier (accounting for about 18 percent of all college students), the shares are 46 and 7 percent, respectively. Only in community colleges is the composition of entering students by family socioeconomic status similar to the composition of all youth of college age.[24]

Patterns of Educational Attainment by Family Permanent Income

These family income–related gaps in higher education attainment rely on estimates of income that are somewhat difficult to interpret, and in some cases are suspect. First, among the national data collected, income values are sometimes for the households in which students reside, and hence do not necessarily pertain to the parents of these children.[25] Second, for some data sources, parental income is supplied by the students themselves in response to survey questions, and these responses are suspect.[26] Third, none of these studies allows for the "income needs" of the families of the youth being studied. It clearly matters whether a student from a family with $50,000 a year of income is an only child or has several siblings who are also competing for family resources. Finally, and most important, the parental or family income data are one-year "snapshot" (or transitory) values and hence fail to reflect the long-term (or "permanent") economic position of students' families.[27]

Robert Haveman and Kathryn Wilson proceeded in a somewhat different way to get a reliable picture of inequalities in higher education attainment for a specific cohort of youth. Using the Michigan Panel Survey of Income Dynamics (PSID), they selected a nationally representative sample of 1,210 children who were born between 1966 and 1970 and followed them from 1968, the first year of the PSID (or their year of birth, if later), until 1999. This cohort would be expected to graduate from high school in the late 1980s and from college in the early 1990s. The authors measured educational outcomes—high school graduation, college attendance, college graduation, and years of schooling—at age twenty-five. For each individual, they also calculated permanent income relative to "needs" and the wealth of the family in which he or she grew up. The ratio of income to needs is the average real value of the family's income while the youths were aged two to

fifteen, divided by the national poverty line (for a family of that
size) and the average wealth (net worth) of the family in 1984,
when the youths ranged in age from fourteen to eighteen.[28]
Table 2.3 summarizes the educational attainment of youth
from the bottom and the top quartiles and deciles of family "permanent" income-to-needs ratios.[29] While only about 22 percent of
youth from the bottom quartile of families attended college,
71 percent from families in the top quartile at least entered a college or university. The gap is nearly 50 percentage points. Among
the youth from the top quartile, 42–44 percent graduated from
college, as against only 6–9 percent of youth in the bottom quartile, a gap of more than 35 percentage points. Transitions from
high school graduation to college attendance and from college
attendance to college graduation are also shown. Again, substantial gaps exist between youth from the highest and lowest quartiles in the probability of making these transitions. The gaps

**Table 2.3 Educational Attainment of 1966–70 Birth Cohort, by
Decile and Quartile of Family Average Income-to-Needs Ratio[a]**

Percent

	Decile		Quartile	
Educational attainment	**Bottom**	**Top**	**Bottom**	**Top**
Share of cohort graduating from high school	56.8	97.7	64.1	96.1
Share of cohort attending college	19.5	78.2	21.6	71.2
Share of high school graduates attending college	34.3	80.0	33.8	74.1
Share of cohort graduating from college	6.3	49.1	5.6	42.1
Share of those attending college who graduate	32.3	62.8	25.9	59.1
Years of schooling	11.2	14.6	11.8	14.2

Source: Robert Haveman and Kathryn Wilson, "Economic Inequality in College Access,
Matriculation, and Graduation," conference on "Economic Inequality and Higher Education: Access, Persistence and Success," Maxwell School of Syracuse University, September
23–24, 2005. Data are from the Michigan Panel Study of Income Dynamics (PSID).

a. The ratio of income to needs is the average real value of the family's income while the
youths were aged two to fifteen, divided by the national poverty line (for a family of that
size) and the average wealth (net worth) of the family in 1984, when the youths ranged
in age from fourteen to eighteen.

between the attainment levels of youth from the top and bottom deciles are even greater, suggesting a continuous relationship between economic status and educational attainment.

The pattern of extreme inequality between youth from the   25
top and bottom quartiles of the family income-to-needs ratio is similar in terms of the allocation of educational services. Table 2.4 shows the distribution of all high school graduates, college attendees, and college graduates in this cohort of youth, by decile and quartile of family income-to-needs ratio. Among high school graduates, nearly 30 percent are from the top income quartile, while about 20 percent are from the bottom quartile. At least in terms of attainment—though not necessarily in terms of quality-adjusted attainment—high school educational services are distributed relatively evenly among children from various economic backgrounds. The pattern for college graduates, however, is quite different. Among all college graduates in this cohort, more than 50 percent are from families with income-to-needs ratios in the top quarter of the nation, while only 7 percent are from the lowest quarter of families. Similarly, the 10 percent of families in the lowest income-to-needs decile yield less than 3 percent of college graduates. Put differently, half of all higher educational services necessary for attaining a college degree are allocated to youth from the richest quarter of the nation's

Table 2.4 Distribution of 1966–70 Birth Cohort at Selected Levels of Educational Attainment, by Decile and Quartile of Family Average Income-to-Needs Ratio[a]

Percent						
Educational attainment	**Decile**		**Quartile**			
	Bottom	**Top**	**Bottom**	**Third**	**Second**	**Top**
High school graduate	6.6	11.6	19.0	25.2	27.1	28.7
Attended college	4.2	17.1	11.8	20.6	28.3	39.2
College graduate	2.9	23.2	6.6	17.4	25.9	50.1

Source: See table 2.3.

a. The ratio of income to needs is the average real value of the family's income while the youths were aged two to fifteen, divided by the national poverty line (for a family of that size) and the average wealth (net worth) of the family in 1984, when the youths ranged in age from fifteen to eighteen.

families, as against only 7 percent allocated to youth from the poorest 25 percent of families and only 3 percent to youth from the poorest 10 percent of families.

How Large Is the Pool of Qualified Low-Income Students?

The question of whether colleges and universities have been making enough effort to admit and enroll qualified students is difficult to answer. The definition of "qualified" is directly related to the selection standards that schools themselves define and impose. Two studies have tried to answer this question for the highest-quality and most selective U.S. colleges and universities, and both have concluded that the available pool of qualified youth is far greater than the group of students admitted and enrolled at these institutions.

The first of these studies, by Carnevale and Rose, uses a simulation approach for 146 top-tier colleges and universities (again, accounting for about 10 percent of all college students). They consider an "SAT equivalent" score above 1,000 as evidence of ability to succeed at these first-tier schools, and then compare the share of low-income students who are qualified with the share of these students who are enrolled. Among students with scores above the cutoff, 5 percent were from the bottom socioeconomic quarter (3 percent of comparable students were enrolled), as against 21 percent from the bottom half (10 percent of comparable students were enrolled). More than 800,000 students had an SAT equivalent score of more than 1,000—four-and-a-half times the total number of student slots at the first-tier schools.[30]

More recently, Gordon Winston and Catharine Hill have used a similar approach to determine whether the nation's most prestigious colleges and universities (twenty-eight of the private colleges participating in the Consortium on Financing Higher Education) could increase their enrollment of low-income students without sacrificing academic standards. Using an SAT equivalent score of 1,420 as the cutoff for "high ability," they show that 12.8 percent of all high-ability students are from the bottom two income quintiles, a total of about 4,300 students. Today these colleges matriculate only about 2,750 such students, leading the authors to conclude that the colleges could enroll more such students without decreasing selection standards.[31]

In focusing on the top-quality colleges and universities, these studies do not address the larger problem of lower-scoring but nevertheless qualified low-income students who attend less selective schools. Indeed, more than three-quarters of all college students attend colleges and universities that do not impose high selectivity standards.[32] Hence, even if the most selective colleges and universities admitted qualified low-income youth, there would still be a nontrivial attendance gap between the rich and the poor.

Indeed, part of the gap between low-income students' popula-   30
tion share and their enrollment in colleges and universities is due to low test scores and other indicators of ability that are indirectly related to family income. For example, although 36 percent of low-income students at high-income high schools were in the top half of the test score distribution, only 24 percent of low-income students at low-income high schools scored at this level.

Although this evidence regarding the effectiveness of higher education's meritocratic filter is not decisive, these gaps are large. More significant, they appear to be growing. Colleges and universities may aspire to weaken the link between family socioeconomic class and life prospects, but their efforts have been discouraging—particularly in the case of the four-year colleges and universities, the traditional heart of the higher education system, producing the highest-quality educational services. In sum, the allocation of educational services (especially services of the highest quality) is concentrated among youth from families with the highest economic status, and the concentration appears to be increasing. This trend has been reinforced by the erosion in state financial support for public higher education over past years, as spending on other priorities, such as medical care for low-income families, criminal justice, and K–12 education has been substituted for support of public colleges and universities.[33]

Slow Growth in College Graduation Rates: Some International Evidence

At a time when the links between U.S. students' economic origins and their attainment of higher education are strengthening, progress in increasing the number of U.S. college graduates has stalled.[34] Indeed, for any given cohort, there has been virtually no change over the past two decades in the share of youth who have been awarded a postsecondary degree. Figure 2.1 compares schooling for two cohorts observed in 2002—one aged twenty-five to thirty-four (born 1966–75), the other aged forty-five to fifty-four (born 1946–55)—in fourteen industrialized nations. With two exceptions—reunified Germany and the United States—the

Figure 2.1 Percentage of the Population that has attained Postsecondary Education, 2002

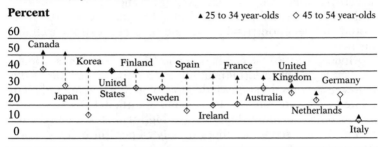

Source: Dirk Pilat, "Canada's Productivity Performance in Comparative Perspective." *International Productivity Monitor* (Ottawa: Center for the Study of Living Standards), no. 10 (2005): 24–40; OECD, *Education at a Glance* (Paris: 2004), table A3.3, p. 71.

share of adults with a postsecondary degree has increased in every country. Although the older U.S. cohort ranked second in the share of adults with a postsecondary degree (about 40 percent), the younger cohort ranked fifth. Four countries had gained parity with the United States or forged ahead, with Canada and Japan outpacing the United States by 10 percentage points. Another five countries had closed the gap to less than 5 percentage points. Only Italy trailed behind by more than 15 percentage points. If U.S. colleges and universities had been able to increase the rate of college graduation over this period, they would likely have been able to serve greater shares of youth from lower-income families, thus weakening the link between family economic origins and postsecondary attainment. The increased concentration of youth from higher-income families in America's colleges and universities, together with the constant rate of college completion, seems consistent with a trend toward zero-sum competition among institutions for a relatively constant stock of the best qualified students—who also are concentrated in the nation's highest-income families.[35]

THE EFFECT OF POSTSECONDARY SCHOOLING ON EARNINGS

Higher education influences social mobility not only because family income affects schooling but also because schooling affects the income of adult children. Research on the link between schooling and earnings is extensive.

In a recent review of research, Orley Ashenfelter, Colm Harmon, and Hessel Oosterbeek compare the findings of several types of studies of the labor market returns to education. They find that across twenty-seven studies in nine countries, the market-based returns to schooling are large and robust, ranging from 6.6 to 9.3 percent. After adjusting for "publication bias" (the tilt inherent in the scholarly publication process leading to a higher probability of acceptance for studies with statistically significant results), they find estimated rates of return between 6.8 and 8.1 percent for the United States.[36]

Building on these overall findings, a few studies have esti-   35
mated how returns to schooling differ by quality and type of institution. Thomas Kane and Cecilia Rouse find that the returns to one credit at a two-year or four-year college are roughly 4–6 percent for every thirty completed credits. They find, further, that the "sheepskin effect" of degree completion over and above the value of the credits completed is small but positive for men who complete a B.A. and for women who complete the associate's degree.[37] Researchers have also estimated returns to the quality of four-year college. One study finds positive effects of elite colleges on earnings.[38] But another finds that students who attend more elite colleges do not earn more than students who were accepted by comparable colleges, but attended less elite colleges.[39]

Similarly, a few studies have sought to identify the lifetime returns to education for youths from different socioeconomic backgrounds. In general, the earnings gains for students from high-income families exceed those for students from low-income families. For example, Jeff Grogger and Eric Eide indicate that, controlling for other characteristics, the discounted present value of income gains over the first nine years of work for white males with high grades in high school is 8 percent greater when family income is in the $70,000 annual income range than for students from families with annual income in the $30,000 range.[40] Similar differences exist for students with other characteristics.

STEPS IN THE COLLEGE PROCESS

Clearly, high-income youth are overrepresented in U.S. colleges. Why they are overrepresented, however, is not well understood. In this section we summarize what is known about how family background affects each of the steps in the process of applying to, securing admission to, and graduating from the nation's colleges and universities.

Preparing for College and Applying for Admission

Students must overcome several hurdles to succeed in postsecondary education, and the overall process is complex. First, students must be well-prepared in elementary and secondary school (see the article by Cecilia Elena Rouse and Lisa Barrow in this issue). High schools in poor and minority neighborhoods, however, tend to be of low quality and to lack the resources, both financial and human, to prepare students adequately for postsecondary schooling.[41] Rigorous courses in all fields, but especially mathematics, are rare in these high schools, as are opportunities for honors course work or advanced placement—making it hard for students to build a proper academic foundation for college work. One study finds that only half of low-income high school graduates in 1992 who applied for admission to a four-year institution were "minimally qualified" to enroll, as against more than 80 percent of students from families with incomes of $75,000 or more.[42] Some observers claim that the nation's secondary schools give students poor signals about the preparation needed to succeed in higher education because advocates and policymakers overemphasize "access" as opposed to "preparation."[43]

Nor do poor-quality high schools support and teach the study and work habits necessary for postsecondary success. Although the reasons for poor student motivation are surely complex and lie in part with the families and neighborhoods in which children are raised, the discipline and standards set by the nation's poorest schools also contribute.

The poor quality of schools in low-income neighborhoods also affects how much students know about how to select colleges, apply for admission, and gain acceptance. A recent study highlights some of the difficulties these students encounter. Thomas Kane reports data from a Boston program showing that inner-city, primarily minority students, report plans to attend college similar to those of their suburban, primarily white, counterparts. But only a third of the inner-city students had taken the SAT exam by October of their senior year, as against 97 percent of the suburban students.[44] Further, the low-income and minority students and their parents were ill-informed about the cost of attending college and were often put off by the high "sticker prices" emphasized by the media.[45] They were also unfamiliar with the availability of needs-based financial aid.

Michael Timpane and Arthur Hauptman provide a comprehensive discussion of academic preparation and performance and offer suggestions for improving both. They recommend that

40

colleges and universities help improve K–12 education (for example, through teacher preparation and partnerships with elementary and secondary schools). They also support moves to help students make the transition from high school to college (for example, through increasing high school graduation standards and providing support services and early interventions), strengthening remediation programs, and improving the performance of low-income students while in college.[46]

Finding and Getting Financial Aid

According to the College Board, financial aid for undergraduates and graduate students totaled more than $122 billion in 2003–04, an 11 percent increase from the previous year, over and above inflation. Federal guaranteed loans account for about half of that total. Other federal support made up another 20 percent, with Pell grants constituting about three-quarters of that. State and institutional support made up the remaining 30 percent. But though financial aid itself is rising, the share targeted on low-income students has been falling, as needs-based assistance has been increasingly replaced by merit-based aid.

According to most recent analyses, trends in family income, tuition, and financial aid policy have most adversely affected those students least able to afford postsecondary schooling. For example, college prices (in real terms, net of inflation) were nearly flat during the 1970s but increased rapidly during the 1980s and 1990s, when tuition rose two and even three times as fast as the price of other consumer goods.[47] This trend, together with the growing inequality of family income, has raised the cost of attending college far more for students in low-income families than for those in well-to-do families. In the early 1970s, paying for a child to attend a public four-year college absorbed 42 percent of the income of a low-income family; by the 2000s, it took nearly 60 percent; for students from high-income families, the increase in income share was from 5 percent to 6 percent.[48] Moreover, students from lower-income families are more sensitive to tuition increases than students from higher-income families.[49]

Although these cost increases have been partially offset by increased student financial aid, the evidence suggests that major disparities continue to exist. In 2001 the Advisory Committee on Student Financial Assistance reported that "unmet need" is substantially higher for low-income students than for others, whether they attend public or private, four-year or two-year, colleges.[50] Several studies have tried to track the recent changes in the effective price of college attendance, taking account of changes in both financial aid and tuition. Amy Schwartz has summarized her own estimates as follows:

> Evidence shows that sticker prices are rising, but increases in financial aid have been significantly offsetting. For two-year colleges, most of which are public institutions, the trend in net prices has been downward and current net prices are, on average, *negative*. Among four-year colleges, the net price of public colleges declined in the last decade with some modest increases in the last few years offsetting a larger decrease in the 1990s. The trend for four-year private colleges, however, has been unambiguously positive—net prices are significantly higher than a decade ago.[51]

Moreover, financial aid has increasingly come in the form of loans, rather than grants.[52] During the early 1980s, for example, grants made up 55 percent of student aid; by 2001, that figure was down to 41 percent. By 2001, loans to students and parents by the federal government totaled nearly $40 billion, more than five times the resources of the Pell grant program that was meant to be the primary source of assistance to low-income students. Although the maximum Pell grant covered about 60 percent of the cost of attending a four-year public institution in the early 1980s, it covered only about 40 percent by 2001.[53]

Michael McPherson and Morton Schapiro have concluded that colleges and universities are increasingly abandoning ability-to-pay principles and using student financial aid both to maximize net tuition revenue and to meet their goals for student quality. Merit scholarships and other forms of non-needs-based assistance have grown over time, resulting in more aid to affluent students.[54]

In more recent work, McPherson and Schapiro track changes in merit and needs-based financial aid and find that at all institutions, low-income students receive more grant aid than high-income students, across the range of SAT scores. But at private colleges and universities, the gap in aid between low- and high-income students increased as aid for low-income students fell, relative to that afforded high-income students. Over the 1990s, among students with the highest SAT scores, low-income students received 4.9 times as much aid during 1992–93, but only 2.8 times as much during 1999–2000. The authors suggest that this movement of grant dollars toward higher-income families reflects not a greater "demand" for students with high SAT scores, but rather an excess supply of places at selective private colleges, leading to a bidding down of the price through greater tuition discounts.[55]

At public colleges and universities, on the other hand, student aid awards rose more rapidly with need, and the "net price" facing low-income students declined during the 1990s. But state budget difficulties since 2000 suggest this trend may be ending. Moreover, more complicated rules about how much interest lenders can charge on student loans have led to new legislation reducing subsidies to lenders, negatively affecting the cost and targeting of federally subsidized student loan programs.[56]

One important issue is the extent to which the increase in merit-based assistance has increased the overall level of college attendance and completion. Susan Dynarski concludes that programs providing a substantial increase in merit-based student aid (thought of as tuition reduction) have increased both college attendance and students' persistence in working toward a degree, especially among women, and in particular, nonwhite women.[57] Her evidence, however, does not effectively account for the possibility that colleges and universities may have offset external increases in student aid by increasing tuition.[58]

Community Colleges

Community colleges and associate's degree programs play an important but as yet poorly understood role in postsecondary education.[59] Indeed, Dan Goldhaber and Gretchen Kiefer show that although about 40 percent of all postsecondary students attend four-year public universities, lower-income children are twice as likely to attend public two-year (community college or associate's degree) programs than are higher-income children, almost exactly in reverse proportion to the share of higher-income children who attend private, four-year colleges (see Figure 2.2).[60]

Community colleges serve several important functions in postsecondary education. First, they provide the key access point to higher education for nonwhite and Latino students.[61] For instance, almost 60 percent of all Latinos enrolled in higher education enroll first in community colleges.[62] These students are highly tuition-price sensitive and often choose part-time instead of full-time enrollment.[63] Still, a full 30 percent of all community college enrollees want to go on to complete a four-year degree. Indeed, community colleges provide remedial education for students who are not yet qualified for four-year colleges and

50

Figure 2.2 Institutional Choice, by Income Level, 1999–2000[a]

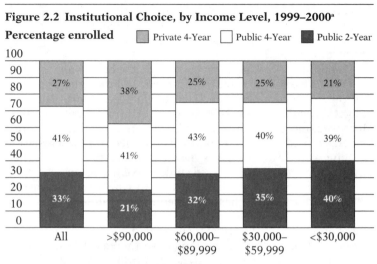

Sources: Reproduced from College Board, *Education Pays 2004* (Washington: College Entrance Examination Board, 2004); Dan Goldhaber and Gretchen Kiefer, "Higher Education and Inequality: The Increasingly Important Role Community Colleges Play in Higher Education," unpublished manuscript, University of Washington, presented to the Maxwell School Conference on Economic Inequality and Higher Education: Access, Persistence and Success, September 23–24, 2005.

a. Values may not sum to 100 percent because of rounding. Percentages include full-time dependent students in the first year of undergraduate study.

universities, though researchers know surprisingly little about this community college function. An estimated 55 percent of all community college students take courses in remedial mathematics or English.[64]

Community colleges also offer technical and occupational training and certificates of competency in some fields, both of which increase the earnings of recipients beyond those of high school graduates.[65] By themselves, however, neither two-year degrees nor certificates lead to additional higher education and baccalaureate degrees. Moreover, students who attend community colleges in search of occupational degrees and certificates are more likely than students at four-year institutions to come from disadvantaged families, to delay enrollment and enroll part time, to interrupt their education, and to cite job skills as the reason for enrolling.[66] The technical training role is not well understood and is complicated by many "nontraditional student" labor market factors. For instance, one recent study estimates that 28 percent of community college enrollees already hold a bachelor's degree and are taking courses to gain a technical certification of competency or for consumption purposes alone.[67]

Still, the primary social mobility role of community colleges lies in their ability to raise college completion rates among low-income children. Indeed, many community colleges are linked to four-year institutions, providing a bridge to a four-year baccalaureate degree, though there is little systematic evidence of such arrangements. Jane Wellman suggests that transfer policies from two- to four-year state colleges, the primary road from community colleges to public institutions granting higher degrees, are not always well articulated by states and that the effectiveness of state policies varies widely.[68] Further development of the National Student Clearinghouse (NSC) database would greatly enhance our ability to gather a more complete picture of this process.[69] According to NSC data, perhaps 30 to 35 percent of community college students transfer to four-year colleges.[70] But Goldhaber and Kiefer suggest that increasing these transfer rates will make capacity in receiving institutions a major policy issue.[71]

In summary, because community colleges are often the initial access point to higher education for disadvantaged students, understanding their role in providing bridges to schools of higher education is essential.

Remediation and Persistence

Being admitted to college does not assure graduation. Indeed Vincent Tinto has noted that "access without support does not ensure equality of opportunity."[72] Low-income students are more likely to be not only academically unprepared, but also psychologically and culturally unprepared, for college. As table 2.3 shows, although 22 percent of youth from the lowest income quartile attend college, only 6 percent graduate. In contrast, half of all students from the highest income quartile who attend college manage to graduate within six years of matriculation. Poorly prepared students tend to be from lower-income backgrounds and are more likely to require remedial courses, additional counseling, and other services, and are therefore less likely to get a degree.[73] For example, in the California State University system, the remediation rate among freshmen is 60 percent, and only

39 percent of remedial students graduate. The problem is similar at community colleges, where 72 percent of students begin expecting to earn a degree and only 23 percent finish.[74]

Nevertheless, remediation efforts appear to be effective. Eric Bettinger and Bridget Long use data from Ohio to assess the effects of remedial programs on students' ultimate success in college. They show that remediation improves educational performance—students who enroll in both math and reading remediation courses are less likely to drop out of school, more likely to complete a bachelor's degree, and less likely to transfer to a lower-level college than similar students not enrolled in these courses. Students in each type of remediation are almost 10 percent less likely to drop out than similar students not in remediation.[75]

SUMMARY AND POLICY OPTIONS

Although overall educational attainment in the United States has risen slightly, the gains are concentrated among high-income children.[76] While the effects of the college selection process have contributed to the substantial and growing concentration of children from higher-income families among the student body, the erosion of public spending for higher education has also played a role. As a result, these institutions have had to rely on some combination of increases in private giving, increased use of own-source funds such as endowments, reductions in costs and services, and increases in tuition and associated fees. This last development works together with the admissions and selection process to reduce access—especially for the offspring of less affluent families—to college and university (and especially community college) education. Finally, public educational assistance has tilted away from youth from low-income families toward the most meritorious and highly qualified youth, and therefore toward those from middle- and higher-income families. These developments come at a time when success in the labor market and in other aspects of social and economic life increasingly requires postsecondary training.

In response to these developments, colleges and universities, together with state governments and secondary schools, must develop financing structures that will both maintain quality and increase access for students from lower-income families. The policies we suggest are premised on the belief that students from high-income families will fare well regardless of ability, so that more of the resources available to secure college admission and matriculation should go to students from lower-income families.

The United States has a uniquely mixed system of public and private higher education. In most other rich nations, where higher education is more universalistic and almost totally public, the cost of higher education is more fully subsidized, but homogeneity may also breed mediocrity. Still, the experiences of these countries can be instructive, as can the U.S. experience. Our policy recommendations are deliberately bold and are designed to increase educational opportunities for low- and middle-income students and therefore to increase intergenerational social and economic mobility. We take as given a pool of high school graduates who want more education, even if they are not fully and equally well prepared for it.

Strengthen Student Preparation

Our first recommendation is to strengthen links between K–12 and postsecondary education and to place a greater emphasis on college preparatory coursework in the former. Students should begin school on a more equal footing, and universal high-quality preschool for all children may be a first step toward that goal. Middle and secondary schools should better prepare their students for higher education in its many forms.

Reducing Scope through Partnering

Colleges and universities should get out of the business of providing services and functions for which they do not have a comparative advantage.[77] These services include remedial education (which at best should be left to community colleges or contract providers), but also dormitories, food services, and back-office operations. Colleges should instead focus on the core competencies in which they specialize. This paring back would be coupled with increased partnering with other service providers—private or public—who specialize in these services. Tuition charges would then be able to reflect the real cost of providing the core educational services, and students and their families could arrange for these related services in separate markets. In addition to reducing the costs of colleges, such a program would probably increase the range of choice available to the potential consumers of these auxiliary services.

Pricing and Performance in Public Higher Education

The vast majority of low-income students will be educated by public universities. Although tuition at public institutions has been rising, it still falls well short of reflecting the real resource cost of the educational services provided. As a result, students who pay the full tuition—largely students from more well-off families—are receiving an implicit subsidy. One somewhat dramatic approach would be for institutions to simultaneously price tuition close to real costs and use the bulk of additional revenue to provide direct student aid targeted at students from low-income families. In addition to addressing the current inequity in the allocation of educational services, such an approach would tend to ration the limited supply of educational services (student slots) to those who value these services the most. Such a solution would also require a heavy advertising plan to make sure that lower-income families understood that the net price of college was far below the sticker price, which is often the only information they have to react to.[78]

Pay for performance is another innovation for public universities to consider. Today, state government financial support to public institutions typically comes in the form of a lump-sum appropriation. As an alternative arrangement, the level of state government support could be tied to the performance of institutions, such as retention rates, graduation rates, the ability to limit cost and tuition increases, or increases in their share of students from below-median-income families. Such an arrangement would have desirable incentive effects and would redistribute resources from low- to high-performing schools. While a number of states have started to set performance benchmarks for state universities, so far they have been reluctant to tie state appropriations to performance. But why not subject postsecondary education to the same pay-for-performance pressures as elementary and secondary education?

Limiting Public Subsidies to Wealthy Private Schools

At present, a substantial amount of federal subsidies (guaranteed student loans, Pell grants, tax subsidies) is made available to students who attend very wealthy institutions. These subsidies could be capped for wealthy universities that are able to increase their available student assistance. The savings of this policy could be redirected to students attending less well-endowed schools, both public and private.

Substituting Public Direct Student Assistance for Institutional Support

As four-year colleges and universities have become increasingly   65
selective in student recruitment, students with the highest qualifications—most often those from the highest-income families—
have been the targets of recruitment efforts and the recipients of
increased merit-based assistance. This trend reflects a variety of
forces, including the desire to increase institutional rankings in
prominent publications, such as *U.S. News and World Report*; the
tastes of faculty and other institutional stakeholders; and the
pursuit of financial gains associated with the rapid increases in
federal merit-based assistance that have been targeted on higher-
income families. These forces are at play in both public and
private higher education.

In response to this trend, state governments (as well as the federal government) could redirect to students the financial support
they now provide to colleges and universities, say, in the form of
higher education vouchers. The direct student assistance could be
targeted toward students from lower-income families. Such an
arrangement would not only enhance equity but also require
schools to compete for students and redirect their attention toward
the tastes and demands of their student constituents and away
from those of other institutional stakeholders, such as faculties.

Lessons from Abroad: Redirecting Public Support for Higher Education

Several countries are experimenting with a relatively new form of
publicly supported student aid, known as income-related loans.
In this system, former students repay debt contingent on their
future incomes, meaning that their ultimate capacity to pay is
given weight, and then only up to a limited point. In other words,
loans are repaid by taxing post-school earnings to recover only
the costs incurred, plus a small interest rate. Australia and New
Zealand, in particular, are in the forefront of these policies. The
especially successful Australian program is being adopted in
Asian nations as well.[79]

CONCLUSION

The U.S. system of higher education reinforces generational patterns of income inequality and is far less oriented toward social
mobility than it should be. If higher education is to improve the

chances for low- and middle-income children to succeed, the current system must be dramatically redirected, and the sooner the better. Big problems, such as those outlined above, require innovative thinking and bold reform.

Notes

1. National Center for Education Statistics, *Digest of Education Statistics* (U.S. Department of Education, 2002), Table 382.
2. M. Lindsay Morris, "Low-Income Women and the Higher Education Act Reauthorization," *On Campus with Women* (Association of American Colleges and Universities) 3, no. 3 (Spring–Summer 2004), www.aacu.org/ocww/volume33_3/national.cfm (accessed on April 25, 2006).
3. Michael Kirst, "Overcoming Educational Inequality: The Role of Elementary and Secondary Education Linkages with Broad Access to Postsecondary Education," paper presented to the conference on Economic Inequality and Higher Education: Access, Persistence and Success, Maxwell School of Syracuse University, September 23–24, 2005 (hereafter, Maxwell School conference on Economic Inequality and Higher Education).
4. National Center for Education Statistics, *The Condition of Education*, NCES 2003–06 (U.S. Department of Education, 2003), Table 18–1.
5. Thomas J. Kane, "College Going and Inequality," in *Social Inequality*, edited by Kathryn Neckerman (New York: Russell Sage Foundation, 2004); Pell Institute, *Indicators of Opportunity in Higher Education* (Washington: Pell Institute, 2004).
6. Thomas G. Mortenson, "Students from Low-Income Families and Higher Educational Opportunity," *Post-secondary Education Opportunity* 78 (1998): 1–2.
7. National Center for Education Statistics, *National Education Longitudinal Study, 1988* (U.S. Department of Education, 2002); National Center for Education Statistics, *The Condition of Education 2000* (U.S. Department of Education, 2002), table 382.
8. Melanie E. Corrigan, "Beyond Access: Persistence Challenges and the Diversity of Low-Income Students," *New Directions for Higher Education* 121 (2003): 25–34.
9. National Center for Education Statistics, *The Condition of Education* (U.S. Department of Education, 2001); John Wirt et al., *The Condition of Education 2004*, NCES 2004–077 (U.S.

Department of Education, National Center for Education Statistics, 2004), Table 19–2, p. 143.

10. John Goldthorpe, "Education-Based Meritocracy: The Barriers to Its Realization," paper presented to the Center for Policy Research, Maxwell School of Syracuse University (April 2002), www.cpr.maxwell.syr.edu/seminar/spring05/goldthorpe.pdf.

11. The effect of higher education on social mobility depends on both the effect of family income on schooling and the effect of schooling on offspring income. In our discussion, we emphasize the first of these components. However, we also provide some evidence on the latter linkage—that between schooling attainment and earnings.

12. Goldthorpe, "Education-Based Meritocracy" (see note 10).

13. Lars Osberg, Timothy M. Smeeding, and Jonathan Schwabish, "Income Distribution and Public Social Expenditure: Theories, Effects, and Evidence," in *Social Inequality*, edited by Kathryn Neckerman (New York: Russell Sage Foundation, 2004). pp. 821–59. See also Susan Mayer, "How Did the Increase in Economic Inequality between 1970 and 1990 Affect American Children's Educational Attainment?" unpublished manuscript, University of Chicago and Russell Sage Foundation (2005), on the effects of economic segregation on educational attainment.

14. Susan Mayer, "How Economic Segregation Affects Children's Educational Attainment," unpublished manuscript, Russell Sage Foundation (2005).

15. While there is no empirical estimate of the effect of the higher education system on social mobility, English social researchers suggest that, relative to parental socioeconomic status, the education sector explains 20 percent of the variance in the status of offspring in that country.

16. While our policy discussion recognizes the possibility that efforts to intervene in the development of human capital before the secondary and postsecondary levels may be more effective in attaining increased social mobility, we conclude that policies targeted on the higher education system are necessary to enable "college-qualified" youth to access and complete postsecondary schooling.

17. Robert D. Mare, "Change and Stability in Educational Stratification," *American Sociological Review* 46 (1981): 72–87; Robert Hauser, "Trends in College Entry among Whites, Blacks, and Hispanics," in *Study of Supply and Demand in Higher Education*, edited by Charles Clotfelter

and Michael Rothschild (University of Chicago Press, 1993), pp. 61–104.

18. For an economic treatment of this issue, see Igal Hendel, Joel Shapiro, and Paul Willen, "Educational Opportunity and Income Inequality," *Journal of Public Economics* 89 (2005): 841–70.

19. Some would argue that in the face of the advantages enjoyed by youth from higher-income families, the higher education sector should target its services on those youth who lack these genetic and family-based advantages. We do not address this issue here, but note that the argument cannot easily be ignored if a goal of the higher education system is to promote social mobility.

20. David Ellwood and Thomas J. Kane, "Who Is Getting a College Education: Family Background and the Growing Gaps in Enrollment," in *Securing the Future: Investing in Children from Birth to College*, edited by Sheldon Danziger and Jane Waldfogel (New York: Russell Sage Foundation, 2000). Ellwood and Kane also report such gaps for students with similar mathematics test scores. For example, while 59 percent of high-income youth in the middle two quartiles of test scores attend a four-year college, only 33 percent of youth from the lowest income quartile and with test scores in this range attend these institutions. See also Paul Barton, "Toward Inequality: Disturbing Trends in Higher Education" (Princeton, N.J.: Educational Testing Service, 1997).

21. Over the period covered by these two cohorts, the earnings return to college-going also increased substantially. It appears that youth from high-income families responded strongly to these increased returns from higher schooling and (of more concern) will reap the gains of these returns in their future careers.

22. The High School and Beyond survey was sponsored by the National Center for Education Statistics to study the educational, vocational, and personal development of young people, beginning with their elementary or high school years and following them over time as they begin to take on adult roles and responsibilities. The survey included two cohorts: the 1980 senior and sophomore classes. Both cohorts were surveyed every two years through 1986, and the 1980 sophomore class was also surveyed in 1992.

23. The Barron indicator of college selectivity is from Barron's *Profiles of American Colleges*.

24. Susan Dynarski finds that even after controlling for ability, as measured by test scores, the college participation gap between youth in families in the top and bottom quartiles is 22 percentage points; without controlling for ability, the gap was 30 percentage points. See Susan Dynarski, "Does Aid Matter? Measuring the Effect of Student Aid on College Attendance and Completion," Working Paper 7422 (Cambridge, Mass.: National Bureau of Economic Research, 1999).

25. The estimates in table 1 reflect the efforts of Ellwood and Kane, "Who Is Getting a College Education?" (see note 20) to measure parental family income in a consistent way across data sources (see p. 320).

26. The family income levels reported on student aid application forms (that is, supplied by parents) are generally substantially higher than the income levels reported by the students themselves in response to survey questions.

27. This distinction is also very important if one wishes to infer more than correlation between family income and higher education attainment. A number of recent studies have found that permanent household income is a significant determinant of both college attendance decisions by youth and the level of family investments in children, while transitory income is not. See Michael P. Keane and Kenneth I. Wolpin, "The Effect of Parental Transfers and Borrowing Constraints on Educational Attainment," *International Economic Review* 42, no. 4 (2001): 1051–103; Steven Cameron and James Heckman, "Life Cycle Schooling and Dynamic Selection Bias: Models and Evidence for Five Cohorts of American Males," *Journal of Political Economy* 106 (1998): 262–332; David Blau, "The Effect of Income on Child Development," *Review of Economics and Statistics* 81, no. 2 (1999): 261–76; Pedro Carneiro and James Heckman, "The Evidence on Credit Constraints in Post-Secondary Schooling," *Economic Journal* 112, no. 482 (2002): 705–34.

28. Robert Haveman and Kathryn Wilson. "Economic Inequality in College Access, Matriculation, and Graduation," paper presented to the Maxwell School conference on Economic Inequality and Higher Education.

29. The estimates are similar when wealth is used as the indicator of economic position.

30. Anthony P. Carnevale and Stephen J. Rose, "Socioeconomic Status, Race/Ethnicity, and Selective College Admissions," in *America's Untapped Resource: Low-Income Students in Higher*

Education, edited by Richard D. Kahlenberg (New York: Century Foundation Press, 2004), pp. 101–56.

31. Cordon Winston and Catharine Hill, "Access to the Most Selective Private Colleges by High-Ability, Low-Income Students: Are They Out There?" paper prepared for the Macalester-Spencer Forum, 2005.

32. Kirst, "Overcoming Educational Inequality" (see note 3).

33. See Thomas Kane and Peter Orszag, "Higher Education Spending: The Role of Medicaid and the Business Cycle," Policy Brief 124 (Brookings, September 2003).

34. Note that the focus here is on the completion of postsecondary schooling, and the data in figure 2.1 refer to degree attainment, not college attendance, per se. There have been increases in the extent of college-going in the United States over past decades. Susan Dynarski reports that "in 1968, 36 percent of 23-year-olds had gone to college. By 2000, that figure had grown to 55 percent. Over the same period, the share of young people with a college *degree* has risen relatively slowly." The reason for the disparity is the growth in college dropouts—students who start but do not complete college. Dynarski states that "in the 2000 Census, just 57 percent of those age 22 to 34 with any college experience had completed an associate's or bachelor's degree." See Susan Dynarski, "Building the Stock of College-Educated Labor," Working Paper 11604 (Cambridge, Mass.: National Bureau of Economic Research, 2005), www.nber.org/papers/w11604.

35. In the future, it may be possible to study the linkage between family economic position and educational attainment using new data sources, for example, the Trends in International Mathematics and Science Study (TIMSS; http://nces.ed.gov/timss/) and the OECD's Program for International Student Assessment (PISA; http://nces.ed.gov/surveys/pisa), in a cross-national context. These data sources have information on the test scores that are a precursor to college-going, thus enabling study of the linkage between family position and test scores. Ludger Woessmann makes an initial foray into these data and finds that although family background has a strong effect on student test scores, there is little variation across countries. However, in France and Flemish Belgium the effect of family background on test scores is smaller than average and in Germany and England it is larger, representing respectively greater and lesser degrees of inequality of

educational opportunity. See Ludger Woessmann, "How Equal Are Educational Opportunities? Family Background and Student Achievement in Europe and the United States," Discussion Paper 1284 (Bonn, Germany: IZA, 2004).

36. Orley Ashenfelter, Colm Harmon, and Hessel Oosterbeek, "A Review of Estimates of the Schooling/Earnings Relationship, with Tests for Publication Bias," *Labour Economics* 6 (1999). Ashenfelter, Harmon, and Oosterbeek distinguished the studies by model, sample, extent of control for relevant variables, and the nature of the labour market (such as country). For example, across all of the studies the estimated rate of return to schooling averages 7.9 percent (S.D. = .036). When direct controls for schooling are employed, the average return drops to 6.6 percent (S.D. = .026); when data using twins are employed, the average return is 9.2 percent (S.D. = .037); when an instrumental variable approach is employed, the average return is 9.3 percent (S.D. = .041).

37. Thomas J. Kane and Cecilia Elena Rouse, "Labor-Market Returns to Two- and Four-Year College," *American Economic Review* 85, no. 3 (1995): 600–14.

38. Dominic Brewer, Eric R. Eide, and Ronald G. Ehrenberg, "Does It Pay to Attend an Elite Private College? Cross-Cohort Evidence on the Effects of College Type on Earnings," *Journal of Human Resources* 34, no. 1 (1999): 104–23. The study controls for selection on unobservables.

39. Stacy Berg Dale and Alan B. Krueger, "Estimating the Payoff to Attending a More Selective College: An Application of Selection on Observables and Unobservables," *Quarterly Journal of Economics* 117, no. 4 (2002), pp. 1491–527.

40. Jeff Grogger and Eric Eide, "Changes in College Skills and the Rise in the College Wage Premium," *Journal of Human Resources* 30, no. 2 (1995): 280–310.

41. Mayer, "How Economic Segregation" (see note 14); Kirst, "Overcoming Educational Inequality" (see note 3).

42. National Center for Education Statistics, *Digest of Education Statistics* (U.S. Department of Education, 2002).

43. Kirst, "Overcoming Educational Inequality" (see note 3); P. Michael Timpane and Arthur M. Hauptman, "Improving the Academic Preparation and Performance of Low-Income Students in American Higher Education," in *America's Untapped Resources: Low-Income Students in Higher Education*, edited by Richard D. Kahlenberg (New York: Century Foundation Press, 2004); Vincent Tinto, "Economic Inequality and Higher

Education: Access, Persistence, and Success," comments delivered at the Maxwell School conference on Economic Inequality and Higher Education.

44. Kane, "College Going and Inequality" (see note 5), contains an excellent discussion of these issues.

45. Thomas Kane and Cecilia Rouse, "The Community College: Educating Students at the Margin between College and Work," *Journal of Economic Perspectives* 13, no. 1 (1999): 63–84; Amanda Pallais and Sarah E. Turner, "Access to Elites: The Growth of Programs to Increase Opportunities for Low Income Students at Selective Universities," paper presented to the Maxwell School conference on Economic Inequality and Higher Education; Michael McPherson, "Comments," presented to the Maxwell School conference on Economic Inequality and Higher Education.

46. Timpane and Hauptman, "Improving the Academic Preparation" (see note 43).

47. Much of the following discussion rests on Lawrence E. Gladieux, "Low-Income Students and the Affordability of Higher Education," in *America's Untapped Resources: Low-Income Students in Higher Education*, edited by Richard D. Kahlenberg (New York: Century Foundation Press, 2004), which includes a number of important recommendations for reform of federal, state, and institutional student financial aid. Many of these focus on increasing the targeting of assistance on students from low-income families.

48. College Board, *Trends in College Pricing, 2001* (New York, 2001).

49. For analysis of the causal impact of college costs on attendance, see Thomas J. Kane, "College Entry by Blacks since 1970: The Role of College Costs, Family Background, and the Returns to Education," *Journal of Political Economy* 102, no. 5 (1994): 878–911; Susan Dynarski, "Hope for Whom? Financial Aid for the Middle Class and Its Impact on College Attendance," *National Tax Journal* 53, no. 3 (2000): 629–61; Susan Dynarski, "Does Aid Matter? Measuring the Effect of Student Aid on College Attendance and Completion," *American Economic Review* 93, no. 1 (2003): 279–88; Susan Dynarski, "The New Merit Aid," in *College Choices: The Economics of Where to Go, When to Go, and How to Pay for It*, edited by Caroline Hoxby (University of Chicago Press, 2004). For a review of this literature, see Susan Dynarski, "The Behavioral and Distributional Implications of Aid for College," *American Economic Review* 92, no. 2 (2002): 279–85.

50. Advisory Committee on Student Financial Assistance, *Access Denied: Restoring the Nation's Commitment to Equal Educational Opportunity* (Washington, 2001).

51. Amy Ellen Schwartz, "The Cost of College and Implications for Income Inequality," paper presented to the Maxwell School conference on Economic Inequality and Higher Education.

52. Leonard E. Burman and others, "The Distributional Consequences of Federal Assistance for Higher Education: The Intersection of Tax and Spending Programs," Discussion Paper 26 (Washington: Urban Institute Tax Policy Center, 2005), summarize the last decade of federal policy developments in this area as follows: "Since 1997, federal higher education subsidies have increasingly been delivered through the tax code rather than through traditional direct spending programs, such as grants, loans, and work study . . . and have been directed toward students from middle- and upper-middle-income families." Using a micro-data simulation model developed for estimating the distributional effects of higher education policies, they find that while two-fifths of Pell program expenditures flow to students in tax units with adjusted gross income (AGI) of less than $10,000, the tax provisions provide little benefit to households at the lower end of the income distribution and concentrate the bulk of their benefits within the broad middle- and upper-middle class, with roughly $50,000 to $100,000 in cash income. They find that tax units in this income range receive almost 42 percent of the benefit from the various tax provisions, and that about one-seventh of the total tax benefit flows to tax units with cash incomes of $100,000 or more.

53. Century Foundation, "Left Behind: Unequal Opportunity in Higher Education" (Washington, 2004).

54. Michael McPherson and Morton Owen Schapiro, *The Student Aid Game: Meeting Need and Rewarding Talent in American Higher Education* (Princeton University Press, 1998).

55. Michael McPherson and Morton Owen Schapiro, "Watch What We Do (and Not What We Say): How Student Aid Awards Vary with Financial Need and Academic Merit," draft paper for presentation at the conference on Opening Opportunity or Preserving Privilege, Chicago, 2005.

56. Congressional Budget Office, "H.R. 609, College Access and Opportunities Act of 2005," presented to the House Committee on Education and the Workplace (July 25, 2005).

57. Dynarski, "Building the Stock" (see note 34).

58. This behavioral response is often referred to as the "Bennett hypothesis," after former secretary of education William Bennett, who argued that "increases in financial aid in recent years have enabled colleges and universities blithely to raise their tuitions." See William J. Bennett, "Our Greedy Colleges," *New York Times*, February 18, 1987, p. A31. For rather different conclusions on this response, see Bridget Long, "The Institutional Impact of the Georgia HOPE," *Journal of Human Resources* 39 (2004): 1045–66; and Benjamin Scafidi and others, "Merit-Based Financial Aid and College Tuition: The Case of Georgia's Hope Scholarships," unpublished manuscript, Georgia State University (2003).

59. Kane and Rouse, "The Community College" (see note 45).

60. Dan Goldhaber and Gretchen Kiefer, "Higher Education and Inequality: The Increasingly Important Role Community Colleges Play in Higher Education," paper presented to the Maxwell School conference on Economic Inequality and Higher Education.

61. Eric P. Bettinger and Bridget Terry Long, "The Role of Institutional Responses to Reduce Inequalities in College Outcomes: Remediation in Higher Education," paper presented to the Maxwell School conference on Economic Inequality and Higher Education.

62. Goldhaber and Kiefer, "Higher Education and Inequality" (see note 60).

63. Ibid.; Kane and Rouse, "The Community College" (see note 45); Thomas Kane, *The Price of Admission: Rethinking How Americans Pay for College* (Brookings, 1999).

64. Bettinger and Long, "The Role of Institutional Responses" (see note 61).

65. Thomas Bailey, Gregory Kienzl, and Dave E. Marcotte, "The Return to a Sub-Baccalaureate Education: The Effects of Schooling, Credentials and Program Study on Economic Outcomes" (Institute on Education and the Economy and the Community College Research Center, Teachers College, Columbia University, 2004).

66. Thomas Bailey et al., "Educational Outcomes of Occupational Postsecondary Students" (Institute on Education and the Economy and the Community College Research Center, Teachers College, Columbia University, 2004).

67. Debbie Sydow, comments presented to the Maxwell School conference on Economic Inequality and Higher Education.

68. Jane Wellman, "State Policy and Community College— Baccalaureate Transfer" (National Center for Public Policy

and Higher Education, Stanford University, August 2002); Kirst, "Overcoming Educational Inequality" (see note 3).

69. Richard Romano and Martin Wisniewski, "Tracking Community College Transfers Using National Student Clearinghouse Data," Working Paper 36 (Cornell Higher Education Research Institute, 2003).

70. Ibid.

71. Goldhaber and Kiefer, "Higher Education and Inequality," Table 1, p. 19 (see note 60), show that nearly half of all community college enrollment is in five large states—California, Florida, Illinois, Texas, and New York—and in all but New York, community college enrollments exceed enrollments in public four-year colleges. California alone has 24.4 percent of the nation's community college students, but only 9.2 percent of the nation's public four-year college enrollees.

72. Tinto, "Economic Inequality" (see note 43).

73. Pallais and Turner, "Access to Elites" (see note 45).

74. Kirst, "Overcoming Educational Inequality" (see note 3). Of course, were we to create policies to promote retention and persistence to a degree for low-income and low-qualification students, per student costs would be likely to increase.

75. Despite the positive impact of remediation on educational outcomes, these authors note that the institutional variation they exploit to obtain their results necessitates excluding from their sample the lowest ability students, who would be in remediation at any institution. The impact of remediation on these students is unknown. Bettinger and Long, "The Role of Institutional Responses" (see note 61); Eric P. Bettinger and Bridget Terry Long, "Addressing the Needs of Under-Prepared Students in Higher Education: Does College Remediation Work?" Working Paper 11325 (Cambridge, Mass.: National Bureau of Economic Research, 2005).

76. Mayer, "How Economic Segregation" (see note 14); Pell Institute, *Indicators of Opportunity* (see note 5); Haveman and Wilson, "Economic Inequality" (see note 28).

77. Thomas Garrett and William Poole, "Stop Paying More for Less: Ways to Boost Productivity in Higher Education," *Regional Economist* (Federal Reserve Bank of St. Louis, January 2006).

78. Pallais and Turner, "Access to Elites" (see note 45); McPherson, "Comments" (see note 45).

79. Bruce Chapman and Chris Ryan, "The Access Implications of Income Contingent Charges for Higher Education: Lessons from Australia," *Economics of Education Review* 24, no. 5

(2005): 491–512. In early 1993, the Clinton administration introduced broad-based reforms to student loan programs, including an option for students to adopt income-contingent repayments for some part of their student loan obligations, up to 20 percent of an agreed income. See Evelyn Brody, "Paying Back Your Country through Income-Contingent Student Loans," *San Diego Law Review* 31 (1994): 449–518.

Thinking About Content

1. According to research cited by Haveman and Smeeding, in what ways is the gap between students in higher socioeconomic classes and lower socioeconomic classes growing when it comes to a college education? Why is this problematic for our country?
2. What are some of the policy recommendations Haveman and Smeeding make at the end of the article? Which ones do you think would be most effective? Why?

Thinking About Strategy

1. Early in the article, the authors provide some background information on the traditional connections between higher education and social mobility in this country. Why would it be important for them to do this for their audience?
2. In addition to citing research on trends in education based on income, the authors offer possible solutions to the problems with equality. Why do you think the authors would propose solutions, especially as that section of the article is quite brief?

Promises to Keep: Working Class Students and Higher Education
MICHELLE M. TOKARCZYK

Michelle M. Tokarczyk is a professor of English and codirector of writing at Goucher College. She is the author of the 1993 book, Working-Class Women in the Academy: Laborers in the Knowledge Factory. *The following essay appeared in a 2001 collection of essays on class entitled* What's Class Got To Do with It? *Edited by Robert Zweig, the book addresses the role of social class in many aspects of our lives.*

———————— ✦ ————————

By now it is widely recognized that, in the words of Michael Bérubé and Cary Nelson, "Where college was once a device for creating tomorrow's leaders, it is now seen as a device for combating socioeconomic inequities." A college education offers the possibility, often the only possibility, that poor youth may escape from poverty and that working class youth may enter the middle class. Indeed, as living-wage union jobs have steadily been replaced by minimum-wage service-industry jobs, a college education is increasingly the only hope young people have for getting work that will support them. College education is important for the working class not only because it gives them entrée into living-wage jobs but also, as important, because it can enable them to become critically thinking adults, which working class primary and secondary schools have often failed to do. Yet there are formidable barriers to working class students' success at colleges at universities. While some barriers are academic, involving college preparedness, many are institutional, resulting from policies and attitudes that are unfriendly to working class students. As a faculty member in a liberal arts college, I have witnessed many of the difficulties working class students experience in this setting. As a working class woman who attended a city university and later worked in city and state universities, I also experienced many of the problems common in these institutions. My own and my students' experiences, coupled with recently published work in the area, illustrate the institutional challenges working class students face. Some innovative programs at a couple of colleges suggest ways to enable working class students to succeed in higher education.

Working class students' needs are unmet because their presence in colleges and universities is largely ignored. For example, a series of articles in the *New York Times* described the experiences of three high school seniors applying to colleges. Each of the students applied to and was finally accepted at a competitive liberal

Special thanks to Goucher's acting dean of students, Gail Edmonds, for sending me to the National Council on Race and Ethnicity Conference in 2000. This chapter also benefited from conversations with my student R. H. A reference librarian at Goucher, Randy Smith, also provided invaluable assistance in helping me track down sources.

arts college or a selective university. Yet as John Alberti notes, "most students in the United States do not attend elite, selective-admissions four-year institutions." College educators often, however, take the relatively elite institutions as the model for higher education: the only real educational environment for faculty and students. What Alberti calls "working-class" colleges and their students are in effect made invisible.

While some faculty resist the notion that an elite institution is the only place where one should teach, some wish that they had positions at these "real" institutions. Certainly there are concrete benefits to teaching at selective colleges and universities: the class sizes and workloads are often more manageable, and at some of the top institutions the pay is certainly better. Yet some faculty who resent their institutions' lack of prestige shift their resentment to their students. Stephen Garger remembers such resentment at the less selective liberal arts college he attended. He especially recalls the faculty member who described his college's mission as "teaching the first generation of immigrant children how to eat with a knife and fork." Some faculty at state and less elite private institutions refuse to acknowledge that their students have unique needs. Rather than try to adapt teaching techniques and school policies to first-generation college students, these faculty behave as though they were indeed teaching in an elite institution. It is thus not surprising that working class students in working class and elite colleges face similar barriers.

A more serious problem for faculty at many state and city colleges is the scarcity of resources. Because schools cannot easily hire more faculty members, they increase the workloads of those they have. Teachers at four-year colleges teach four courses a semester; at community colleges the load is often five courses a semester. Over twenty-five students may be enrolled in a developmental writing class; professional organizations such as the National Council of Teachers of English recommend a cutoff of fifteen in these classes. Content courses are likewise overenrolled. Publication requirements for tenure continue to increase. Given such heavy workloads, it is difficult for faculty to devote much time to mentoring.

As important, there is little time to develop techniques and programs for first-generation students. While many colleges and universities—even the elite ones—offer developmental and study skills classes for under-prepared students, they often do nothing to help working class students adapt to college expectations. College freshmen nationwide are frequently surprised at how much more challenging college courses are than high school ones. Students from mediocre high schools at which little was demanded of them are especially hard hit. In an article on working class students in higher education, one student was paraphrased as saying that college is a very unforgiving place. It is unforgiving not of those who don't learn the rules, but rather of those who did not know the rules before arriving on campus. Faculty at schools with few resources and large numbers of working class students may become exasperated. Rather than teach students the rules of the game—the study habits necessary for success—exasperated faculty sometimes dumb down their courses. In effect, the faculty inadvertently perpetuate the class-based education begun in elementary schools: working class students are taught the basics and given information to absorb, while middle and upper class students are taught critical thinking.

Working class students often have difficulty in their studies partially because many colleges and universities—elite and nonelite—refuse to recognize that many students must work. According to the National Center for Education Studies, "In 1995–96, four out of five undergraduates reported working while they were enrolled in postsecondary education. One half reported that the primary reason they worked was to pay for their education. . . . Students who worked to pay expenses reported working an average of 25 hours per week while enrolled." In addition to working many hours, working class students frequently take heavy course loads in order to graduate early, thereby minimizing tuition costs. At Northern Kentucky University, for example, a semester load of fifteen to eighteen credits, five or six courses, is common. Since working class students do not have the sense of entitlement to a college education that those in upper classes do, and since parents, school personnel, and peers have not continually reinforced their aspirations, when these students' grades suffer, they often do not blame their extraordinary workload, but believe they are just not smart enough to succeed. Not only do students fear failing out, but those who have merit scholarships perpetually worry that their grade point averages will drop below the required level and they will then be unable to afford college.

Often there are no mentors to advise students. Even if mentors are assigned, many do little more than advise on graduation requirements. At the city college I attended I was placed in an honors English program and a selective experimental curricular program. I was assigned advisers, yet none thought to tell me how difficult it would be to complete an honors course of study, with some classes requiring twenty readings, and work sixteen to thirty hours a week. None even asked me if I worked. Perhaps more important, none thought to advise me as to which courses would prepare me for graduate study.

In reading accounts of former working class students, one is repeatedly struck by the number of policies and behaviors that ignore the realities of working class lives. Elizabeth A. Grant tells of having to walk two miles to the Oswego campus during the rough upstate New York winters. When, concerned about her very cold feet, she took off her boots in French class, the teacher ordered her to put them on, get out of class, and not return until she was "civilized." As a freshman in an introductory music history course, I, along with a large proportion of the class, did very poorly on the midterm. It was 1971, the first year of the open enrollment policy at the City University of New York, and my teacher asked how many of us had come in under open enrollment. I wasn't sure how to answer; I had come in that year, but my grades would have gotten me in anyway. Still, I ashamedly raised my hand as the teacher surveyed the raised hands in disgust.

Professors at private colleges, especially liberal arts colleges, rarely show such open disdain for students, mainly because they must recruit students and, to some extent, satisfy them as consumers to ensure that the students will continue to pay the schools' hefty tuitions. Of course, the majority of students at these schools are relatively prepared, middle class students with whom the faculty can identify. The small classes and emphasis on teaching of many liberal arts colleges offer promise to working class students who can manage the tuition there, often through a combination of working, scholarships, and living with family. Yet the fact that working class students are such a minority at these schools poses special challenges.

For one, working class students are often an anomaly to their peers. A working class student at Goucher told me that students did not understand her living at home and working three part-time jobs. Because she did not have a car, she had to continually arrange for rides to and from campus. Students just looked at her as though she were strange, so she stopped talking about her situation, stopped trying to make friends, and kept to herself.

School personnel can be as uncomprehending as undergraduates. Some colleges require internships or other off-campus experiences that can be extremely time consuming, especially for students who do not have cars. At my college now one of the heated debates is whether to require four January programs in which students would go abroad or engage in an intercultural experience, possibly in another locale. Several faculty have pointed out that working class students could not afford the travel costs, and even if the costs were compensated, working class students could not afford to take that much time off from their jobs. It remains to be seen whether the proposed January semester will be designed to meet the needs of all our students.

Many working class students, of course, do succeed. Their success can often be partially traced to a mentor who went out of his or her way to encourage and provide for students. Mike Rose repeatedly praises Jack MacFarland, the high school teacher who encouraged Rose, a boy from south Los Angeles, to attend Loyola College. When Rose was struggling, MacFarland contacted faculty to ensure that Rose got the help he needed. It is difficult to institutionalize such mentoring, because, while people will acknowledge racial or gender difference, they often are only vaguely aware of class inequity. Many unconsciously embrace the American myth that everyone is middle class, that anyone who tries can succeed, and thus may be reluctant to acknowledge the impact of working class status. In her writing Caroline Pari relates the challenges of discussing class at the community college where she teaches. Some students insisted the United States is a classless society; others argued that class was not a meaningful marker, only race was. In my own composition course on class and upward mobility, in any given semester I have one or two students who announce, either to me or to the class, that they have realized they are working class. Such realizations come only after several weeks of learning about the existence of class in this country and the stigma of lower class status. Some students may talk to me or write about their class background but refrain from discussing it publicly. I take care not to out them. Mentoring is crucial to working class students, but it must be part of a program that increases knowledge of class and is attuned to students' needs and fears.

Despite such challenges, some colleges are developing programs to assist first-generation students in their transition to college. The University of La Verne in California has an approach that focuses on "loci of interventions" for students. These involve interactions with the students' families, including some home visits, and institutional adaptations, such as changes in campus processes and structures. The program takes into account that many first-generation students are students of color, so some community intervention may be necessary. For example, college officials met with the local police department to discuss the officers' repeatedly stopping and questioning African American males.

The program at La Verne, sponsored by a James Irvine Foundation grant, recognizes the profound implications of lower socioeconomic class. Not only do students need financial aid for tuition and housing but they also, since they have no cash reserves, need emergency funds to pay for unexpected books, delayed checks, and the like. An especially impressive feature of the program at La Verne is its emphasis on continual research to learn how the program is faring and how it can be improved. Thus faculty are learning how mentoring needs vary along race and ethnic lines. When probed about the most important attributes of a mentor, African American students stressed race. Latinos and Latinas emphasized that mentors, regardless of race, should be friends and nurturers. Asian Americans were relatively indifferent to race, and rather than nurturers, they wanted mentors who were older and accomplished in their fields. That the paper reporting these results makes no mention of what white students prefer may reflect the small number of working class white students at this college, or it may reflect a societal assumption that whites are not represented in the lower socioeconomic classes. Nonetheless, the information this college gathered about its students' mentoring preferences undoubtedly enabled it to set up better mentorships.

Mount San Antonio College, a community college also in California, has a similar program for first-generation students that focuses on establishing learning communities consisting of students, faculty, and counselors. These communities not only enable learning but also combat the isolation and alienation many working class students feel when beginning college. 15

The two institutions I've discussed with programs for first-generation students have significant numbers of students of color, whose class issues are compounded by that of race. Thus these colleges may have felt an acute impetus to develop programs. However, there is no reason why other colleges cannot develop similar programs that would assist working class students— financially, educationally, and socially. The educational effort might begin with faculty and administration. Many colleges have made attempts to enlighten personnel about the specific challenges facing particular ethnic or racial groups, but leave out questions of class. It is striking to me and to many other working class academics that faculty who would never utter a racial slur will casually refer to "trailer trash" or "white trash." Clearly some faculty education is in order.

Similarly, many colleges require first-year students to take a transition-to-college course that includes a component on diversity. Race, ethnicity, sexual orientation, and religion are discussed, but often class is not a part of the curriculum. If such courses had a component on class, upper and middle class students might begin to be more sensitive to economic difference, and working class students might feel less stigmatized.

It is important that colleges acknowledge that the typical student is no longer an eighteen-year-old middle class white male. Students of diverse backgrounds are more likely to be working class, and colleges must work to meet these students' needs. Institutions could begin to do so by considering the implications of policies such as required time abroad or internships for working class students. They could recruit faculty on campus who, often from working class backgrounds themselves, are interested in advising working class students. Institutions could also explore setting aside sums of money for emergency student needs—books, baby-sitting, car repairs, and the like.

In the spring of 2002, Goucher students organized a series of workshops on ethnicity and race. Here a Puerto Rican student complained that minorities are often admitted into colleges, businesses, and other institutions with the provision that they play by white mainstream rules. I would argue that we behave similarly toward working class students of all races and ethnic backgrounds in colleges and universities, admitting them with the tacit understanding that they can and will behave like middle or upper middle class young people. It is time for us to find a way to teach to all students.

My father was a toll collector on first the Whitestone Bridge, then the Henry Hudson Bridge in New York City; my mother worked for about eighteen years in various clerical positions before becoming a homemaker, and she never accumulated more than would fit in the back of a car. I am very grateful that my life is easier than my parents' was. I am further pleased that my work is rewarding. But I am most pleased that I have had the opportunity to hone the critical thinking and verbal skills I saw in my parents. When I was an undergraduate at Lehman College, I heard a student ask a question that has bothered me for years. To paraphrase, "Where do the poor go to get an understanding of themselves and their world? We know where the rich people go; they go to Harvard.

Where do the poor go?" Higher education not only promises a chance for upward mobility. It also promises a fuller understanding of and interaction with one's self, community, and society. These are the promises we've made that we must keep, that we can keep, if only we acknowledge to whom we've made the promises.

Thinking About Content

1. Tokarczyk asserts that there are institutional barriers for working class students who enter college. What are some of these barriers? Can you think of others that she does not mention?
2. In what ways are some colleges making the transition easier for first-generation college students? Can you think of ideas of your own?

Thinking About Strategy

1. Tokarczyk concludes this essay by describing her own background. How does this affect her credibility on this topic?
2. How do you blend personal writing—like personal narrative—in a public writing like an essay that is meant to inform or explore a topic? How does this blending affect your thesis statement?

Prompts for Extended Writing Assignments

Personal Response
What does it mean to be educated? Is being educated different from having skills? Write an extended essay focusing on *your* definition of education that takes difference in class into consideration.

From Another's Perspective
What are your experiences with education? You and a writing partner will develop comparative autobiographies in which you examine your experiences with school and explain how those experiences are reflected in your definition of a good education.

Call for Social Action
Describe the conditions of the schools you have attended. Write a letter to the editor of a newspaper, to the president of the local school board, or to your congressional representative that addresses inequities in school conditions.

Research Opportunity
Research some of the ways social class affects educational access. Explore some of the research studies in this area. Then write an essay in which you summarize some of the most significant struggles for students from lower classes.

Are We There Yet? Gender Equality in America's Schools

Is education an equal opportunity endeavor? Are boys and girls treated differently in school, and does their education suffer as a result? Do women have equal access to higher education? These are important questions that we, as a culture, continually ask ourselves. The important role that gender plays in educational experiences is currently the topic of much research and debate, and the questions about gender equality resurface continually as we thoughtfully examine the reality of our public schools and higher education system.

As you read this chapter on education and gender, we want you to think about what role gender plays in our educational system, and what obstacles exist for girls and boys and for men and women in the different levels of our educational system. What can we do to eliminate some of these obstacles?

Higher Education: Colder by Degrees

Myra Sadker and David Sadker

Professors Myra and David Sadker offered insight into two decades of research on differences in education for boys and girls in their 1994 book, Failing at Fairness: How America's Schools Cheat Girls. *The following essay exploring women's roles in higher education classrooms is taken from* Failing at Fairness.

──────────── ✦ ────────────

A t the highest educational level, where the instructors are the most credentialed and the students the most capable, teaching is the most biased. We discovered this during a two-year grant in which we and a staff of trained raters observed and coded post-secondary classrooms. When we analyzed the data, we discovered how hidden lessons, rooted in elementary school and exacerbated in high school, emerged full-blown in the college classroom. Drawn from our research files, the following classroom scene offers more than a discussion of the Constitution; it shows how earlier subtle sexism has evolved and intensified.

> The course on the U.S. Constitution is required for graduation, and more than fifty students, approximately half male and half female, file in. The professor begins by asking if there are questions on next week's midterm. Several hands go up.

BERNIE: Do we have to memorize names and dates in the book? Or will the test be more general?
PROFESSOR: You do have to know those critical dates and people. Not every one but the important ones. If I were you, Bernie, I would spend time learning them. Ellen?
ELLEN: What kind of short-answer questions will there be?
PROFESSOR: All multiple choice.
ELLEN: Will we have the whole class time?
PROFESSOR: Yes, we'll have the whole class time. Anyone else?
BEN (calling out): Will there be an extra-credit question?
PROFESSOR: I hadn't planned on it. What do you think?
BEN: I really like them. They take some of the pressure off. You can also see who is doing extra work.
PROFESSOR: I'll take it under advisement. Charles?
CHARLES: How much of our final grade is this?
PROFESSOR: The midterm is 25 percent. But remember, class participation counts as well. Why don't we begin?

> The professor lectures on the Constitution for twenty minutes before he asks a question about the electoral college. The electoral

college is not as hot a topic as the midterm, so only four hands are raised. The professor calls on Ben.

BEN: The electoral college was created because there was a lack of faith in the people. Rather than have them vote for the president, they voted for the electors.

PROFESSOR: I like the way you think. (He smiles at Ben, and Ben smiles back.) Who could vote? (Five hands go up, five out of fifty.) Angie?

ANGIE: I don't know if this is right, but I thought only men could vote.

BEN *(calling out):* That was a great idea. We began going downhill when we let women vote. (Angie looks surprised but says nothing. Some of the students laugh, and so does the professor. He calls on Barbara.)

BARBARA: I think you had to be pretty wealthy, own property—

JOSH *(not waiting for Barbara to finish, calls out):* That's right. There was a distrust of the poor, who could upset the democracy. But if you had property, if you had something at stake, you could be trusted not to do something wild. Only property owners could be trusted.

PROFESSOR: Nice job, Josh. But why do we still have electors today? Mike?

MIKE: Tradition, I guess.

PROFESSOR: Do you think it's tradition? If you walked down the street and asked people their views of the electoral college, what would they say?

MIKE: Probably they'd be clueless. Maybe they would think that it elects the Pope. People don't know how it works.

PROFESSOR: Good, Mike. Judy, do you want to say something? (Judy's hand is at "half-mast," raised but just barely. When the professor calls her name, she looks a bit startled.)

JUDY *(speaking very softly):* Maybe we would need a whole new constitutional convention to change it. And once they get together to change that, they could change anything. That frightens people, doesn't it? (As Judy speaks, a number of students fidget, pass notes, and leaf through their books; a few even begin to whisper.)

A visit to the typical college class, which is a stop on the campus tour that most parents never make, shows that students behave as if they, too, are visitors. While 80 percent of pupils in elementary and secondary classes contribute at least one comment in each of their classes, approximately half of the college class says nothing at all. One in two sits through an entire class without ever answering a question, asking one, or making a comment. Women's silence is loudest at college, with twice as many females voiceless. Considering the rising cost of college tuition, the female rule of speech seems to be: The more you pay, the less you say.

At the other end of the college speech spectrum are the salient students who monopolize the discussion. Their hands shoot up for attention even before the professor finishes the question. Others don't bother to wave for recognition; they blurt out answers, sometimes way off the mark, before other students formulate their ideas. As in the class we described, these aggressive, Jeopardy-like players are usually male. In our research we have found that men are twice as likely to monopolize class discussions, and women are twice as likely to be silent. The college classroom is the finale of a twelve-year rehearsal, the culminating showcase for a manly display of verbal dominance.

Studying classrooms at Harvard, Catherine Krupnick also discovered this gender divide, one where males perform and females watch. Here were the most academically talented women in the nation, and even they were silenced. When they did speak, they were more likely to be interrupted. Males talked more often, and they talked longer. When the professor as well as most of the students were male, the stage was set for women to be minor players, a virtual Harvard underclass.

Bernice Sandler and Roberta Hall found that professors give 5 males more nonverbal attention as well. They make more eye contact with men, wait longer for them to answer, and are more likely to remember their names. The result, Sandler and Hall concluded, is a "chilly classroom climate," one that silently robs women of knowledge and self-esteem.

When females do volunteer comments, the impact of years of silence and self-devaluation becomes evident. In our class scenario above, Angie showed this loss. Like many women, she has learned to preface her speech with phrases like "I'm not sure if this is what you want" or "This probably isn't right but . . . " These female preambles of self-deprecation are a predictable part of the college classroom. In our coding system we called them "self-putdowns." In class after class we were disheartened at how many times women compromised superb comments: "I'm not really sure," "This is just a guess," "I don't know, but could the answer be . . . " Or like Judy they spoke in such a soft and tentative manner that their classmates don't even bother to listen.

When we asked college women why they neutralized the power of their own speech, they offered revealing explanations:

> I do it to lower expectations. If my answer is wrong, so what? I don't lose anything. I already said it might be wrong.

> I don't want to seem like I'm taking over the class or anything. If I disguise that I know the answers, then the other students won't resent me.

> I say I'm not sure because I'm really not sure. I'm not certain that I'm following the professor, and I'm just being honest about it.

> I didn't know I was talking like that.

The last one is the reaction we hear most frequently. Self-doubt has become part of women's public voice, and most are unaware it has happened. This pattern of uncertain speech is reminiscent of the standardized science test taken in elementary and middle school, the exam where many girls selected the "I don't know" option rather than take a guess at the correct response. By the time these schoolgirls become college women, the "I don't know" option, the only one guaranteed not to garner any points, has insinuated itself into speech, a tacit acknowledgment of diminished status.

We also found that one-third of the college classrooms that contain both males and females are characterized by informally sex-segregated seating, patterns formed by the students themselves. The salient students, usually male, are well versed in the concept of strategic seating; they choose places where they can be spotted quickly by the professor. Those who want to hide, the silent students, who are more likely to be female, prize the corners, the unobtrusive areas, and the anonymity that grows with distance. It is as if a transparent gender divide was erected within the classroom.

While not as stark, the parallel with the sex segregation of elementary school is obvious. And teachers continue their patterns, too. The subtle bias in teacher reactions that we detected in lower grades resurfaces in college. Professors usually respond to student answers with neutral silence or a vague "Okay." But when praise is awarded, when criticism is leveled, or when help is given, the male student is more likely to be on the receiving end. In the class scene we described, Mike was challenged to improve his answer and then rewarded for the correction. In fact, the professor praised three male students: Ben, Josh, and Mike. Women's comments never received the professor's stamp of approval. At best they were merely acknowledged, at worst interrupted or ridiculed. So, like boys in elementary school, men in college receive not only more attention from the professor but better attention as well.

The professor in the previous example did not intervene   10
when Ben poked fun at women and at Angie's comment, but he did not say anything sexist or sexual himself. But many professors do. At Iowa State, 65 percent of female students said they had been the target of sexist comments, and 43 percent said professors flirted with them. At Harvard University, almost half the women graduate students reported sexual harassment. This is how women described the incidents:

> He came into class, looked directly at me, and announced to everyone, "Your sweater is too tight." I felt terrible. The next week he whispered to me, "You look like you had a tough night." I just dropped his course and had to go to summer school.

> One day this professor requested that I come to his office to discuss a paper. When I arrived, he escorted me to a chair and closed the office door. He walked over to me, put his hands on either side of my face, and told me I was a very beautiful woman. Then he kissed my forehead. We never discussed any of my academic work. . . . I disregarded his constant requests to visit his office and hurriedly left his class. I received my lowest grade in his course.

Joseph Thorpe, a professor at the University of Missouri, knows just how bad it can get. He sent questionnaires to over one thousand women who were recent recipients of psychology doctorates and were members of the American Psychological Association. Thorpe found that many students had been propositioned by their professors. Most of these overtures were turned down, but almost half said they suffered academic penalties for refusing. The survey also revealed that one in every four or five women studying for their psychology doctorates was having sex with the teacher, adviser, or mentor responsible for her academic career.

"These figures seem terribly high," we said in an interview with Thorpe. "Do you think they're inflated?"

"I think they underpredict what's going on," he said. "The study did not interview any of the women who dropped out, the ones who became so emotionally devastated that they never finished their programs. If we knew those numbers, the figures would be higher. In fact, for subgroups in our sample, the numbers were higher. When we looked at the responses from single, separated, or divorced female students, the sex-with-adviser rate climbed to 33 percent."

Senior professors are overwhelmingly male and critically important. These professors distribute funds in the form of assistantships and fellowships. They can offer coauthorships on publications crucial to a fledgling career. With the right phone calls, they can land prestigious jobs for their students. Male students are more likely to be part of this mentoring relationship, but when women are mentored, the dynamics sometimes become sexual.

With grades and professional careers at stake, female students may feel vulnerable and powerless to object. If a professor is a senior faculty member and distinguished in his field, it becomes even more difficult. When one of our students at The American University told us of harassment she was experiencing in a course, we urged her to bring charges. "It's useless," she told us. "This professor is a nationally known scholar. When I said I was going to report him, he laughed. 'No one would believe you,' he said. 'Do you know how many awards I have won? I'm like a god on this campus.'" This young woman did not report the professor; she dropped the course instead.

The alienation of female students on the male campus emerges even in the quiet alcoves of the university library. Surrounded by books with few if any females, women continue to learn they are worth less.

Thinking About Content

1. Sadker and Sadker link the cost of education with the kinds of education girls receive by saying "the more you pay, the less you say." What have your experiences been in college? How are classes set up? Who gets to talk and who doesn't? Is this fair?

2. Do you think the climate of sexual harassment on college campuses has changed since this research was conducted in the 1970s and 1980s?

Thinking About Strategy

1. Sadker and Sadker begin this excerpt describing their research process and use primary research—transcribed interviews and self-reported writings—to support their findings. Do you find this strategy effective? How does it contribute to the credibility of the text? How can you use primary research to enhance your writing?

2. There are many citation systems available to show the secondary research a writer has conducted. This excerpt uses a system that includes notes at the end of the completed document. In what ways does this change your experience of the text? How will you incorporate secondary research into your texts?

Boy Problems

Ann Hulbert

Ann Hulbert is the author of Raising America, *a book addressing the debates and trends in raising children in America, and a frequent contributor to* The New York Review of Books *and the* New Republic. *The following essay appeared in* New York Times Magazine *in 2005.*

✦

"It's her future. Do the math," instructs a poster that is part of the Girl Scouts of the U.S.A.'s two-year-old "Girls Go Tech" campaign. Accompanying the message—which belongs to a series of public service announcements also sponsored by the Ad Council—is a photograph of an adorable little girl reading a book called "Charlotte's Web Site." The cover of the E.B. White takeoff shows Fern and Wilbur looking intently at Charlotte on a computer screen. The text below warns that "by sixth grade, an alarming number of girls lose interest in math, science and technology. Which means they won't qualify for most future jobs."

But they don't lose interest in reading, this particular ad presumes—nor do girls lose interest in school, certainly not at the rate boys do. The recent controversy over comments made by Lawrence Summers, the president of Harvard, about the gender gap in science and engineering has eclipsed a different educational disparity: boys perform consistently below girls on most tests of reading and verbal skills and lag in college enrollment and degree attainment. After dominating postsecondary education through the late 1970's, young American men now earn 25 percent fewer bachelor's degrees than young women do.

Who knows what Summers would say about this phenomenon, which is the flip side of the underrepresentation of female scientists at the top that he was addressing. Male achievement, as he explained, tends toward the extremes when it comes to testing, while females' scores are more concentrated in the middle of the range. What Summers didn't spell out is that boys owe their edge in math to the unusually high performance of a relatively small number of boys in a pool that also has more than its share of low-scoring students. In assessments of verbal literacy, the clumping of boys toward the bottom is more pronounced.

The gender disparity widens among low-income and minority students. And it is especially dramatic among African-Americans, a recent Urban Institute study shows. Black women now earn twice as many college degrees as black men do. They also receive double the number of master's degrees. But the female lead isn't just a black phenomenon; among whites, women earn 30 percent more bachelor's degrees than men and some 50 percent more master's degrees.

It's his future. Do the math—but, as the Boy Scouts warn, be   5
prepared. This trend doesn't lend itself to clear-cut treatment. Ignore the male lag, some advocates of girls are inclined to argue, on the grounds that men on average still end up outearning women. Bring back old-fashioned competition and more hard-boiled reading matter, urge advocates for boys like Christina Hoff Sommers, who in "The War Against Boys: How Misguided Feminism Is Harming Our Young Men" (2000) denounces a touchy-feely, cooperative, progressive ethos that she says undermines boys' performance and school engagement. Males come from Mars and thrive instead on no-nonsense authority, accountability, clarity and peer rivalry.

What both of these views—feminist and antifeminist alike— fail to appreciate is how much patient attentiveness (in the Venus vein) it takes to boost stragglers rather than strivers. In the "do the math" mission under way with girls, the overarching goal has been surprisingly competitive: to maintain the momentum of female math students (who do just as well as boys early on in school) and to keep the top achievers in the academic pipeline for those "future jobs" in our technological world. The payoff for efforts that have been directed toward school performance has been gratifying. Girls are taking more math and science courses in high school and majoring with greater frequency in those fields in college. (Look at the 40 Intel finalists: this year 38 percent of them were girls.)

The educational predicament of boys is fuzzier by comparison and likely to elude tidy empirical diagnosis and well-focused remedies. At the National Bureau of Economic Research (under whose auspices Summers delivered his remarks about women), analysts have been puzzling over the whys behind "Where the Boys Aren't," the title of one working paper. There are some obvious explanations: men in the Army and in prison and more job options for males (in construction and manufacturing) that don't require a college education but pay relatively well.

Yet there are also murkier social and behavioral—and biological—issues at stake that don't augur well for a quick-fix approach. On the front end, boys appear to be later verbal bloomers than girls, which sets them up for early encounters with academic failure—and which makes early-intervention gambits like the Bush administration's push to emphasize more literacy skills in preschool look misdirected. Down the road, there is evidence that poorer "noncognitive skills" (not academic capacity but work habits and conduct) may be what hobble males most, and that growing up in single-parent families takes more of an educational toll on boys than girls.

Those are challenges that beg for more than school-based strategies. To give her credit, Laura Bush hasn't shied away from them as she starts a boy-focused youth initiative, which runs the gamut from dealing with gangs to financing fatherhood programs to improving remedial English programs. Rewards for such efforts aren't likely to be prompt and aren't aimed at the top—two reasons they deserve the spotlight. Females have yet more strides to make in the sciences, but they're building on success. A boost-the-boys educational endeavor faces the challenge of dealing with downward drift. Clearly the nation needs an impetus to tackle the larger problem of growing social inequality. Worries that it is boys who are being left behind could be the goad we need.

Thinking About Content

1. What is the new gender disparity in education that Hulbert describes?
2. What are some of the theories on why boys are lagging when it comes to education that Hulbert mentions? Which seem most plausible to you, based on your experiences?

Thinking About Strategy

1. What is Hulbert's purpose in this essay? Who do you think is her target audience?
2. Go online or to your campus library to examine a few issues of *New York Times Magazine*. What is the purpose of this periodical? Does Hulbert's purpose and tone in "Boy Problems" fit well within other works appearing in this periodical? Explain.

The Truth About Boys and Girls
SARA MEAD

The following essay by Sara Mead was published by Education Sector *in June 2006. In the essay, Mead responds to the several articles and television programs which assert that boys are falling behind in public schools and higher education systems. Mead counterargues that boys are not necessarily doing worse than girls but that girls are closing some of the gaps that have existed historically. Mead is a senior policy analyst at* Education Sector, *an independent education think tank.*

———————— ✦ ————————

If you've been paying attention to the education news lately, you know that American boys are in crisis. After decades spent worrying about how schools "shortchange girls,"[1] the eyes of the nation's education commentariat are now fixed on how they shortchange boys. In 2006 alone, a *Newsweek* cover story, a major *New Republic* article, a long article in *Esquire*, a "Today" show segment, and numerous op-eds have informed the public that boys are falling behind girls in elementary and secondary school and are increasingly outnumbered on college campuses. A young man in Massachusetts filed a civil rights complaint with the U.S. Department of Education, arguing that his high school's homework and community service requirements discriminate against boys.[2] A growth industry of experts is advising educators and policymakers how to make schools more "boy friendly" in an effort to reverse this slide.

It's a compelling story that seizes public attention with its "man bites dog" characteristics. It touches on Americans' deepest insecurities, ambivalences, and fears about changing gender roles and the "battle of the sexes." It troubles not only parents of boys, who fear their sons are falling behind, but also parents of girls, who fear boys' academic deficits will undermine their daughters' chances of finding suitable mates.

But the truth is far different from what these accounts suggest. The real story is not bad news about boys doing worse; it's good news about girls doing better.

In fact, with a few exceptions, American boys are scoring higher and achieving more than they ever have before. But girls have just improved their performance on some measures even faster. As a result, girls have narrowed or even closed some academic gaps that previously favored boys, while other long-standing gaps that favored girls have widened, leading to the belief that boys are falling behind.

There's no doubt that some groups of boys—particularly His-   5
panic and black boys and boys from low-income homes—are in real trouble. But the predominant issues for them are race and class, not gender. Closing racial and economic gaps would help poor and minority boys more than closing gender gaps, and focusing on gender gaps may distract attention from the bigger problems facing these youngsters.

The hysteria about boys is partly a matter of perspective. While most of society has finally embraced the idea of equality for women, the idea that women might actually surpass men in some areas (even as they remain behind in others) seems hard for many people to swallow. Thus, boys are routinely characterized as "falling behind" even as they improve in absolute terms.

In addition, a dizzying array of so-called experts have seized on the boy crisis as a way to draw attention to their pet educational, cultural, or ideological issues. Some say that contemporary classrooms are too structured, suppressing boys' energetic natures and tendency to physical expression; others contend that boys need more structure and discipline in school. Some blame "misguided feminism" for boys' difficulties, while others argue that "myths" of masculinity have a crippling impact on boys.[3] Many of these theories have superficially plausible rationales that make them appealing to some parents, educators, and policymakers. But the evidence suggests that many of these ideas come up short.

Unfortunately, the current boy crisis hype and the debate around it are based more on hopes and fears than on evidence. This debate benefits neither boys nor girls, while distracting attention from more serious educational problems—such as large racial and economic achievement gaps—and practical ways to help both boys and girls succeed in school.

A NEW CRISIS?

"The Boy Crisis. At every level of education, they're falling behind. What to do?"

—*Newsweek* cover headline, Jan. 30, 2006

Newsweek is not the only media outlet publishing stories that suggest boys' academic accomplishments and life opportunities are declining. But it's not true. Neither the facts reported in these articles nor data from other sources support the notion that boys' academic performance is falling. In fact, overall academic achievement and attainment for boys is higher than it has ever been.

Long-Term Trends

Looking at student achievement and how it has changed over time can be complicated. Most test scores have little meaning themselves; what matters is what scores tell us about how a group of students is doing relative to something else: an established definition of what students need to know, how this group of students performed in the past, or how other groups of students are performing. Further, most of the tests used to assess student achievement are relatively new, and others have changed over time, leaving relatively few constant measures.

10

The National Assessment of Educational Progress (NAEP), commonly known as "The Nation's Report Card," is a widely respected test conducted by the U.S. Department of Education using a large, representative national sample of American students. NAEP is the only way to measure national trends in boys' and girls' academic achievements over long periods of time.[4] There are two NAEP tests. The "main NAEP" has tracked U.S. students' performance in reading, math, and other academic subjects since the early 1990s. It tests students in grades four, eight, and 12. The "long-term trend NAEP" has tracked student performance since the early 1970s. It tests students at ages 9, 13, and 17.

Reading

The most recent main NAEP assessment in reading, administered in 2005, does not support the notion that boys' academic achievement is falling. In fact, fourth grade boys did better than they had done on both the previous NAEP reading assessment, administered in 2003, and the earliest comparable assessment, administered in 1992. Scores for both fourth- and eighth-grade boys have gone up and down over the past decade, but results suggest that the reading skills of fourth- and eighth-grade boys have improved since 1992.[5]

The picture is less clear for older boys. The 2003 and 2005 NAEP assessments included only fourth- and eighth-graders, so the most recent main NAEP data for 12th-graders dates back to 2002. On that assessment, 12th-grade boys did worse than they had in both the previous assessment, administered in 1998, and the first comparable assessment, administered in 1992. At the 12th-grade level, boys' achievement in reading does appear to have fallen during the 1990s and early 2000s.[6]

Even if younger boys have improved their achievement over the past decade, however, this could represent a decline if boys' achievement had risen rapidly in previous decades. Some commentators have asserted that the boy crisis has its roots in the mid- or early-1980s. But long-term NAEP data simply does not support these claims. In fact, 9-year-old boys did better on the most recent long-term reading NAEP, in 2004, than they have at any time since the test was first administered in 1971. Nine-year-old boys' performance rose in the 1970s, declined in the 1980s, and has been rising since the early 1990s.

Like the main NAEP, the results for older boys on the long-term NAEP are more mixed. Thirteen-year-old boys have improved their performance slightly compared with 1971, but for the most part their performance over the past 30 years has been flat. Seventeen-year-old boys are doing about the same as they did in the early 1970s, but their performance has been declining since the late 1980s.[7]

The main NAEP also shows that white boys score significantly better than black and Hispanic boys in reading at all grade levels. These differences far outweigh all changes in the overall performance of boys over time. For example, the difference between white and black boys on the fourth-grade NAEP in reading in 2005 was 10 times as great as the improvement for all boys on the same test since 1992.

And while academic performance for minority boys is often shockingly low, it's not getting worse. The average fourth-grade NAEP reading scores of black boys improved more from 1995 to 2005 than those of white and Hispanic boys or girls of any race.

Math

The picture for boys in math is less complicated. Boys of all ages and races are scoring as high—or higher—in math than ever before. From 1990 through 2005, boys in grades four and eight improved their performance steadily on the main NAEP, and they scored significantly better on the 2005 NAEP than in any previous year. Twelfth-graders have not taken the main NAEP in math since 2000. That year, 12th-grade boys did better than they had in 1990 and 1992, but worse than they had in 1996.[8]

Both 9- and 13-year-old boys improved gradually on the long-term NAEP since the 1980s (9-year-old boys' math performance did not improve in the 1970s). Seventeen-year-old boys' performance declined through the 1970s, rose in the 1980s, and remained relatively steady during the late 1990s and early 2000s.[9] As in reading, white boys score much better on the main NAEP in math than do black and Hispanic boys, but all three groups of boys are improving their math performance in the elementary and middle school grades.[10]

Other Subjects

In addition to the main and long-term NAEP assessments in reading and math, the NAEP also administers assessments in civics, geography, science, U.S. history, and writing. The civics assessment has not been administered since 1998, but the geography and U.S. history assessment were both administered in 1994 and 2001; the writing assessment in 1998 and 2002; and the science assessment in 1996, 2000, and 2005.

In geography, there was no significant change in boys' achievement at any grade level from 1994 to 2001. In U.S. history, fourth- and eighth-grade boys improved their achievement, but there was no significant change for 12th-grade boys. In writing, both fourth- and eighth-grade boys improved their achievement from 1998 to 2002, but 12th-grade boys' achievement declined. In science, fourth-grade boys' achievement in 2005 improved over their performance in both 1996 and 2000, eighth-grade boys showed no significant change in achievement, and 12th-grade boys' achievement declined since 1996.

Overall Long-Term Trends

A consistent trend emerges across these subjects: There have been no dramatic changes in the performance of boys in recent years, no evidence to indicate a boy crisis. Elementary-school-age boys are improving their performance; middle school boys are either improving their performance or showing little change, depending on the subject; and high school boys' achievement is declining in most subjects (although it may be improving in math). These trends seem to be consistent across all racial subgroups of boys, despite the fact that white boys perform much better on these tests than do black and Hispanic boys.

Evidence of a decline in the performance of older boys is undoubtedly troubling. But the question to address is whether this is a problem for older boys or for older students generally. That can be best answered by looking at the flip side of the gender equation: achievement for girls.

The Difference Between Boys and Girls

To the extent that tales of declining boy performance are grounded in real data, they're usually framed as a decline relative to girls. That's because, as described above, boy performance is generally staying the same or increasing in absolute terms.

But even relative to girls, the NAEP data for boys paints a complex picture. On the one hand, girls outperform boys in reading at all three grade levels assessed on the main NAEP. Gaps between girls and boys are smaller in fourth grade and get larger in eighth and 12th grades. Girls also outperform boys in writing at all grade levels. 25

In math, boys outperform girls at all grade levels, but only by a very small amount. Boys also outperform girls—again, very slightly—in science and by a slightly larger margin in geography. There are no significant gaps between male and female achievement on the NAEP in U.S. history. In general, girls outperform boys in reading and writing by greater margins than boys outperform girls in math, science, and geography.

But this is nothing new. Girls have scored better than boys in reading for as long as the long-term NAEP has been administered. And younger boys are actually catching up: The gap between boys and girls at age 9 has narrowed significantly since 1971—from 13 points to five points—even as both genders have significantly improved. Boy-girl gaps at age 13 haven't changed much since 1971—and neither has boys' or girls' achievement.

At age 17, gaps between boys and girls in reading are also not that much different from what they were in 1971, but they are significantly bigger than they were in the late 1980s, before achievement for both genders—and particularly boys—began to decline.

The picture in math is even murkier. On the first long-term NAEP assessment in 1973, 9- and 13-year-old girls actually scored better than boys in math, and they continued to do so throughout the 1970s. But as 9- and 13-year-olds of both genders improved their achievement in math during the 1980s and 1990s, boys *pulled ahead* of girls, opening up a small gender gap in math achievement that now favors boys. It's telling that even though younger boys are now doing better than girls on the long-term NAEP in math, when they once lagged behind, no one is talking about the emergence of a new "girl crisis" in elementary- and middle-school math.

Seventeen-year-old boys have always scored better than girls   30
on the long-term NAEP in math, but boys' scores declined slightly
more than girls' scores in the 1970s, and girls' scores have risen
slightly more than those of boys since. As a result, older boys'
advantage over girls in math has narrowed.

Overall, there has been no radical or recent decline in boys'
performance relative to girls. Nor is there a clear overall trend—
boys score higher in some areas, girls in others.

The fact that achievement for older students is stagnant or
declining for both boys and girls, to about the same degree, points
to another important element of the boy crisis. The problem is
most likely not that high schools need to be fixed to meet
the needs of boys, but rather that they need to be fixed to meet the
needs of *all* students, male and female.

The need to accurately parse the influence of gender and
other student categories is also acutely apparent when we examine the issues of race and income.

We Should Be Worried About Some Subgroups of Boys

There are groups of boys for whom "crisis" is not too strong a term.
When racial and economic gaps combine with gender achievement
gaps in reading, the result is disturbingly low achievement for poor,
black, and Hispanic boys.

But the gaps between students of different races and classes   35
are much larger than those for students of different genders—
anywhere from two to five times as big, depending on the grade.
The only exception is among 12th-grade boys, where the achievement gap between white girls and white boys in reading is the
same size as the gap between white and black boys in reading and
is larger than the gap between white and Hispanic boys. Overall,
though, poor, black, and Hispanic boys would benefit far more
from closing racial and economic achievement gaps than they
would from closing gender gaps. While the gender gap picture is
mixed, the racial gap picture is, unfortunately, clear across a wide
range of academic subjects.

In addition to disadvantaged and minority boys, there are
also reasons to be concerned about the substantial percentage of
boys who have been diagnosed with disabilities. Boys make up
two-thirds of students in special education—including 80 percent
of those diagnosed with emotional disturbances or autism—and
boys are two and a half times as likely as girls to be diagnosed with
attention deficit hyperactivity disorder (ADHD).[11] The number of
boys diagnosed with disabilities or ADHD has exploded in the

past 30 years, presenting a challenge for schools and causing concern for parents. But the reasons for this growth are complicated, a mix of educational, social, and biological factors. Evidence suggests that school and family factors—such as poor reading instruction, increased awareness of and testing for disabilities, or over-diagnosis—may play a role in the increased rates of boys diagnosed with learning disabilities or emotional disturbance. But boys also have a higher incidence of organic disabilities, such as autism and orthopedic impairments, for which scientists don't currently have a completely satisfactory explanation. Further, while girls are less likely than boys to be diagnosed with most disabilities, the number of girls with disabilities has also grown rapidly in recent decades, meaning that this is not just a boy issue.

Moving Up and Moving On

Beyond achievement, there's the issue of attainment—student success in moving forward along the education pathway and ultimately earning credentials and degrees. There are undeniably some troubling numbers for boys in this area. But as with achievement, the attainment data does not show that boys are doing worse.

Elementary-school-age boys are more likely than girls to be held back a grade. In 1999, 8.3 percent of boys ages 5–12 had been held back at least one grade, compared with 5.2 percent of girls. However, the percentage of boys retained a grade has declined since 1996, while the percentage of girls retained has stayed the same.[12]

Mirroring the trends in achievement noted above, racial and economic differences in grade retention are as great as or greater than gender differences. For example, white boys are more likely than white girls to be retained a grade, but about equally likely as black and Hispanic girls. Black and Hispanic boys are much more likely to be held back than either white boys or girls from any racial group. Similarly, both boys and girls from low-income homes are much more likely to be held back, while boys from high-income homes are less likely to be held back than are girls from either low- or moderate-income families.[13]

Boys are also much more likely than girls to be suspended or expelled from school. According to the U.S. Department of Justice, 24 percent of girls have been suspended from school at least once by age 17, but so have fully 42 percent of boys.[14] This is undeniably cause for concern.

Boys are also more likely than girls to drop out of high school. Research by the Manhattan Institute found that only

40

about 65 percent of boys who start high school graduate four years later, compared with 72 percent of girls. This gender gap cuts across all racial and ethnic groups, but it is the smallest for white and Asian students and much larger for black and Hispanic students. Still, the gaps between graduation rates for white and black or Hispanic students are much greater than gaps between rates for boys and girls of any race.[15] These statistics, particularly those for black and Hispanic males, are deeply troubling. There is some good news, though, because both men and women are slightly more likely to graduate from high school today than they were 30 years ago.[16]

Aspirations and Preparation

There is also some evidence that girls who graduate from high school have higher aspirations and better preparation for postsecondary education than boys do. For example, a University of Michigan study found that 62 percent of female high school seniors plan to graduate from a four-year-college, compared with 51 percent of male students.[17] Girls are also more likely than boys to have taken a variety of college-preparatory classes, including geometry, algebra II, chemistry, advanced biology, and foreign languages, although boys are more likely to have taken physics.

But this is another case where boys are actually improving, just not as fast as girls. The percentages of both boys and girls taking higher-level math and science courses in high school have increased dramatically in the past 20 years. For example, the percentages of both boys and girls taking precalculus have more than quadrupled since 1982, and the percentages of students taking calculus have more than doubled. But, particularly in the sciences, the percentage of girls taking advanced courses in high school has increased more rapidly than the percentage of boys, so that girls are now more likely than boys to take such classes.[18]

Similarly, the percentages of both boys and girls taking AP exams, which measure whether students have mastered rigorous, college-level curricula in various subjects, have increased dramatically in the past 20 years: Four and a half times as many students took AP tests in 2002 as did so in 1985. But girls have increased their AP test-taking more rapidly than boys, so that more girls than boys now take AP tests. In 2002, girls took 54 percent of AP exams, compared with 46 percent for boys. But while girls take the majority of AP exams in some subjects—social sciences, English, and especially foreign languages—boys dominate in other subjects, including calculus, the sciences, and computer science.[19]

It is also the case that more girls than boys take college   45
entrance exams—the SAT and the ACT. But boys have higher average scores than girls do, on both. In fact, boys score significantly
higher than girls on both the verbal and math subtests of the SAT,
and they have done so throughout most of the exam's history (girls
scored slightly higher than boys on the verbal portion of the exam
in the late 1960s), although boys' average score advantage is much
greater on the math than the verbal section.[20]

The male advantage on the SAT also appears to contradict
the notion of a boy crisis, but it should not really be interpreted
that way. Girls' average SAT scores are lower than those of boys
at least in part because more girls than boys take the SAT. Since
the SAT is taken only by students who intend to go to college,
most high-performing students of both genders take it. The
larger population of girls taking the SAT means more girls than
boys from lower on the achievement distribution are taking
the test, resulting in lower average scores for girls. In addition, the SAT verbal section has historically relied heavily on
analogies, an area of abilities in which psychological research
finds that men consistently outperform women.[21] Changes to
the SAT in 2005, which eliminated analogies and added a writing section, are likely to result in improved scores for women
relative to men.

The Allegedly Disappearing Big Man on Campus

*"Forty-two men for every 58 women go to college now,
undergrad and grad. That means 1 in 4 female students
can't find a male peer to date."*

—*Esquire*, July 2006

*"Women now significantly outnumber men on college cam-
puses, a phenomenon familiar enough to any sorority sister seeking a date to the next formal."*

—Richard Whitmire, *The New Republic*, Jan. 23, 2006

To hear commentators tell it, college campuses are becoming all-
female enclaves, suffering from a kind of creeping Wellesleyfica-
tion. But men are enrolling in college in greater numbers than
ever before and at historically high rates.

This is undeniably good news for the nation, as more and
more future workers will need college credentials to compete in

the global economy. Why, then, all the anxiety? Because women are increasing college enrollment at an even faster rate.

Of men graduating from high school in spring 2001, 60 percent enrolled in college in the following fall, compared with 64 percent of women. The gap is smaller among those enrolling in four-year institutions: 41 percent of men, compared with 43 percent of women.

Women are, however, more likely to graduate from college once they get there. Sixty-six percent of women who enrolled in college as freshmen seeking a bachelor's degree during the 1995–96 school year had completed a bachelor's degree by 2001, compared with 59 percent of men.[22] As with high school graduation rates, this appears to be the area in which gender-focused concerns are most justified, with men less likely to stay in school and earn a degree.

Because men are less likely to go to college and more likely to drop out, the share of college students who are men has declined. From 1970 to 2001, men's share of college enrollment fell from 58 to 44 percent, while women's share blossomed from 42 to 56 percent. And fully 57 percent of bachelor's degrees in 2001 were awarded to women.[23]

But these numbers don't necessarily indicate an emerging crisis. Like many other trends in gender and education, they're nothing new. In fact, nearly two-thirds of the increase in women's share of college enrollment occurred more than two decades ago, between 1970 and 1980.

Overall trends, moreover, can be misleading. Women are overrepresented among both nontraditional students—older students going back to college after working or having a family—and students at two-year colleges. Among students enrolled in four-year colleges right out of high school, or traditional college students, the percentages of men and women are closer—and the dating situation is not as dire as Whitmire and *Esquire* suggest.

More important, even as their share of enrollment on college campuses declines, young men are actually more likely to attend and graduate from college than they were in the 1970s and 1980s. The share of men 25 to 29 who hold a bachelor's degree has also increased, to 22 percent—a rate significantly higher than that for older cohorts of men.[24] But the number of women enrolling in and graduating from college has increased much more rapidly during the same time period. The proportion of women enrolling in college after high school graduation, for example, increased nearly 50 percent between the early 1970s

50

and 2001, and nearly 25 percent of women ages 25 to 29 now hold bachelor's degrees.

While it's possible to debate whether men's college attendance 55 is increasing fast enough to keep up with economic changes, it's simply inaccurate to imply that men are disappearing from college campuses or that they are doing worse than they were 10 or 20 years ago. Men's higher-education attainment is not declining; it's increasing, albeit at a slower rate than that of women.

In addition, while women have outstripped men in undergraduate enrollment, women still earn fewer than half of first professional degrees, such as law, medicine, and dentistry, and doctorates. Women do earn more master's degrees than men, but female graduate students are heavily concentrated in several traditionally female fields, most notably education and psychology.[25]

Outcomes of Education

With women attending and graduating from college at higher rates than men, we might expect young women, on average, to be earning more than men. But the reality is the opposite.

Female college degrees are disproportionately in relatively low-paying occupations like teaching. As a result, women ages 25–34 who have earned a bachelor's degree make barely more money than men of the same age who went to college but didn't get a bachelor's degree.[26] Further, recent female college graduates earn less than their male counterparts, even after controlling for choice of field.[27]

In other words, the undeniable success of more women graduating from high school, going to college, and finishing college ultimately results in women remaining behind men economically—just by not as much as before. Far from surging ahead of men, women are still working to catch up.

THE SOURCE OF THE BOY CRISIS: A KNOWLEDGE DEFICIT AND A SURPLUS OF OPPORTUNISM

It's clear that some gender differences in education are real, and 60 there are some groups of disadvantaged boys in desperate need of help. But it's also clear that boys' overall educational achievement and attainment are not in decline—in fact, they have never been better. What accounts for the recent hysteria?

It's partly an issue of simple novelty. The contours of disadvantage in education and society at large have been clear for a long time—low-income, minority, and female people consistently fall short of their affluent, white, and male peers. The idea that historically privileged boys could be at risk, that boys could be shortchanged, has simply proved too deliciously counterintuitive and "newsworthy" for newspaper and magazine editors to resist.

The so-called boy crisis also feeds on a lack of solid information. Although there are a host of statistics about how boys and girls perform in school, we actually know very little about why these differences exist or how important they are. There are many things—including biological, developmental, cultural, and educational factors—that affect how boys and girls do in school. But untangling these different influences is incredibly difficult. Research on the causes of gender differences is hobbled by the twin demons of educational research: lack of data and the difficulty of drawing causal connections among multiple, complex influences. Nor do we know what these differences mean for boys' and girls' future economic and other opportunities.

Yet this hasn't stopped a plethora of so-called experts— from pediatricians and philosophers to researchers and op-ed columnists—from weighing in with their views on the causes and likely effects of educational gender gaps. In fact, the lack of solid research evidence confirming or debunking any particular hypothesis has created fertile ground for all sorts of people to seize on the boy crisis to draw attention to their pet educational, cultural or ideological issues.

The problem, we are told, is that the structured traditional classroom doesn't accommodate boys' energetic nature and need for free motion—or it's that today's schools don't provide enough structure or discipline. It's that feminists have demonized typical boy behavior and focused educational resources on girls—or it's the "box" boys are placed in by our patriarchal society. It's that our schools' focus on collaborative learning fails to stimulate boys' natural competitiveness—or it's that the competitive pressures of standardized testing are pushing out the kind of relevant, hands-on work on which boys thrive.

The boy crisis offers a perfect opportunity for those seeking an   65
excuse to advance ideological and educational agendas. Americans' continued ambivalence about evolving gender roles guarantees that stories of "boys in crisis" will capture public attention. The research base is internally contradictory, making it easy to find superficial support for a wide variety of explanations but difficult

for the media and the public to evaluate the quality of evidence cited. Yet there is not sufficient evidence—or the right kind of evidence—available to draw firm conclusions. As a result, there is a sort of free market for theories about why boys are under-performing girls in school, with parents, educators, media, and the public choosing to give credence to the explanations that are the best marketed and that most appeal to their pre-existing preferences.

Unfortunately, this dynamic is not conducive to a thoughtful public debate about how boys and girls are doing in school or how to improve their performance.

Hard-Wired Inequality?

One branch of the debate over gender and education has focused on various theories of divergence between male and female brains. Men and women are "wired differently," people say, leading to all kinds of alleged problems and disparities that must be addressed. There's undoubtedly some truth here. The difficulty is separating fact from supposition.

The quest to identify and explain differences between men's and women's mental abilities is as old as psychology itself. Although the earliest work in this genre began with the assumption that women were intellectually inferior to men, and sought both to prove and explain why this was the case, more recent and scientifically valid research also finds differences in men's and women's cognitive abilities, as well as in the physiology of their brains.

It's important to note that research does not find that one gender is smarter than the other—on average, men and women score the same on tests of general intelligence.[28] But there are differences between men's and women's performance in different types of abilities measured by intelligence tests. In general, women have higher scores than men on most tests of verbal abilities (verbal analogies being an exception), while men have higher scores on tests of what psychologists call "visual-spatial" abilities—the ability to think in terms of nonverbal, symbolic information, measured through such tasks as the ability to place a horizontal line in a tilted frame or to identify what the image of an irregular object would look like if the object were rotated. Quantitative or mathematical abilities are more even, with men performing better on some types of problems—including probability, statistics, measurement and geometry—while women perform better on others, such as computation, and both genders perform equally well on still others.

Much of this research is based on studies with adults— 70
particularly college students—but we know that gender differences in cognitive abilities vary with development. Differences in
verbal abilities are among the first to appear; vocabulary differences, for example, are seen before children are even 2 years old,
and by the time they enter kindergarten, girls are more likely than
boys to know their letters and be able to associate letters with
sounds.[29] Male advantages in visual-spatial abilities emerge later
in childhood and adolescence.[30]

The research identifying these differences in male and female
cognitive abilities does not explain their cause, however. There
may be innate, biologically based differences in men and women.
But gender differences may also be the result of culture and
socialization that emphasize different skills for men and women
and provide both genders different opportunities to develop their
abilities.

Researchers have investigated a variety of potential biological
causes for these differences. There is evidence that sex hormones
in the womb, which drive the development of the fetus's sex
organs, also have an impact on the brain. Children who were
exposed to abnormal levels of these hormones, for example, may
develop cognitive abilities more like those of the opposite sex.
Increased hormone levels at puberty may again affect cognitive
development. And performance on some types of cognitive tests
tends to vary with male and female hormonal cycles.[31]

In addition, new technologies that allow researchers to look
more closely into the brain and observe its activities have shown
that there are differences between the sexes in the size of various
brain structures and in the parts of the brain men and women use
when performing different tasks.[32]

But while this information is intriguing, it must be interpreted
with a great deal of caution. Although our knowledge of the brain
and its development has expanded dramatically in recent years, it
remains rudimentary. In the future, much of our current thinking
about the brain will most likely seem as unsophisticated as the
work of the late 19th and early 20th century researchers who
sought to prove female intellectual inferiority by comparing the
size of men's and women's skulls.

In particular, it is notoriously difficult to draw causal links 75
between observations about brain structure or activity and
human behavior, a point that scientists reporting the findings of
brain research often take great pains to emphasize. Just as correlation does not always signify causation in social science

research, correlations between differences in brain structure and observed differences in male and female behavior do not necessarily mean that the former leads to the latter.

But these caveats have not prevented many individuals from confidently citing brain research to advance their preferred explanation of gender gaps in academic achievement.

Proponents of different educational philosophies and approaches cherry-pick findings that seem to support their visions of public education. And a growing boys industry purports to help teachers use brain research on gender differences to improve boys' academic achievement. But many of these individuals and organizations are just seizing on the newest crisis—boys' achievement—to make money and promote old agendas. Scientific-sounding brain research has lent an aura of authority to people who see anxiety about boys as an opportunity for personal gain. Many have also added refashioned elements of sociology to their boys-in-crisis rhetoric.

DUBIOUS THEORIES AND OLD AGENDAS

"Girl behavior becomes the gold standard. Boys are treated like defective girls."

—Psychologist Michael Thompson, as quoted in *Newsweek*

Thompson is just one of many commentators who argue that today's schools disadvantage boys by expecting behavior—doing homework, sitting still, working collaboratively, expressing thoughts and feelings verbally and in writing—that comes more naturally to girls. These commentators argue that schools are designed around instructional models that work well with girls' innate abilities and learning styles but do not provide enough support to boys or engage their interests and strengths. While female skills like organization, empathy, cooperativeness, and verbal agility are highly valued in schools, male strengths like physical vigor and competitiveness are overlooked and may even be treated as problems rather than assets, the argument goes.

Building from this analysis, a wealth of books, articles, and training programs endeavor to teach educators how to make schools more "boy friendly." Many of these suggestions—such as allowing boys to choose reading selections that appeal to their interests—are reasonable enough.

But many other recommendations are based on an inappro-   80
priate application of brain research on sex differences. Many of these authors draw causal connections between brain research findings and stereotypical male or female personality traits without any evidence that such causality exists. These analyses also tend to ignore the wide variation among individuals of the same sex. Many girls have trouble completing their homework and sitting still, too, and some boys do not.

Members of the growing "boys industry" of researchers, advocates, and pop psychologists include family therapist Michael Gurian, author of *The Minds of Boys, Boys and Girls Learn Differently!*, and numerous other books about education and gender; Harvard psychologist William Pollack, director of the Center for Research on Boys at McLean Hospital and author of *Real Boys*; and Michael Thompson, clinical psychologist and the author of *Raising Cain*. All of these authors are frequently cited in media coverage of the boy crisis. A quick search on Amazon.com also turns up Jeffrey Wilhelm's *Reading Don't Fix No Chevys*, Thomas Newkirk's *Misreading Masculinity: Boys, Literacy and Popular Culture*, Christina Hoff Sommers' *The War On Boys*, Leonard Sax's *Why Gender Matters*, and *Hear Our Cry: Boys in Crisis*, by Paul D. Slocumb. A review of these books shows that the boys industry is hardly monolithic. Its practitioners seem to hold a plethora of perspectives and philosophies about both gender and education, and their recommendations often contradict one another.

Some focus on boys' emotions and sense of self-worth, while others are more concerned with implementing pedagogical practices—ranging from direct instruction to project-based learning—that they believe will better suit boys' learning style. Still others focus on structural solutions, such as smaller class sizes or single-sex learning environments. But all are finding an audience among parents, educators, and policymakers concerned about boys.

It would be unfair to imply that these authors write about boys for purely self-serving motives—most of these men and women seem to be sincerely concerned about the welfare of our nation's boys. But the work in this field leaves one skeptical of the quality of research, information, and analysis that are shaping educators' and parents' beliefs and practices as they educate boys and girls. Perhaps most tellingly, ideas about how to make schools more "boy friendly" align suspiciously well with educational and ideological beliefs the individuals promoting them had long before boys were making national headlines. And some of these prescriptions are diametrically opposed to one another.

A number of conservative authors, think tanks, and journals have published articles arguing that progressive educational pedagogy and misguided feminism are hurting boys.[33] According to these critics, misguided feminists have lavished resources on female students at the expense of males and demonized typical boy behaviors such as rowdy play. At the same time, progressive educational pedagogy is harming boys by replacing strict discipline with permissiveness, teacher-led direct instruction with student-led collaborative learning, and academic content with a focus on developing students' self-esteem. The boy crisis offers an attractive way for conservative pundits to get in some knocks against feminism and progressive education and also provides another argument for educational policies—such as stricter discipline, more traditional curriculum, increased testing and competition, and single-sex schooling—that conservatives have long supported.

Progressive education thinkers, on the other hand, tend to see boys' achievement problems as evidence that schools have not gone far *enough* in adopting progressive tenets and are still forcing all children into a teacher-led pedagogical box that is particularly ill-suited to boys' interests and learning styles. Similarly, the responses progressive education writers recommend—more project-based and hands-on learning, incorporating kinetic and other learning styles into lessons, making learning "relevant," and allowing children more self-direction and free movement—simply sound like traditional progressive pedagogy.[34]

More recently, critics of the standards movement and its flagship federal legislation, the No Child Left Behind Act (NCLB), have argued that the movement and NCLB are to blame for boys' problems. According to *Newsweek*, "In the last two decades, the education system has become obsessed with a quantifiable and narrowly defined kind of academic success, and that myopic view, these experts say, is harming boys." This is unlikely, because high-school-age boys, who seem to be having the most problems, are affected far less by NCLB than elementary-school-age boys, who seem to be improving the most.

Further, many of the arguments NCLB critics make about how it hurts boys—by causing schools to narrow their curriculum or

85

eliminate recess—are not borne out by the evidence. A recent report from the Washington, D.C.-based Center for Educational Policy showed that most schools are not eliminating social studies, science, and arts in response to NCLB.[35] And, a report from the U.S. Department of Education found that over 87 percent of elementary schools offer recess and most do so daily.[36] More important, such critics offer no compelling case for why standards and testing, if harmful, would have more of a negative impact on boys than on girls.

In other words, few of these commentators have anything new to say—the boy crisis has just given them a new opportunity to promote their old messages.

HOW SHOULD PARENTS, EDUCATORS, AND POLICYMAKERS RESPOND?

To be sure, there are good reasons to be concerned about boys— particularly low-income, urban, rural, and minority boys as well as those with disabilities. Whether or not our schools are to blame for causing these boys' problems, they need to do a better job of working to address them. In particular, the disproportionate number of boys being identified with learning and emotional disabilities, suspended from school, and dropping out suggests that what our schools are doing doesn't work very well for some boys. But with so much ideological baggage and so little real evidence influencing the public debate on boys' achievement, how are policymakers, educators, and parents to know what to do?

It's likely that there is at least a grain of truth in all the different explanations being offered. The boy industry would not have the success it does if its arguments did not, to some degree, resonate with the experiences of parents and educators. But the many questions left unanswered by the research on these issues— as well as the ideological agendas of many participants in these discussions—make it difficult to draw practical conclusions about how to respond.

But there are several things parents, educators, and policymakers could and should do.

The first is to not panic. Boys' educational achievement is improving overall, some gender gaps are less significant than press reports make them out to be, and many boys are doing fine despite the averages.

Second, we need to realize that many areas in which we see boys struggling are connected to larger educational and social problems and are not just a function of gender. Fortunately, we know more about these larger problems—and some of the steps we can take to address them—than we do about gender gaps. Low-income, black, and Hispanic boys, in the aggregate, are not doing well. Focusing on closing these racial and economic achievement gaps would do more to help poor, black, and Hispanic boys than closing gender gaps, and it would also help girls in these groups.

Similarly, while boys seem to be doing pretty well in elementary school, their achievement in high school appears to be declining. But so is the achievement of high school girls. The past decade of school reform—in which we have seen elementary-school-age boys make a lot of progress—focused heavily on the elementary school years and particularly on building early literacy skills. But national policymakers have realized, in the past few years, that America's public high schools are also in need of significant reforms. It makes sense to expand these reforms—which should help both boys and girls to achieve—and see if they reverse high school boys' academic achievement declines and narrow gender gaps before we go too far down the boy-crisis road.

Educators, parents, and policymakers should therefore be skeptical of simplistic proposals aimed at fixing the boy crisis, such as expanding single-sex schooling, implementing gender-based instructional techniques, or funding new federal programs aimed at improving boys' achievement. The close relation between the difficulties facing some boys and complex educational challenges such as racial and economic achievement gaps, high school reform, and special education suggests that silver-bullet approaches are unlikely to solve the problems facing many boys. Each of these ideas may have a modicum of merit, but there is little sound research evidence for their effectiveness.

In addition, we need to recognize the role that choices play in producing different educational outcomes for men and women. Although some achievement gaps emerge early and appear to have a developmental component, those about which we are the most worried occur later, when the choices young people make have a significant impact on their educational results. Over the past 25 years, economic opportunities for women have increased dramatically, but many require a bachelor's degree. Families and education systems have been very clear in conveying this message to young women and encouraging them to get the education they need to be economically successful. Less educated men, however, historically have more economic opportunities than less educated women, so their incentives to get a good education are not as strong as those facing women. Many jobs traditionally held by less educated men are disappearing, or now require more education than they did a generation ago, but boys may not understand this. We need to look carefully at the messages that pop culture, peer culture, and the adults who are involved in young people's lives send to boys about the importance of education to their future opportunities, and make sure that these messages are conveying accurate information to young men about their economic opportunities and the education they need to take advantage of them.

Finally, policymakers should support and fund more research about differences in boys' and girls' achievement, brain development, and the culture of schools to help teachers and parents better understand why boys' achievement is not rising as fast as that of girls. Such research should include studies that use proper methodological and analytic tools to look into the cause of gender achievement gaps, as well as experimental evaluations of different approaches that seek to close them. To support research, policymakers should make sure that data systems are collecting quality information about boys' and girls' school experiences and academic achievement and men's and women's educational attainment and workforce outcomes. In addition, policymakers should fund research on some of the specific problems—learning disabilities, autism, and disciplinary or emotional problems—that disproportionately affect boys.

These steps can help establish a more reasonable conversation and lead to effective responses to the achievement problems facing some boys, without unfairly undermining the gains that girls have made in recent decades.

Endnotes

1. *How Schools Shortchange Girls* (Washington, D.C.: American Association of University Women, 1992), http://www.aauw.org/research/girls_education/hssg.cfm.
2. Adrienne Mand Lewin, "Can Boys Really Not Sit Still in School?" ABCnews.com, January 26, 2006.

3. See Christina Hoff Sommers, *The War Against Boys* (New York: Simon & Schuster, 2000) and William Pollack, *Real Boys: Protecting Our Sons from the Myths of Boyhood* (New York: Random House, 1998).

4. Individual states also administer their own assessments, but none can be used to gauge long-term trends as well as the NAEP, nor do they offer the advantage of a national sample. Overall, differences between boys' and girls' performance on NAEP assessments match those found on state assessments—girls tend to do better than boys on tests of English/language arts, and boys tend to do slightly better in math.

5. Marianne Perie, Wendy S. Grigg, and Patricia L. Donahue, *The Nation's Report Card: Reading 2005* (Washington, D.C.: U.S. Department of Education, Institute of Education Sciences, National Center for Education Statistics, 2005), http:// nces.ed.gov/nationsreportcard/reading/.

6. *Ibid.*

7. M. Perie, R. Moran, and A. D. Lutkus, *NAEP 2004 Trends in Academic Progress: Three Decades of Student Achievement in Reading and Mathematics* (Washington, D.C.: U.S. Department of Education, Institute of Education Sciences, National Center for Education Statistics, 2005), http://nces.ed.gov/nationsreportcard/ltt/results2004/.

8. Marianne Perie, Wendy S. Grigg, and Gloria S. Dion, *The Nation's Report Card: Math 2005* (Washington, D.C.: U.S. Department of Education, National Center for Education Statistics, 2005).

9. The main NAEP and long-term trend NAEP are different assessments, so it is not necessarily inconsistent that older boys' performance rose on the main NAEP from 1992 to 1996 while it did not rise on the long-term trend NAEP.

10. *2004 Trends in Academic Progress, op. cit.;* author analysis using NAEP data explorer, http://nces.ed.gov/nationsreportcard/nde/.

11. Office of Special Education Programs, *25th Annual Report to Congress* (Washington, D.C.: U.S. Department of Education, 2003), http://www.ed.gov/about/offices/list/osers/osep/research.html; Centers for Disease Control and Prevention, "Mental Health in the United States: Prevalence of and Diagnosis and Medication Treatment for Attention Deficit/Hyperactivity Disorder—United States, 2003," *MMWR Weekly*, September 2, 2005. http://www.cde.gov/mmwr/preview/mmwehtml/mm5434a2.htm.

12. Catherine Freeman, *Trends in Educational Equity of Girls and Women* (Washington, D.C.: U.S. Department of Education, National Center for Education Statistics, 2004), http://nces.ed.gov/pubsearch/pubsinfo.asp?pubid=2005016.

13. *Trends in Educational Equity of Girls and Women, op. cit.*

14. Office of Juvenile Justice and Delinquency Prevention, *Juvenile Offenders and Victims: 2006 National Report* (Washington, D.C.: U.S. Department of Justice, Office of Justice Programs, 2006), http://ojjdp.ncjrs.org/ojstatbb/nr2006/indes.html.

15. Jay P. Greene and Marcus Winters, *Leaving Boys Behind: Public High School Graduation Rates* (Manhattan Institute, April 2006), http://www.manhattan-institute.org/html/cr_48.htm#05; research published by the Urban Institute reaches similar findings. See Christopher B. Swanson, *Who Graduates? Who Doesn't? A Statistical Portrait of Public High School Graduation 2001* (Washington, D.C.: The Urban Institute, 2003). http://www.urban.org/publications/410934.html.

16. *Trends in Educational Equity of Girls and Women: 2004, op. cit.*

17. As cited in *Trends in Educational Equity of Girls and Women: 2004, op. cit.* and Richard Whitmire, "Boy Trouble," *The New Republic*, January 23, 2006.

18. *Trends in Educational Equity of Girls and Women: 2004, op. cit.*

19. *Trends in Educational Equity of Girls and Women: 2004, op. cit.*

20. *2005 College-Bound Seniors: Total Group Profile Report* (New York: The College Board, August 2005), http://www.collegeboard.com/prod_downloads/about/news_info/cbsenior/yr2005/2005-college-bound-seniors.pdf. This report focuses on data from SAT exams administered before spring 2005, when a new SAT was launched that replaced the previous verbal section with critical reading and essay portions.

21. Diane Halpern, *Sex Differences in Cognitive Abilities* (Mahwah, N.J.: Lawrence Erlbaum Associates, 2000).

22. *Trends in Educational Equity of Girls and Women: 2004, op. cit.*

23. Katharin Peter and Laura Horn, *Gender Differences in Participation and Completion of Undergraduate Education and How They Have Changed Over Time* (Washington, D.C.: U.S. Department of Education, Institute of Education Sciences, National Center for Education Statistics, February 2005), http://nces.ed.gov/pubsearch/pubsinfo.asp?pubid=2005169.

24. *Trends in Educational Equity of Girls and Women: 2004, op. cit.*

25. *Ibid.*

26. *Highlights of Women's Earnings in 2004* (Washington, D.C.: U.S. Department of Labor, U.S. Bureau of Labor Statistics, September 2005).

27. *Trends in Educational Equity of Girls and Women: 2004, op. cit.*

28. Many intelligence tests are deliberately designed to eliminate any "gender bias"—essentially to ensure that male and female averages are the same. But research by Arthur Jensen, using tests that were not specifically written to eliminate sex differences, also found no significant differences between male and female general intelligence. See Arthur R. Jensen, *The g Factor: The Science of Mental Ability* (New York: Praeger, 1998).

29. Nicholas Zill and Jerry West, *Entering Kindergarten: A Portrait of American Children When They Begin School* (Washington, D.C.: U.S. Department of Education, Institute of Education Sciences, National Center for Education Statistics, 2000). http://nces.ed.gov/pubs2001/2001035.pdf

30. For a comprehensive summary of the evidence on gender differences in cognitive abilities, see Halpern, *op. cit.*

31. Halpern, *op. cit.*

32. Halpern, *op. cit*; See Jay N. Giedd, F. Xavier Castellanos, Jagath C. Rajapakse, A. Catherine Vaituzis, and Judith L. Rapoport, "Sexual Dimorphism of the Developing Human Brain," *Progress in Neuropsychopharmacology and Biological Psychiatry*, 1997; Sarah Durston, Hilleke Hulshoff Pol, B. J. Casey, Jay N. Giedd, Jan K. Buitelaar, and Herman Van Engeland, "Anatomical MRI of the Developing Human Brain: What Have We Learned?" *Journal of the American Academy of Adolescent Psychiatry*, 40: 9, September 2001.

33. See, for example, Christina Hoff Sommers, *op. cit.*; Krista Kafer, "Boys Lag Behind But Extra Help Goes to Girls," *School Reform News*, August 30, 2002; Mark Bauerlein and Sandra Stotsky, "Why Johnny Won't Read," *The Washington Post*, January 25, 2005.

34. See Michael Gurian, Patricia Henley, and Terry Trueman, *Boys and Girls Learn Differently* (Hoboken, N.J.: Jossey-Bass, 2001).

35. Diane Stark Rentner, Caitlin Scott, Nancy Kober, Naomi Chudowsky, Victor Chudowsky, Scott Joftus, Dalia Zabala, *From the Capital to the Classroom: Year 4 of the No Child Left Behind Act* (Washington, D.C.: Center for Education Policy, 2006), http://www.ctredpol.org/nclb/Year4/Press/.

36. Basmat Parsad and Laurie Lewis, *Calories In, Calories Out: Food and Exercise in Public Elementary Schools 2005* (Washington, D.C.: U.S. Department of Education, National Center for Education Statistics, 2006), http://nces.ed.gov/ pubsearch/ pubsinfo.asp?pubid=2006057.

Thinking About Content

1. What are some of the examples Mead uses to support her argument that there is no such thing as a "boy crisis"?

2. In this essay, Mead takes issue with those who use current brain research about the differences between male and female cognitive abilities to draw conclusions about educational success. What are her concerns? Why does she caution her readers to be careful about drawing "causal connections between brain research findings and stereotypical male or female personality traits"?

Thinking About Strategy

1. Throughout this essay, Mead quotes passages from some of the recent articles on the "boy crisis" in schools. She then goes on to explain the problems with the quotes, citing current research. Do you think this is an effective

strategy for a counterargument? Why or why not? Would you use a similar strategy if you were trying to develop a counterargument of your own? Explain your answer.

2. Mead ends her essay with a "call to action" in which she explains how parents, educators, and policy makers should respond to the "boy crisis." What does she say should be done? Is this call to action effective or ineffective and why?

Sex Bias Cited in Vocational Ed
THE WASHINGTON POST

The following news story appeared in the Washington Post, *one of our nation's top newspapers, on June 6, 2002. The brief article raises important questions about the continued discrimination against girls in our educational system.*

――――――――― ✦ ―――――――――

Pervasive sex segregation persists in high school vocational programs around the country—including in Maryland and Virginia—30 years after Congress passed a law barring such discrimination in education, according to a study released today.

The D.C.-based National Women's Law Center plans to file legal petitions today in all 12 regions of the Department of Education's Office of Civil Rights, requesting investigations into whether vocational and technical high schools and classes violate Title IX and demanding that action be taken to remedy all conduct that does not comply with federal law.

"There are just stunning patterns of sex segregation in schools across the country," said Jocelyn Samuels, vice president and director of educational opportunities for the law center. "The primary problems in career ed are inattention and lack of perception that there is a problem."

The center's survey on vocational programs marks the 30th anniversary of the federal law—Title IX of the Education Amendments—that bars sex discrimination in schools and other educational programs receiving federal funds. That includes almost all public elementary and secondary schools and most colleges and universities.

The survey found that girls still are clustered in classes that   5
lead to traditionally female jobs in cosmetology, child care and
other low-paying fields, while boys dominate classes that lead to
traditionally male—and high-paying—careers in technology and
the trades. Young women enrolled in such programs earn a
median hourly wage of $8.49 as a hairdresser, for example, com-
pared with $30.06 an hour in the traditionally male career of
plumbing and pipe fitting.

The pattern was consistent in all states surveyed, including
California and New York. In Maryland, for example, data showed
that female students make up 99 percent of the student body in
cosmetology courses, 84 percent in child care courses, 93 percent
in courses that prepare students to work as assistants in the
health-care field, and 89 percent in courses that prepare students
for other health-care occupations.

Male students make up 84 percent of those in drafting courses,
84 percent in computer installation and repair courses, 95 percent
in carpentry courses and 95 percent in automotive classes.

Maryland education officials said they could not comment
because they had not seen the report.

In Fairfax County, one of the richest counties in the country,
boys outnumber girls in every technology class in every high
school, according to research by the Fairfax County Office for
Women.

In 2000–01, girls accounted for only 5 percent of students in   10
design and technology courses, 10 percent in network administration courses and 27 percent in computer science classes, the
data showed. Only 5 percent of students in courses given by
CISCO Networking Academies at three Fairfax high schools
were girls.

Lesley Persily, program analyst for the county's Office
for Women, said the Fairfax Board of Education requested
information in 1998 on how well schools were complying with
Title IX.

"We released the data in 1998 in computer technology, and it
showed that every single class had a majority of boys," she said.
"Really, the numbers haven't changed since then."

Marty Abbott, director of high school instruction in Fairfax,
said: "This is an issue we have always been concerned with. . . .
We felt we had made some strides with our middle schools
and some of our high school courses, and we know that still at
some of the very top-level courses we need to see more girls

enrolling in those courses. But we have put a lot of effort into this, and we were hoping those numbers would appear stronger at this point."

One problem discovered by the investigators for the law center was there is no systematic requirement for data collection on vocational schools and programs. Some states keep data haphazardly, and some don't keep any at all. Furthermore, the law center said Virginia and a number of other states, as well as the District of Columbia, do not have Title IX coordinators, a violation of the law.

Girls are still not advised about the possibilities in different   15
trades, and they face harassment once they enter these fields, said Melissa Barbier, director of girls programs for Chicago Women in Trades, a 20-year organization dedicated to promoting women and girls in the trades.

She said it is vital for teachers and counselors to not only help women understand their options but to advocate for them.

"A shop teacher, for example, plays a big role in referring students to certain employers they have relationships with. What we are finding is that even teachers who support students inside the classroom are not helping them make the next link because they are not willing to advocate for their female students."

Supporters of Title IX recently have become alarmed by some Bush administration proposals that they regard as turning the clock back on educational opportunities for women.

The administration announced its intention recently to support single-sex schools and classes. And last week, it declined to comment on the merits of a lawsuit filed by the National Wrestling Coaches Association and other groups challenging Title IX athletic protections. It argued instead that the suit should be dismissed on procedural grounds.

Though Title IX applies to all aspects of education, it is best   20
known for opening the door to athletics for females. The number of college women participating in competitive athletics is now four times the pre-Title IX rate, and the number of high school girls playing competitive sports has risen from 300,000 before Title IX to 2.65 million by 1999.

Still, women in Division I colleges represent more than half of the student body, yet they receive only 41 percent of athletic scholarship dollars, 30 percent of recruiting dollars and 33 percent of overall athletic budgets, according to the law center.

Thinking About Content

1. There is a tendency to believe that although gender bias has happened in the past, it is no longer the case that girls or women are discriminated against. Does this report fit into that belief?
2. The article states that "it is vital for teachers and counselors to not only help women understand their options but to advocate for them." What does this suggest about the roles teachers play in students' lives? Are teachers role models for students?

Thinking About Strategy

1. What kinds of transitions exist between paragraphs in this text?
2. How does this article end? What kind of effect does that ending have on the reader? How do different types of endings encourage readers to different actions?

Are All-Girls Schools Best? The Continuing Controversy Over Single-Gender Education

LYNETTE LAMB

Lynette Lamb has authored many articles on girls and education. The following essay addressing both sides of the single-gender school issue originally appeared in September 2000 in New Moon Network, *a magazine whose target audience is parents of young girls.*

◆

Last fall there was an energetic discussion on the Care About Girls listserv concerning the pros and cons of single gender schools, which have become far more popular in the last decade. Thanks in part to the work of Carol Gilligan and the AAUW in pointing out how adolescent girls are at risk, applications at girls' schools have increased a dramatic 69 percent in Manhattan since 1991, the *New York Times* reported last year, with applications going up significantly at schools outside New York as well.

Lisa kicked off the listserv conversation by asking for input on whether to enroll her 5-year-old daughter in an all-girls school or a coeducational one.

The result? An overwhelmingly enthusiastic response in favor of single-sex schools. Greta wrote to praise the "superior education" she'd received at a secular all-girls school, and the far weaker one she found when she transferred in her junior year to a public school. A bank officer at 22, Greta wrote that she now realizes "a single-sex environment afforded me the confidence to try anything and the ignorance of sexual biases. I forged ahead without fear."

Alison, a veteran of 13 years of Manhattan all-girls schools, wrote to say she'd received a "fabulous education." Now enrolled in an elite medical school, she's certain that her superior grounding in science and math helped get her there. But despite being a "huge fan of single-sex education," she cautioned parents that such settings are not "guaranteed to teach self-confidence and feminist ideals, any more than coed schools are certain to turn out shy, self-effacing young women." She suggested that listserv members come up with an equity index, the score of which would be determined by a list of questions they could pose to school administrators concerning a school's gender equity.

Another listserv member, Jennifer, writes that despite having always attended coed schools, she remained an "outspoken character, thanks to parents who always taught me to question things and to boldly state my opinion." Don't underestimate the power of parents to help their girls remain unafraid to speak out, she reminded listserv members.   5

Finally, Susannah—while admitting that her thoughts were based mostly on a few personal examples—pointed out that her friends who had attended all-girl schools were actually "more gendered in their outlook, more likely to view boys in superficial and stereotypical terms, and to view dating and relationships the same way."

As interesting as this anecdotal evidence might be, at some point it helps to look at actual research. Just what do the studies say about the superiority of a single-sex education?

Well, as usual, it depends on whose studies you're looking at. The AAUW's 1998 report, *Separated by Sex: A Critical Look at Single-Sex Education for Girls*, challenged the notion that single-sex education is always better for girls. Their findings, gleaned from an extensive literature review and a roundtable of the country's foremost researchers in the area, concluded that "separating by sex is not the solution to gender inequity in education," according to Maggie Ford, AAUW Educational Foundation president.

To summarize their findings—discussed at far greater length in their 95-page report—the AAUW found the following:

- There is no evidence in general that single-sex education works or is better for girls than coeducation.
- When elements of a good education are present, girls and boys succeed. Elements include small classes and schools, equitable teaching practices, and focused academic curriculum.
- Some kinds of single-sex programs produce positive results for some students, including a preference for math and science among girls. While girls' achievement has improved in some single-sex schools, there is no significant improvement in girls' achievement in single-sex classes.
- There is no escape from sexism in single-sex schools and classes.
- Single-sex classes in particular disrupt the coeducational public school environment.

Although the researchers conceded that single-sex schools   10 often had more girls enrolled in math and science classes, more girls taking academic risks, and more girls confident in their academic competence, they weren't certain whether those advantages derived from factors unique to single-sex programs or from factors common to all good schools (such as small classes, an intense academic curriculum, and a disciplined environment).

Not surprisingly, the National Coalition of Girls' Schools has come to a different conclusion. In its more recent report, issued in January, the organization takes issue with how the media has reported the topic. The AAUW's *Separated by Sex* report, they say, has been particularly misinterpreted, spun by the media as a negative commentary on girls' schools when it is actually anything but that.

The NCGS argues that "largely absent from the debate has been hard, scientific data assessing the defining characteristics of girls' schools," which the group says includes raising girls' academic achievement, increasing the numbers of females in science and math classes, benefiting female career aspirations, and leading to more positive sex-role attitudes and self-esteem.

Also absent from the debate, the NCGS argues, have been the actual voices of the girls' school graduates themselves.

The NCGS set out to rectify that lapse in its report, *Achievement, Leadership & Success: A Report on Educational, Professional, and Life Outcomes at Girls' Schools in the United States.* In a six-page survey, the group polled more than 4,000 alumni from the classes of 1983, 1987, 1991, and 1995 at 64 NCGS schools.

The results were resoundingly positive. Most alumni (85 per- 15 cent) rated their schools as excellent or very good, and 88 percent would repeat the experience. Three-fourths agreed that girls' schools are more relevant to young women's personal and social needs; while 90 percent said such schools were more relevant to their academic needs.

Nearly three-fourths of the alumni felt they were better prepared for college than were their counterparts from coed high schools, while 85 percent believed they were better prepared academically.

Further, girls' school alumni enter college with higher test scores and once there, major in science and math at a higher rate than females or males nationwide, the NCGS report found.

Finally, once they enter the work world, NCGS graduates are overwhelmingly found as leaders at work and in their communities, with more of them (78 percent versus 62 percent nationwide) pursuing managerial and professional fields, and far more volunteering in community organizations (86 percent versus 39 percent of adults nationwide). Fully 80 percent held leadership positions, especially in college and in the workplace.

The advantages sound pretty convincing, although naturally each family has to balance these advantages with the availability and cost of such schools in their own community, as well as their daughters' opinions on the subject.

Studies are important, of course, but perhaps the words of 20 Tony-award winning playwright Wendy Wasserstein (*The Heidi Chronicles*, *The Sisters Rosenszweig*) might make a bigger impression on the girl in your life. After writing in the *New York Times* that girls' school students strike her as "not only fearless but also genuinely interested in one another," and that "the security of a single-sex environment gives young women the confidence to create their own image instead of buying into a cookie cutter world," Wasserstein, a graduate of a single-sex high school and college, concludes with this resounding line: "I truly believe the reason I have enough confidence in my own voice to write or even raise my daughter is because I went to girls' schools."

Thinking About Content

1. What are some of the anecdotal experiences of girls who attended all-girls schools? What disagreements exist?
2. What research does Lamb cite in her essay? How does the research differ?

Thinking About Strategy

1. The research on single-gender education in Lamb's essay is contradictory at times. How does Lamb handle this contradiction? What can you do if you are writing an essay on a social issue, and there is contradictory evidence? Can you model Lamb's technique, or can you think of others?
2. How does Lamb's strategy of opening with anecdotal evidence and then transitioning into her research work for you as a reader? Do you find the use of anecdotal evidence effective? Explain why or why not.

Prompts for Extended Writing Assignments

Personal Response
Popular movies and music often depict education. Write about a movie and/or song lyrics that reflect your attitude about the gender differences or the lack thereof in schools.

From Another's Perspective
Is education in the United States an equal opportunity enterprise? Why or why not? Interview at least three other people and combine this information with evidence from the readings in this chapter as well as Chapters One and Two to support your assertion.

Call for Social Action
College education was not always accessible to women. Make a poster or a timeline that shows women's access to college at your school, your state, or your region. Present this poster at your school or within your local community.

Research Opportunity
Research how gender affects education. Write an essay that argues for or against single-sex schools.

Progressive Education? Race and Education in America

There is no doubt that the United States has made substantial progress in our education system when it comes to race. We have moved beyond the abuse many non-English speakers, such as Native American children, faced in the past. And with the 1954 Brown versus the Board of Education of Topeka decision, the Supreme Court ended segregation in public schools. But many argue that we have much room for improvement as we debate the best way to provide quality education to immigrants and students attending poor, largely nonwhite schools.

The issue of education and race continues to remain a hot political and social topic, as affirmative action is questioned and "English only" educational programs are developed. We thus ask you to question assumptions about education, race, and equality. As you explore the readings and consider the writing assignments in this chapter, think about your own experiences in education and how your race or ethnicity affects your experiences. We also ask you to consider the experiences of others through the readings and ask important questions about the equality of education in our country.

Education in a Multicultural Society: Our Future's Greatest Challenge
LISA DELPIT

Lisa Delpit, an award-winning educator, received much acclaim for her 1995 book, Other People's Children, *in which the following essay originally appeared. Hailed as a visionary look at the ways culture and education intersect,* Other People's Children *addresses the academic consequences of cultural miscommunication.*

——————————— ✦ ———————————

In any discussion of education and culture, it is important to remember that children are individuals and cannot be made to fit into any preconceived mold of how they are "supposed" to act. The question is not necessarily how to create the perfect "culturally matched" learning situation for each ethnic group, but rather how to recognize when there is a problem for a particular child and how to seek its cause in the most broadly conceived fashion. Knowledge about culture is but one tool that educators may make use of when devising solutions for a school's difficulty in educating diverse children.

THE CULTURAL CLASH BETWEEN STUDENTS AND SCHOOL

The clash between school culture and home culture is actualized in at least two ways. When a significant difference exists between the students' culture and the school's culture, teachers can easily misread students' aptitudes, intent, or abilities as a result of the difference in styles of language use and interactional patterns. Secondly, when such cultural differences exist, teachers may utilize styles of instruction and/or discipline that are at odds with community norms. A few examples: A twelve-year-old friend tells me that there are three kinds of teachers in his middle school: the black teachers, none of whom are afraid of black kids; the white teachers, a few of whom are not afraid of black kids; and the largest group of white teachers, who are *all* afraid of black kids. It is this last group that, according to my young informant, consistently has the most difficulty with teaching and whose students have the most difficulty with learning.

I would like to suggest that some of the problems may certainly be as this young man relates. Yet, from my work with teachers in many settings, I have come to believe that a major portion of the problem may also rest with how these three groups of teachers interact and use language with their students. These differences in discourse styles relate to certain ethnic and class groups. For instance, many African-American teachers are likely to give directives to a group of unruly students in a direct and explicit fashion, for example, "I don't want to hear it. Sit down, be quiet, and finish your work NOW!" Not only is this directive explicit, but with it the teacher also displays a high degree of personal power in the classroom. By contrast, many middle-class European-American teachers are likely to say something like, "Would you like to sit down now and finish your paper?", making use of an indirect command and downplaying the display of power. Partly because the first instance is likely to be more like the statements many African-American children hear at home, and partly because the second statement sounds to many of these youngsters like the words of someone who is fearful (and thus less deserving of respect), African-American children are more likely to obey the first explicit directive and ignore the second implied directive.

The discussion of this issue is complex, but, in brief, many of the difficulties teachers encounter with children who are different in background from themselves are related to this underlying attitudinal difference in the appropriate display of explicitness and personal power in the classroom.

If teachers are to teach effectively, recognition of the importance of student perception of teacher intent is critical. Problems arising from culturally different interactional styles seem to disproportionately affect African-American boys, who, as a result of cultural influences, exhibit a high degree of physicality and desire for interaction. This can be expressed both positively and negatively, as hugging and other shows of affection or as hitting and other displays of displeasure. Either expression is likely to receive negative sanction in the classroom setting.

Researcher Harry Morgan documents in a 1990 study what most of us who have worked with African-American children have learned intuitively: that African-American children, more than white, and boys more than girls, initiate interactions with peers in the classroom in performing assigned tasks. Morgan concludes that a classroom that allows for greater movement and interaction will better facilitate the learning and social styles of African-American boys, while one that disallows such activity will unduly penalize them. This, I believe, is one of the reasons that there recently has been such a movement toward developing schools specifically for African-American males. Black boys *are* unduly penalized in our regular classrooms. They *are* disproportionately assigned to special education. They do not have to be, and would not be, if our teachers were taught how to redesign classrooms so that the styles of African-American boys are accommodated.

I would like to share with you an example of a student's ability being misread as a result of a mismatch between the student's and teacher's cultural use of language. Second-grader Marti was reading a story she had written that began, "Once upon a time, there was an old lady, and this old lady ain't had no sense." The teacher interrupted her, "Marti, that sounds like the beginning of a wonderful story, but could you tell me how you would say it in Standard English?" Marti put her head down, thought for a minute, and said softly, "There was an old lady who didn't have any sense." Then Marti put her hand on her hip, raised her voice and said, "But this old lady ain't had *no* sense!" Marti's teacher probably did not understand that the child was actually exhibiting a very sophisticated sense of language. Although she clearly knew the Standard English form, she chose a so-called nonstandard form for emphasis, just as world-class writers Charles Chesnutt, Alice Walker, Paul Lawrence Dunbar, and Zora Neale Hurston have done for years. Of course, there is no standardized test presently on the market that can discern that level of sophistication. Marti's misuse of Standard English would simply be assessed as a "mistake." Thus, differences in cultural language patterns make inappropriate assessments commonplace.

Another example of assessment difficulties arising from differences in culture can be found in the Latino community. Frequently, Latino girls find it difficult to speak out or exhibit academic prowess in a gender-mixed setting. They will often defer to boys, displaying their knowledge only when in the company of other girls. Most teachers, unaware of this tendency, are likely to insist that all groups be gender-mixed, thus depressing the exhibition of ability by the Latino girls in the class.

A final example involves Native Americans. In many Native American communities there is a prohibition against speaking for someone else. So strong is this prohibition that to the question, "Does your son like moose?," an adult Native American man responded to what should have been asked instead: "*I* like moose." The consequence of this cultural interactional pattern may have contributed to the findings in Charlotte Basham's study of a group of Native American college students' writing. The students appeared unable to write summaries and, even when explicitly told not to, continued to write their opinions of various works rather than summaries of the authors' words. Basham concludes that the prohibition against speaking for others may have caused these students considerable difficulty in trying to capture in their own words the ideas of another. Because they had been taught to always speak for themselves, they found doing so much more comfortable and culturally compatible.

STEREOTYPING

There is a widespread belief that Asian-American children are the   10
"perfect" students, that they will do well regardless of the academic setting in which they are placed. This stereotype has led to a
negative backlash in which the academic needs of the majority of
Asian-American students are overlooked. I recall one five-year-old
Asian-American girl in a Montessori kindergarten class. Cathy
was dutifully going about the task assigned to her, that of placing
a number of objects next to various numerals printed on a cloth.
She appeared to be thoroughly engaged, attending totally to the
task at hand, and never disturbing anyone near her. Meanwhile,
the teacher's attention was devoted to the children who
demanded her presence in one form or another or to those she
believed would have difficulty with the task assigned them. Small,
quiet Cathy fit neither category. At the end of work time, no one
had come to see what Cathy had done, and Cathy neatly put away
her work. Her behavior and attention to task had been exemplary.
The only problem was that at the end of the session no numeral
had the correct number of objects next to it. The teacher later told
me that Cathy, like Asian-American students she had taught previously, was one of the best students in the class. Yet, in this case,
a child's culturally influenced, nondisruptive classroom behavior,
along with the teacher's stereotype of "good Asian students," led
to her not receiving appropriate instruction.

Another example of stereotyping involves African-American
girls. Research has been conducted in classroom settings which
shows that African-American girls are rewarded for nurturing
behavior while white girls are rewarded for academic behavior.
Though it is likely true that many African-American girls are
excellent nurturers, having played with or helped to care for
younger siblings or cousins, they are penalized by the nurturing
"mammy" stereotype when they are not given the same encouragement as white girls toward academic endeavors.

Another example of stereotyping concerns Native American
children. Many researchers and classroom teachers have
described the "nonverbal Indian child." What is often missed in
these descriptions is that these children are as verbal and eager to
share their knowledge as any others, but they need appropriate
contexts—such as small groups—in which to talk. When asked
inappropriate questions or called on to talk before the entire class,
many Native American children will refuse to answer, or will
answer in as few words as possible. Thus, teachers sometimes

refrain from calling on Native American students to avoid causing them discomfort, and these children subsequently miss the opportunity to discuss or display their knowledge of the subject matter.

A primary source of stereotyping is often the teacher education program itself. It is in these programs that teachers learn that poor students and students of color should be expected to achieve less than their "mainstream" counterparts.

CHILD DEFICIT ASSUMPTIONS THAT LEAD TO TEACHING LESS INSTEAD OF MORE

We say we believe that all children can learn, but few of us really believe it. Teacher education usually focuses on research that links failure and socioeconomic status, failure and cultural difference, and failure and single-parent households. It is hard to believe that these children can possibly be successful after their teachers have been so thoroughly exposed to so much negative indoctrination. When teachers receive that kind of education, there is a tendency to assume deficits in students rather than to locate and teach to strengths. To counter this tendency, educators must have knowledge of children's lives outside of school so as to recognize their strengths.

One of my former students is a case in point. Howard was in first grade when everyone thought that he would need to be placed in special education classes. Among his other academic problems, he seemed totally unable to do even the simplest mathematics worksheets. During the unit on money, determining the value of nickels and dimes seemed hopelessly beyond him. I agreed with the general assessment of him until I got to know something about his life outside of school. Howard was seven years old. He had a younger sister who was four and afflicted with cerebral palsy. His mother was suffering from a drug problem and was unable to adequately care for the children, so Howard was the main caretaker in the family. Each morning, he would get his sister up, dressed, and off to school. He also did the family laundry and much of the shopping. To do both those tasks, he had become expert at counting money and knowing when or if the local grocer was overcharging. Still, he was unable to complete what appeared to his teachers to be a simple worksheet. Without teachers having knowledge of his abilities outside of school he was destined to be labeled mentally incompetent.

This story also exposes how curriculum content is typically presented. Children who may be gifted in real-life settings are often at a loss when asked to exhibit knowledge solely through decontextualized paper-and-pencil exercises. I have often pondered that if we taught African-American children how to dance in school, by the time they had finished the first five workbooks on the topic, we would have a generation of remedial dancers!

If we do not have some knowledge of children's lives outside of the realms of paper-and-pencil work, and even outside of their classrooms, then we cannot know their strengths. Not knowing students' strengths leads to our "teaching down" to children from communities that are culturally different from that of the teachers in the school. Because teachers do not want to tax what they believe to be these students' lower abilities, they end up teaching less when, in actuality, these students need *more* of what school has to offer. This is not a new concept. In 1933 Carter G. Woodson discussed the problem in *The Mis-Education of the Negro*:

> The teaching of arithmetic in the fifth grade in a backward county in Mississippi should mean one thing in the Negro school and a decidedly different thing in the white school. The Negro children, as a rule, come from the homes of tenants and peons who have to migrate annually from plantation to plantation, looking for light which they have never seen. The children from the homes of white planters and merchants live permanently in the midst of calculation, family budgets, and the like, which enable them sometimes to learn more by contact than the Negro can acquire in school. Instead of teaching such Negro children less arithmetic, they should be taught much more of it than white children.

Teaching less rather than teaching more can happen in several ways. Those who utilize "skills-based" approaches can teach less by focusing solely on isolated, decontextualized bits. Such instruction becomes boring and meaningless when not placed in any meaningful context. When instruction allows no opportunity for children to use their minds to create and interpret texts, then children will only focus on low-level thinking and their school-based intellect will atrophy. Skills-oriented approaches that feature heavy doses of readiness activities also contribute to the "teaching less" phenomenon. Children are typically assigned to these activities as a result of low scores on some standardized test. However, they end up spending so much time matching circles and triangles that no one ever introduces them to actually learning how to read. Should anyone doubt it, I can guarantee you that no amount of matching circles and triangles ever taught anyone how to read. Worse, these activities take time away from real kinds of involvement in literacy such as listening to and seeing the words in real books.

Teaching less can also occur with those who favor "holistic" or "child-centered" approaches. While I believe that there is much of value in whole language and process writing approaches, some teachers seem almost to be using these methodologies as excuses for not teaching. I am reminded of a colleague who visited a classroom in California designed around the state-mandated whole language approach. My colleague witnessed one child in a peer reading group who clearly could not read. When she later asked the teacher about this child, the teacher responded that it was "OK" that this fourth-grader could not read, because he would understand the content via the subsequent discussion. While it is great that the child would have the opportunity to learn through a discussion, it is devastating that no one was providing him with what he also needed—explicit instruction in learning how to read.

In some "process writing" classrooms, teachers unfamiliar with the language abilities of African-American children are led to believe that these students have no fluency with language. They therefore allow them to remain in the first stages of the writing process, producing first draft after first draft, with no attention to editing or completing final products. They allow African-American students to remain at the level of developing fluency because these teachers do not understand the language competence their students already possess. The key here is not the kind of instruction but the attitude underlying it. When teachers do not understand the potential of the students they teach, they will underteach them no matter what the methodology.

IGNORANCE OF COMMUNITY NORMS

Many school systems have attempted to institute "parent training" programs for poor parents and parents of color. While the intentions of these programs are good, they can only be truly useful when educators understand the realities with which such parents must contend and why they do what they do. Often, middle-class school professionals are appalled by what they see of poor parents, and most do not have the training or the ability to see past surface behaviors to the meanings behind parents' actions.

In a preschool I have often visited, four-year-old David's young mother once came to his class to provide a birthday party for her son. I happened to hear the conversation of the teachers that afternoon. They said she came to school in a "bum costume" yelling, "Let's party!" and running around the room. She had presents for all the children and a cake she or someone else had baked for the occasion. The teachers were horrified. They said they could smell alcohol on her breath, that the children went wild, and that they attempted to get the children out to recess as quickly as possible.

From an earlier conversation, I happened to know that this woman cares deeply for her son and his welfare. She is even saving money to put him in private school—a major sacrifice for her—when he enters kindergarten. David's teachers, however, were not able to see that, despite her possible inappropriateness, his mother had actually spent a great deal of effort and care in putting together this party for her son. She also probably felt the need to bolster her courage a bit with a drink in order to face fifteen four-year-olds and keep them entertained. We must find ways for professionals to understand the different ways in which parents can show their concern for their children.

Another example of a cultural barrier between teacher understandings and parental understandings occurred at a predominantly Latino school in Boston. Even though the teachers continually asked them not to, the parents, primarily mothers, kept bringing their first graders into their classroom before the school day officially began. The teachers wanted all children to remain on the playground with a teacher's aide, and they also wanted all parents to vacate the school yard as soon as possible while the teachers readied the classrooms for the beginning of the day. When the parents continued to ignore the request, the teachers began locking the school doors. Pretty soon feelings escalated to the point of yelling matches, and the parents even approached the school board.

What the teachers in this instance did not understand was that the parents viewed six-year-olds as still being babies and in need of their mother's or their surrogate mother's (the teacher's) attention. To the parents, leaving children outside without one of their "mothers" present was tantamount to child abuse and exhibited a most callous disregard for the children's welfare. The situation did not have to have become so highly charged. All that

25

was needed was some knowledge about the parents and community of the children they were teaching, and the teachers could have resolved the problem easily—perhaps by stationing one of the first-grade teachers outside in the mornings, or by inviting one of the parents to remain on the school grounds before the teachers called the children in to class.

INVISIBILITY

Whether we are immediately aware of it or not, the United States is surely composed of a plethora of perspectives. I am reminded of this every time I think of my friend Martha, a Native American teacher. Martha told me how tired she got of being asked about her plans for Thanksgiving by people who seemed to take no note that her perspective on the holiday might be a bit different than their own. One year, in her frustration, she told me that when the next questioner asked, "What are you doing for Thanksgiving?", she answered, "I plan to spend the day saying, 'You're welcome!'"

If we plan to survive as a species on this planet we must certainly create multicultural curricula that educate our children to the differing perspectives of our diverse population. In part, the problems we see exhibited in school by African-American children and children of other oppressed minorities can be traced to this lack of a curriculum in which they can find represented the intellectual achievements of people who look like themselves. Were that not the case, these children would not talk about doing well in school as "acting white." Our children of color need to see the brilliance of their legacy, too.

Even with well-intentioned educators, not only our children's legacies but our children themselves can become invisible. Many of the teachers we educate, and indeed their teacher educators, believe that to acknowledge a child's color is to insult him or her. In her book *White Teacher*, Vivian Paley openly discusses the problems inherent in the statement that I have heard many teachers—well-intentioned teachers—utter, "I don't see color. I only see children." What message does this statement send? That there is something wrong with being black or brown, that it should *not* be noticed? I would like to suggest that if one does not see color, then one does not really see children. Children made "invisible" in this manner become hard-pressed to see themselves worthy of notice.

ADDRESSING THE PROBLEMS OF EDUCATING POOR AND CULTURALLY DIVERSE CHILDREN

To begin with, our prospective teachers are exposed to descriptions of failure rather than models of success. We expose student teachers to an education that relies upon name calling and labelling ("disadvantaged," "at-risk," "learning disabled," "the underclass") to explain its failures, and calls upon research study after research study to inform teachers that school achievement is intimately and inevitably linked with socioeconomic status. Teacher candidates are told that "culturally different" children are mismatched to the school setting and therefore cannot be expected to achieve as well as white, middle-class children. They are told that children of poverty are developmentally slower than other children.

Seldom, however, do we make available to our teacher initiates the many success stories about educating poor children and children of color: those institutions like the Nairobi Day-School in East Palo Alto, California, which produced children from poor African-American communities who scored three grade levels above the national average. Nor do we make sure that they learn about those teachers who are quietly going about the job of producing excellence in educating poor and culturally diverse students: teachers like Marva Collins of Chicago, Illinois, who has educated many African-American students considered uneducable by public schools; Jaime Escalante, who has consistently taught hundreds of Latino high school students who live in the poorest *barrios* of East Los Angeles to test their way into advanced-placement calculus classes; and many other successful unsung heroes and heroines who are seldom visible in teacher education classrooms.

Interestingly, even when such teaching comes to our consciousness, it is most often not by way of educational research but via the popular media. We educators do not typically research and document this "power pedagogy" (as Asa Hilliard calls it), but continue to provide, at worst, autopsies of failure and, at best, studies in minimalist achievement. In other words, we teach teachers rationales for failure, not visions of success. Is there any wonder that those who are products of such teacher education (from classroom teachers to principals to central office staff) water down the curriculum for diverse students instead of challenging them with more, as Woodson says, of what school has to offer?

A second reason problems occur for our culturally diverse students is that we have created in most schools institutions of isolation. We foster the notion that students are clients of "professional" educators who are met in the "office" of the classroom where their deficiencies are remediated and their intellectual "illnesses" healed. Nowhere do we foster inquiry into who our students really are or encourage teachers to develop links to the often rich home lives of students, yet teachers cannot hope to begin to understand who sits before them unless they can connect with the families and communities from which their students come. To do that, it is vital that teachers and teacher educators explore their own beliefs and attitudes about nonwhite and non-middle-class people. Many teachers—black, white, and "other"—harbor unexamined prejudices about people from ethnic groups or classes different from their own. This is partly because teachers have been so conditioned by the larger society's negative stereotypes of certain ethnic groups, and partly because they are never given the opportunity to learn to value the experiences of other groups.

I propose that a part of teacher education include bringing parents and community members into the university classroom to tell prospective teachers (and their teacher educators) what their concerns about education are, what they feel schools are doing well or poorly for their children, and how they would like to see schooling changed. I would also like to see teacher initiates and their educators go out to community gatherings to acquire such firsthand knowledge. It is unreasonable to expect that teachers will automatically value the knowledge that parents and community members bring to the education of diverse children if valuing such knowledge has not been modelled for them by those from whom they learn to teach.

Following a speech I made at a conference a few years ago, I have been corresponding with a very insightful teacher who works at a prestigious university lab school. The school is staffed by a solely European-American faculty, but seeks to maintain racial and cultural balance among the student body. They find, however, that they continue to lose black students, especially boys. The teacher, named Richard, wrote to me that the school often has problems, both behavioral and academic, with African-American boys. When called to the school to discuss these problems, these children's parents typically say that they do not understand, that their children are fine at home. The school personnel interpret these statements as indications of the parents "being defensive," and presume that the children are as difficult at home as at school, but that the parents do not want to admit it.

When Richard asked for some suggestions, my first recom-   35
mendation was that the school should work hard to develop a multicultural staff. Of course, that solution would take a while, even if the school was committed to it. My next and actually most important suggestion was that the school needed to learn to view its African-American parents as a resource and not as a problem. When problems arise with particular African-American children, the school should get the parents of these children involved in helping to point out what the school might do better.

Richard wrote back to me:

> The change though that has made me happiest so far about my own work is that I have taken your advice and I am asking black parents about stuff I never would have brought up before. . . . We do a lot of journal writing, and with the 6- to 8-year-olds I teach, encourage them to draw as well as write, to see the journal as a form of expression. I was having a conference with the mother of one black boy. . . . We looked at his journal and saw that he was doing beautiful intricate drawings, but that he rarely got more than a few words down on the page. I talked to his mother about how we were trying to encourage C. to do the writing first, but that he liked to draw.
>
> During the conversation I started to see this as something like what you were talking about, and I asked C.'s mom how she would handle this at home. I only asked her about how she herself might deal with this, but she said, "In black families, we would just tell him write the words first." I passed that information on to C.'s reading teacher, and we both talked to him and told him he had to get the words down first. Suddenly he began making one-and two-page entries into his journal.
>
> While this is pleasing in and of itself, it is an important lesson to us in terms of equity. C. is now getting equal access to the curriculum because he is using the journal for the reasons we intended it. All we needed was a culturally appropriate way to tell him how to do it.

I am not suggesting that excellent teachers of diverse students *must* be of their students' ethnicity. I have seen too many excellent European-American teachers of African-American students, and too many poor African-American teachers of African-American students to come to such an illogical conclusion. I do believe, however, that we should strive to make our teaching force diverse, for teachers who share the ethnic and cultural backgrounds of our increasingly diverse student bodies may serve, along with parents and other community members, to provide insights that might otherwise remain hidden.

The third problem I believe we must overcome is the narrow and essentially Eurocentric curriculum we provide for our teachers. At the university level, teachers are not being educated with the broad strokes necessary to prepare them properly for the twenty-first century. We who are concerned about teachers and teaching must insist that our teachers become knowledgeable of the liberal arts, but we must also work like the dickens to change liberal arts courses so that they do not continue to reflect only, as feminist scholar Peggy McIntosh says, "the public lives of white Western men." These new courses must not only teach what white Westerners have to say about diverse cultures, they must also share what the writers and thinkers of diverse cultures have to say about themselves, their history, music, art, literature, politics, and so forth.

If we know the intellectual legacies of our students, we will gain insight into how to teach them. Stephanie Terry, a first-grade teacher I have recently interviewed, breathes the heritage of her students into the curriculum. Stephanie teaches in an economically strapped community in inner-city Baltimore, Maryland, in a school with a 100 percent African-American enrollment. She begins each year with the study of Africa, describing Africa's relationship to the United States, its history, resources, and so forth. As her students learn each new aspect of the regular citywide curriculum, Stephanie connects this knowledge to aspects of their African ancestry: while covering a unit about libraries she tells them about the world's first libraries, which were established in Africa. A unit on health presents her with the opportunity to tell her students about the African doctors of antiquity who wrote the first texts on medicine. Stephanie does not replace the current curriculum; rather, she expands it. She also teaches about the contributions of Asian-Americans, Native Americans, and Latinos as she broadens her students' minds and spirits. All of Stephanie's students learn to read by the end of the school year. They also learn to love themselves, love their history, and love learning.

Stephanie could not teach her children the pride of their ancestry and could not connect it to the material they learn today were it not for her extraordinarily broad knowledge of the liberal arts. However, she told me that she did not acquire this knowledge in her formal education, but worked, read, and studied on her own to make such knowledge a part of her pedagogy.

Teachers must not merely take courses that tell them how 40 to treat their students as multicultural clients, in other words, those that tell them how to identify differences in interactional or communicative strategies and remediate appropriately. They must also learn about the brilliance the students bring with them "in their blood." Until they appreciate the wonders of the cultures represented before them—and they cannot do that without extensive study most appropriately begun in college-level courses—they cannot appreciate the potential of those who sit before them, not can they begin to link their students' histories and worlds to the subject matter they present in the classroom.

If we are to successfully educate all of our children, we must work to remove the blinders built of stereotypes, monocultural instructional methodologies, ignorance, social distance, biased research, and racism. We must work to destroy those blinders so that it is possible to really see, to really know the students we must teach. Yes, if we are to be successful at educating diverse children, we must accomplish the Herculean feat of developing this clear-sightedness, for in the words of a wonderful Native Alaskan educator: "In order to teach you, I must know you." I pray for all of us the strength to teach our children what they must learn, and the humility and wisdom to learn from them so that we might better teach.

Thinking About Content

1. Delpit contends that cultural misunderstandings lead to problems for students. What are some of the examples she gives?
2. What problems does Delpit see with teacher-education programs? What solutions does she propose?

Thinking About Strategy

1. How does Delpit open this essay? What purpose does such an opening serve?
2. What strategies does Delpit employ to establish credibility for her argument?

What Color Is an A?

PETER SCHMIDT

The following reading was published in The Chronicle of Higher Education *in June 2007.* The Chronicle of Higher Education *is a print and online periodical addressing a wide variety of issues focused on America's colleges and universities. The author, Peter Schmidt, is a deputy editor at* The Chronicle *who covers issues related to affirmative action and academic diversity.*

— ✦ —

Chantrice Ollie is an all-too-rare find at most predominantly white, selective colleges: a black student with a high grade-point average.

She applied to Skidmore College with weaker academic credentials than most of the students it admits. Her public high school, in Cleveland, offered few advanced courses. She had earned mostly A's, but her SAT scores were well below Skidmore's usual standards.

Had Ms. Ollie enrolled at a different elite college, there is a good chance her grade-point average would be well below the 3.6 she has earned at Skidmore in her freshman year. But Skidmore— a small, private, liberal-arts college in a town known for its horse tracks—has committed itself to taking in academic long shots and turning them into winners. On the whole, the black students admitted through Skidmore's special programs for subpar applicants from economically and educationally disadvantaged backgrounds earn higher grades than those who enroll through the regular admissions process. The same holds true for other racial and ethnic groups.

Ms. Ollie attributes much of her academic success so far to the emotional support she receives from the programs' staff and her fellow participants. "It's a family," she says.

In finding ways to increase the share of its minority 5 students who perform at high levels, Skidmore is itself exceptional. After more than five decades of racial integration and four decades of affirmative action, most of the nation's colleges and universities have not come close to eliminating the performance gap that separates many black, Hispanic, and Native American students from their white and Asian-American counterparts.

Although some colleges say they are working on the problem, few have any proof that their strategies are effective. The paucity of minority undergraduates earning high grade-point averages remains one of the chief obstacles to diversifying the enrollments of advanced-degree programs.

The crisis could grow more dire. As legal and legislative assaults on affirmative action continue, more graduate and professional schools may have to stop considering applicants' race and ethnicity. Unless colleges can find ways to improve minority undergraduates' academic performance, there is likely to be a drop in the percentage of black, Hispanic, and Native American students becoming doctors, lawyers, professors, and engineers.

Susan B. Layden, who oversees Skidmore's efforts to promote minority achievement as associate dean of student affairs, is among a growing group of educators and researchers who believe that colleges must do far more to help minority students earn high grades.

"This is not rocket science," she says. "We can do this across higher education, especially at the elites."

WORSE THAN EXPECTED

In seeking to increase their numbers of high-achieving black, Hispanic, and Native American students, colleges face two formidable problems: Such students are substantially underrepresented among applicants with high grades and SAT scores. And even those who perform well in high school tend to do worse in college than white and Asian-American students with comparable SAT scores and grades—a problem known as "the overprediction phenomenon."

The underrepresentation of black, Hispanic, and Native American students among highly qualified college applicants is often blamed on disparities in family education and income, as well as on inequities in elementary and secondary education. But the children of many affluent professionals in those same groups are struggling, too—tending, on average, to score lower on the SAT and academic-achievement tests than white and Asian-American students who attend inferior schools and have parents with less education and money.

Education researchers and other social scientists have offered a host of explanations for such performance gaps, including the residual effects of slavery and segregation, the stigmatization of high academic achievers by their minority peers, and the lack of minority role models among college administrators and professors. All those theories are the subject of vigorous debate.

Whatever the reasons, the fact is that white and Asian-American students continue to outperform black, Hispanic, and Native American students by a significant degree. According to the National Postsecondary Student Aid Study, the percentage of the nation's white undergraduates earning mostly A's is about twice the proportion of black undergraduates doing so.

Researchers with access to the transcripts of students at selective colleges say the performance gaps are even more pronounced there, especially at the highest achievement levels and among students majoring in mathematics, engineering, the sciences, and technology-related fields.

Such gaps exist in advanced-degree programs as well.   15 Studies of law schools conducted since the early 1990s have found that about half of black students rank in the bottom fourth, or even the bottom tenth, of their classes (the variation mainly reflects differences in the law schools and student populations being studied). One of the chief goals of programs such as Skidmore's is to ensure that minority students are better represented among students ranked in the middle and near the top.

ACADEMIC BOOT CAMP

In an attempt to compensate for the short supply of black, Hispanic, and Native American students who meet its regular admissions standards, Skidmore, with a total enrollment of about 2,400, annually admits about 40 freshmen whose failure to make the cut seems related to their disadvantaged backgrounds. Once they matriculate, the college provides them with support services intended to help them succeed academically.

Skidmore has two intertwined efforts under way: the Higher Education Opportunity Program, which receives state support and serves only New Yorkers, and the Academic Opportunity Program, for students from other states.

The programs assist students who have high high-school grades and other traits signaling strong long-term academic potential, but who have low SAT scores or come from schools that offered few advanced courses.

One of those students is Uriel Salcedo, a sophomore whose parents are working-class Mexican immigrants. The teachers at his Denver public high school lavished high grades on him and praised his writing ability. But when he arrived at Skidmore, he says, he got C's and D's on his papers: "It was like I had been living a lie most of my life."

The Skidmore programs are designed to ease that transition, starting before the freshman year even begins. Each incoming student must attend a four-and-a-half-week academic boot camp. Students spend their days taking an intensive writing course, an intensive math course, and a course in which they must digest— and write analytically about—the ideas of figures like Plato and Darwin. They are required to study for three hours a night, with the help of professional tutors.

Bobby Langford, a black freshman from Worcester, Mass., says the summer program pushed him "to the limit," but that his writing skills improved substantially. Moreover, the philosophers he studied are so firmly implanted in his head that often, he jokes, "I think I am thinking too much."

Vaughn Greene, a black junior who enrolled through the Higher Education Opportunity Program and has served as a head resident in the dormitories during the past two summer institutes, says many students at first fail to take the summer program seriously. After getting slammed with D's and F's on their first papers, however, "they realize it is time to switch gears and actually do something because these people aren't playing."

The lesson appears to sink in. As of last fall, 78, or nearly 60 percent, of the 133 students involved in the two Skidmore programs had grade-point averages of at least 3.0, and more than a fourth had at least 3.5.

In trying to close the academic performance gap between the races, Skidmore is taking on one of academe's touchiest subjects. Officials of colleges and universities generally refuse to disclose the median grade-point averages of their minority students. Many are hesitant to even discuss the performance gap, for fear that doing so would stigmatize minority students or provide ammunition to those seeking an end to race-conscious admissions.

Critics of affirmative action say the academic performance gap is simply a result of colleges' willingness to lower their standards for the sake of diversity. "If you systematically admit students with lower academic qualifications, then those students are going perform below the level" of regularly admitted students, says Roger B. Clegg, president of the Center for Equal Opportunity, an advocacy group. The center has produced several reports citing the lower achievement of minority students as evidence that admissions offices give substantial preferences to certain minority candidates.

"AN IGNORED ISSUE"

Some college leaders argue that the performance gap merits discussion regardless of the political ramifications. "There are people who are just waiting to pounce" on any bad news about minority achievement to make a point, says Joseph A. Tolliver, St. Lawrence University's vice president for student life. But "if you don't talk about it, how are you going to solve it?"

Freeman A. Hrabowski III is president of the University of Maryland–Baltimore County, which has attracted national attention by successfully fighting the overprediction phenomenon and getting black and Hispanic students with high SAT scores to perform at least as well as those scores would predict. He calls the performance gap "an ignored issue." College leaders, he says, "should be more concerned about seeking the truth and less concerned about what sounds popular or even politically correct."

Discussions of the possible causes of the performance gap can easily veer toward subjects that are controversial, even taboo. Glenn C. Loury, a professor of social sciences and economics at Brown University who previously directed Boston University's Institute on Race and Social Division, observes that some academics fault the cultures associated with certain minority groups or even suggest that genetics may be at work. He can feel uncomfortable even entertaining the idea that cultural forces play a role because, in doing so, he says, "you are presuming there is something wrong with African-American kids, and now you are undertaking to fix them."

The discussion is further complicated by the effectiveness of many historically black and predominantly Hispanic colleges. Many of them produce large numbers of minority graduates with academic records strong enough to easily gain admission to most graduate programs and law and medical schools. Their relative success suggests that predominantly white colleges may place a distinct set of obstacles in the paths of minority students, an idea that can put campus administrators on the defensive.

TALKS UNDER WAY

Many college officials who are working to close the performance   30
gap say the initial impetus for their efforts was the 1998 publication of William G. Bowen and Derek Bok's *The Shape of the River: Long-Term Consequences of Considering Race in College and University Admissions* (Princeton University Press). Based on their analyses of data from 28 selective colleges, Mr. Bowen, a former president of Princeton University, and Mr. Bok, a former president of Harvard University, extensively documented race- and ethnicity-linked differences in achievement, including those attributable to the overprediction phenomenon. They also found a strong correlation between undergraduate grades and future earnings, with black students who earn low grades suffering more, in terms of their future earnings, than white students with comparable academic records.

Since then dozens of colleges have joined efforts to study and discuss the academic performance gap, although most have yet to bear fruit.

Among the efforts under way is the Consortium on High Achievement and Success, comprising more than 30 private liberal-arts colleges and small universities, including Amherst, Brandeis, Oberlin, Pomona, St. Lawrence, and Swarthmore. Established in 2001 and based at Trinity College, in Hartford, Conn., the group has adopted a statement of principles declaring that "all students who matriculate to our campuses are capable of succeeding," and that member institutions intend to focus on "promoting high educational achievement, not remediation."

So far the consortium has collected data from member colleges to determine what approaches are working, encouraged its members to replicate any programs shown to remedy the especially severe education problems of black and Hispanic men or to academically challenge highly talented minority students, and worked to design academic support programs aimed at helping students perform well in difficult entry-level courses. It plans to. hold meetings in the coming months on effective approaches to educating freshmen, teaching writing, and advising students who wish to enter the health professions.

"We are trying all sorts of things. Some things are succeeding, some are not," says Mr. Tolliver, of St. Lawrence, who is a member of the consortium's Steering Board.

As part of a separate effort, scientists from 18 higher-education 35 institutions, including Bowdoin College, Harvard University, the University of Maryland–Baltimore County, and the University of Washington, have been meeting since late 2005 in symposia on improving diversity in the sciences. Member institutions have agreed to submit data on grade-point averages, retention rates, and other measures of success, to establish a basis for long-term studies seeking to identify effective strategies for improving minority achievement.

Wendy E. Raymond, an associate professor of biology at Williams College who helps to lead the effort, says the federal government has spent millions of dollars on programs that "have had very little statistical success" in getting more minority students to become scientists. "Let's encourage funding for programs that actually work," she says.

Elsewhere on the research front, Mr. Bowen is gathering data on the performance gap as part of a study of 21 major public universities. The Council on Aid to Education's Collegiate Learning Assessment is seeking to measure how much undergraduates at various colleges are learning. And the National Action Council for Minorities in Engineering is gauging member colleges' progress in getting minority students to earn high grades.

FEW PROVEN STRATEGIES

From 2002 to 2005, L. Scott Miller, then executive director of the Consortium for High Academic Performance, at the University of California at Berkeley, led a three-member team in evaluating more than 100 efforts to improve the educational achievement of minority or disadvantaged undergraduates. The researchers found many programs and strategies that focused on increasing graduation rates, but very few that explicitly sought to help more minority students earn high grades.

Moreover, the team found, few of the programs examined had undergone any sort of rigorous evaluation of their effectiveness. As a result, its report concluded, selective colleges "have few programs and strategies with strong empirical evidence showing that they help increase the number of high-achieving undergraduates from underrepresented groups."

Among the few exceptions cited were Skidmore's two pro-   40
grams and the Meyerhoff Scholars Program at the University of
Maryland–Baltimore County.

Established by Mr. Hrabowski in 1988, the Meyerhoff program recruits high-achieving, well-prepared students interested
in science, engineering, and mathematics and takes steps to
ensure that they perform academically every bit as well as
might be predicted based on their high-school grades and SAT
scores. Among its key components, the program urges faculty
members to act as mentors, monitors students' progress, and
encourages students in the program to help each other in study
groups.

The university has compiled data showing that participants
have much higher grade-point averages, and are much more
likely to get admitted to graduate programs in science, engineering, and math than are students of the same minority
groups who emerged from high school with similar academic
profiles.

Unfortunately for other colleges, the Meyerhoff program's
success depends largely on its ability to bring high-achieving
minority students together. Because the nation's high schools
annually produce only a few thousand black and Hispanic graduates with Meyerhoff-caliber academic profiles, there is a limit on
the number of colleges that can duplicate the approach.

EXPENSIVE PROPOSITION

Mr. Miller and his fellow researchers concluded that the Skidmore programs would be easier for colleges to copy. Both the
Skidmore and Meyerhoff programs are costly, however. The Skidmore programs had a total budget of $4 million in the 2006–7
academic year.

Much of the money that is not used for financial aid pays the   45
salaries of the educators who advise and provide the intensive
tutoring to the students involved.

The office that houses the Skidmore programs has a wel-
coming feel. Students are free to drop in to seek academic help
or simply banter and chat with staff members. On a recent
Friday morning, Monica D. Minor, director of the Higher Education Opportunity Program, helped Eilin Nunez, a sophomore
from the Dominican Republic, plan a term paper about politics
in the Middle East. In another room, Lewis Rosengarten, the

associate director, worked with Linda Leandre, a black freshman, to revise a paper that she had written for an English-composition class.

It is not as if Skidmore's minority students are completely happy with the college. The freshman class is just 3 percent black and 3.7 percent Hispanic. In April students here staged a protest demanding that the college do more to promote diversity and fight racial bias.

"There are a lot of people here who have no idea where we come from, the struggles we have had to get to college," says Ms. Ollie, the freshman from Cleveland.

The program's advisers make a point of urging students not let their studies suffer by getting overinvolved in minority-student organizations or efforts to transform the college. Ms. Layden, the associate dean of student affairs, says she occasionally intervenes with administrators when she determines that they are distracting minority students from their studies by asking them to help with minority recruitment or public-liaison efforts.

The conventional wisdom in academe is that students will   50
perform better academically if they feel good about themselves socially and personally. The Skidmore programs operate on the assumption that doing well academically helps students feel good about themselves, says Ms. Layden. To help minority students feel they can achieve at higher levels regardless of what is going on around them, she says, "we create a smaller environment within this place where students feel safe."

Race, Ethnicity, and Mean Grade-Point Averages

Mean grade-point averages of applicants to U.S medical schools in 2004, by race and ethnicity:

Race/Ethnicity	Mean GPA
White	3.53
Asian	3.47
Cuban American	3.44
Puerto Rican	3.36
Native American	3.3
Mexican-American	3.27
Black	3.17

Source: Association of American Medical Colleges, "Facts and Figures," 2005

Race, Ethnicity, and Undergraduate Grades

Proportion of each racial and ethnic group earning high or low grades as undergraduates, based on 2003–4 data for all U.S. colleges:

	Percentage earning...	
	mostly A's	mostly C's or lower
Black	9.6%	40.7%
Hispanic	12.7%	34.6%
American Indian	13.2%	32.5%
Pacific Islander	14.4%	32%
Asian	16.9%	25.6%
White	19.3%	24%

Source: U.S. Department of Education, Profile of Undergraduates in U.S. Postsecondary Education Institutions, 2003–4

Thinking About Content

1. What is the problem Schmidt defines at the beginning of the essay? Why, according to the author, is this situation with minority students so serious?

2. Schmidt points out that there are "few proven strategies" to help with the "performance gap" he writes about. What makes this issue so complicated? What are some things being done to address the issue? What ideas do you have?

3. What are some of the controversies surrounding additional support for minorities in higher education? Why do you think these controversies exist?

Thinking About Strategy

1. Peter Schmidt opens his essay with a story about one particular student and then concludes his essay with tables showing national data related to minority success rates at undergraduate schools. What would be the purpose of this opening and this closing? Explain whether or not you find these strategies effective.

2. Go online and find out a little more about *The Chronicle of Higher Education* and any articles related to issues of affirmative action or general minority issues. How do your personal experiences inform your opinion on these issues? Did what you found online confirm what you already knew or make you question it? Explain.

Are America's Schools Leaving Latinas Behind?

AMERICAN ASSOCIATION OF UNIVERSITY WOMEN

This press release from the American Association of University Women, an organization promoting education and equality for women and girls, reports findings from a study of Hispanic children and their success in K–12 schools.

———————— ◆ ————————

WASHINGTON DC U.S. schools are not meeting the educational needs of America's fastest-growing female minority population—Latinas—according to a new report released today by the American Association of University Women (AAUW) Education Foundation.

This comprehensive report, *¡Si, Se Puede! Yes, We Can: Latinas in Schools*, reviews the educational (K–12) status and progress of Latinas. It explores the cultural interaction between America's Hispanic children and the schools they attend. Authored by Angela B. Ginorio and Michelle Huston, the report looks at Latinas and how their futures—or "possible selves"—are influenced by their families, their culture, their peers, their teachers, and the media.

The report found that Latinas bring many personal strengths and cultural resources to the schools they attend. For them to become successful, the report contends, schools need to view bilingualism and other values as assets rather than liabilities. For example, "going away to college" is often a high school counselor's definition to success, but some Latinas, because of family responsibilities, believe it is important to stay close to home.

"Instead of making all students fit into a single educational box, schools need to move out of the box to meet the needs of its changing student population," said Jacqueline Woods, executive director of AAUW.

In spite of the importance of education to the Latino community, family needs and peer pressure often clash with school expectations for Latinas. For example, the report finds that "many Latinas face pressure about going to college from boyfriends and fiancees who expect their girlfriends or future wives not to be 'too educated' and from peers who accuse them of 'acting White' when they attempt to become better educated or spend time on academics."

5

"Contrary to popular beliefs about Hispanic communities," said Ginorio, "most parents hope that their children will excel in school, yet Latino families' economic and social position often defer the realization of those dreams. Moreover, school practices such as tracking impose low expectations that create self-fulfilling prophecies."

According to the report, Latinas are lagging behind other racial and ethnic groups of girls in several key measures of educational achievement and have not benefited from gender equity to the extent that other groups of girls have. Analyzing the differences in educational achievement between Latinas and other groups of girls, the report finds that:

- The high school graduation rate for Latinas is lower than for girls in any other racial or ethnic group.
- Latinas are less likely to take the SAT exam than their White or Asian counterparts, and those who do score lower on average than those groups of girls.
- Compared with their female peers, Latinas are under-enrolled in Gifted and Talented Education (GATE) courses and underrepresented in AP courses.
- Latinas are the least likely of any group of women to complete a bachelor's degree.

Although Latinas fare worse than other racial and ethnic groups of girls on most measures of educational performance, they perform better than their male peers on many measures. In reviewing educational data comparing Latinas to Latinos, the report finds that:

- In the fourth grade, Latinas score higher than Latinos in reading and history; by eighth grade, they score higher in mathematics and reading; and by the 12th grade, they score higher in science and reading.
- Latinas outnumber Latinos in taking the SAT exam (58 percent to 42 percent in 1999), yet score lower than Latinos who do take the exam on both the math and verbal section. The gender gap among Hispanics is greater than among any other group.
- Latinas take the same number of or more AP exams than Latinos, but score lower in AP math and science exams.
- Latinas are almost three times less likely to be suspended and less likely to be referred for special education as Latinos.

According to the report, Hispanic girls and boys suffer similar educational challenges in the schools they attend compared to their White and Asian counterparts, and urges schools to pay closer attention to the problems faced by both Latinas and Latinos. The report also notes variations within the Latina community according to culture of origin and region.

"America's public schools must address the psychological, 10 social, cultural, and community factors that affect the education of Hispanic students," said Woods. "Otherwise, Latinas and Latinos will too often continue to be victims of a second-rate education that can change the American dream into a nightmare. We rely on our schools to open the doors for Latinas and Latinos to higher education and better paying jobs."

The report provides clear and compelling evidence that both Latinas and Latinos face stereotyping and other obstacles that discourage success in school. Some obstacles are different for Latinas than for Latinos. Latinas are three times as likely to fear for their personal safety in school as other girls. And Latinos are often assumed to be gang members by teachers and counselors simply because they speak Spanish.

"If we want Latinas to succeed as other groups of girls have," continued Ginorio, "schools need to work with and not against their families and communities and the strengths that Latinas bring to the classroom. We need to recognize cultural values and help Latinas harmonize these values with girls' aspirations to education and learning."

The report offers a number of strong recommendations and new approaches:

- *All adults need to encourage academic success.* Latinas need to hear from all the adults in their lives that college and professional careers are rewarding options and ones that they can achieve. Advisors must curtail tendencies to promote gender- and racially stereotyped careers as well as ensure that Latinas are not under-represented in college-preparatory classes.
- *Recruit and train teachers from the Hispanic community* so that we can have educators who can serve as role models and who can better connect the educational goals of the school to the cultural background of its students.
- *Involve the whole family in the process of college preparation.* College requirements need to be demystified and families need to understand longer-term benefits of attending college even if it means moving away from home.
- *Deal meaningfully with stereotypes and societal issues such as teen pregnancy that impact school performance.* This includes offering childcare and alternative scheduling and therefore recognizing

that being a young mother and a student intent on completing her education are not incompatible.

Thinking About Content

1. What are the competing definitions of success? How does this imply that education and educational opportunities need to change?
2. What are some of the school practices that are cited as causing problems for Latinas?
3. What connections can be made between this study and the excerpt from Myra and David Sadker's book *Failing at Fairness*? in Chapter 3? How do race and gender work together in the educational system?

Thinking About Strategy

1. What are the genre conventions of a press release? How does it differ from an essay or a newspaper article or a personal narrative?
2. This writing uses bulleted text in three different places. How does bulleting text change the reading of it? How can you use formatting techniques to make your own writing stronger?

Stereotypes of Asian American Students

ANGELA KIM AND CHRISTINE J. YEH

Angela Kim and Christine J. Yeh actively research issues associated with Asian Americans and Asian-American culture. Yeh is an assistant professor of Psychology and Education at the renowned Teacher's College at Columbia University. Kim is a student/researcher at the same school. The following essay was created for ERIC, the Educational Resources Information Center, in 2002.

──────────── ✦ ────────────

In 1995, 268,000 of the 720,000 new immigrants that came to the United States were from Asia and the Pacific Islands. The Asian American population doubled between 1980 and 1990, and it will double again between 1990 and 2020. "Asian American" as a racial group represents 29 distinct ethnic categories (Atkinson,

Morten, & Sue, 1993). Further, there is considerable social and economic variation between recent Asian immigrants and Asian American communities that have been in the United States for generations. The number of Asian American school age children and youth increased from 212,900 in 1980 to almost 1.3 million in 1990, creating a significant influx in many of the nation's public school systems, especially cities along the East and West coasts.

This digest discusses the various negative and positive Asian American stereotypes. It also explores how school practices and individual educators—consciously or unconsciously—may reinforce them. Doing so has important negative social, political, and economic ramifications for Asian Americans. Indeed, while Asian Americans are often characterized as the "model minority" (Lee, 1997, p. 442), many have serious psychological and emotional concerns which are not being addressed.

GENERAL STEREOTYPES

The various stereotypes assigned to Asian American students cause them emotional distress and create conflicts with their peers, both those of different races and those in their own racial group. Even more important, stereotyping limits students' opportunities and access to resources (Fisher, Wallace, & Fenton, 2000; S. Lee, 1996). Indeed, Fisher et al. (2000) found higher levels of distress from peer discrimination (being threatened, called racially insulting names, and excluded from activities) in Chinese and Korean students than in African Americans, Hispanics, and whites.

S. Lee (1996) reported that high- and low-achieving Asian-identified students experienced anxiety to uphold the expectations of the model minority stereotypes. The students who were unable to perform well academically felt depressed and were embarrassed to seek help. Moreover, dispelling the Asian American universal academic success myth, the Educational Testing Service (1997) found that twelfth grade students from six major ethnic groups (Chinese, Japanese, Korean, Filipino, South Asian, and Southeast Asian) had significant variations in their educational backgrounds and achievement. ETS also demonstrated how stereotyping has led to the neglect of the development of student services and support for the many Asian American students who are undereducated and have low socioeconomic status.

Some of the educational stereotypes identify Asian Americans 5 as "geniuses," "overachievers," "nerdy," "great in math or science," "competitive," "uninterested in fun," and "4.0 GPAs" (S. Lee, 1996). Some personality and behavior stereotypes assert that Asians are "submissive," "humble," "passive," "quiet," "compliant," "obedient," "stoic," "devious," "sneaky," "sly," "tend to hang out in groups," "stay with their own race," "condescend to other races," and are "racist," "not willing to mesh with American culture," "try to be like Americans," "want to be Caucasian," and "act F.O.B. [fresh off the boat]" (S. Lee, 1994; 1996; Yeh, 2001). The physical appearance and mannerism stereotypes include "short," "slanted eyes," "eyeglass wearing," "poor or non-English speaking," and "poor communicators" (S. Lee, 1996; Siu, 1996). Stereotypes related to the socioeconomic status of Asian Americans and their attitudes about money identify them as "stingy," "greedy," "rich," "poor," "grocery store owners," "dry cleaners," "restaurant owners," and "chefs" (S. Lee, 1996; Yin, 2000).

MODEL MINORITY STEREOTYPES

The model minority stereotypes attribute educational and economic success to all Asian Americans, with the danger that they ignore the between- and within-group differences of assimilation/acculturation, social, political, economic, and education backgrounds (Educational Testing Service, 1997; E. Lee, 1997; Siu, 1996; Yin, 2000). By focusing on exceptional "success stories" and generalizing to all Asian Americans, the model minority myth does not take into consideration the large number of Asian American students and their families who suffer from poverty and illiteracy (Educational Testing Service, 1997; Siu, 1996; Yin, 2000). For example, while only 5.6 percent of Japanese Americans have only an elementary education or less, 61 percent of the Hmong Americans fall into this category (Siu, 1996). Further, although the poverty rates for Japanese and Filipino Americans are 3.4 percent and 5.2 percent respectively, 24 percent of Vietnamese, 42 percent of Cambodians, and 62 percent of Hmong Americans live below the poverty line (Yin, 2000).

Within a group, Chinese American parents, for example, who are well-educated, English-speaking, wealthy professionals from Hong Kong will have different experiences and needs for their children in the United States than will a poorly-educated, non-English speaking, financially-troubled laborer from the countryside in China (Siu, 1996). In addition, Southeast Asian (Vietnamese, Laotian, Cambodian, and Hmong) students and their families—whose backgrounds may include war trauma, relocation experiences, family separation, and education disruptions—will have different psychological and academic needs from East Asian (Chinese, Filipino, Koreans, and Japanese) students and their families (Boehnlein, Leung, & Kinzie, 1997; E. Lee, 1996; S. Lee, 1994; 1996; Leung, Boehnlein, & Kinzie, 1997; Moore, Keopraseuth, Leung, & Chao, 1997; Siu, 1996).

SOCIAL AND PSYCHOLOGICAL CONCERNS

The model minority stereotype that Asian American students are "whiz kids" (Brand, 1987) and immune from behavioral or psychological distresses prevents them from acknowledging academic and emotional problems and seeking help. S. Lee (1996) reports on a Cambodian student named Ming who was failing his classes but refused to seek help for his academic difficulties, believing that admitting his academic failure would cause his family to lose face (be ashamed). He was trying to live within the boundaries of the model minority stereotype, and as a result was perpetuating his academic problems, leaving him feeling isolated and depressed.

Whether the Asian American students are excelling academically or having problems, it is essential to recognize and acknowledge that they experience school, social, and familial stresses to uphold their "model minority" image (Chung, 1997; Fisher et al., 2000; Haung, 1997; S. Lee, 1996; Siu, 1996). In fact, a study (Lorenzo, Frost, & Reinherz, 2000) found that although Asian American students did better academically and had fewer delinquent behaviors than Caucasian Americans, the Asian American youth reported more depressive symptoms, withdrawn behavior, and social problems. They also had poorer self-images and reported more dissatisfaction with their social support.

In addition, Asian American students have reported experiencing racial and ethnic discrimination by their peers (Fisher et al., 2000; Kohatsu et al., 2000; Phinney & Chavira, 1995; Siu, 1996). Siu's (1996) study of literate Asian American students at risk demonstrates the social and psychological struggles resulting from the model minority stereotypes that foster discrimination and anti-Asian sentiments from their peers. The review found that a large proportion (63 percent) of Vietnamese, Hmong, and Korean elementary and secondary students reported that American students were "mean" to them. Being insulted or

10

laughed at by classmates were cited as reasons for not liking school and lacking friends. In addition, commonly mentioned concerns of Vietnamese, Chinese, and Cambodian refugee school age children were physical altercations with peers in school and in social interactions.

S. Lee (1996) discusses how Korean students distanced themselves from Southeast Asian students because they did not want to be associated and be perceived as "welfare sponges." It was, further, found by Siu that the proportion of suspensions for fighting was much higher for Filipino and Southeast Asian students than for all other ethnic groups, including whites, Latinos, and African Americans. These fights were attributed to cultural barriers and prejudice against Asians, especially Southeast Asians. Such racial tensions and a hostile school environment may divert students' focus from their studies to less productive or even destructive activities, and spur some Asian American youths to join gangs for their own protection and for a sense of belonging (Siu, 1996).

The increase in the number of Asian American students in schools highlights the importance of understanding how Asian American stereotypes are reinforced in the school context and contribute to a biased and limited perspective of Asian Americans that does not reflect their within group heterogeneity. In order to serve the social, psychological, and educational needs of Asian American students, teachers, counselors, and administrators must be able to address their own assumptions about this growing group, understand how those assumptions shape their interactions with the students, and effectively communicate that they care and want to help.

References

Atkinson, D. R., Morten, G., & Sue, D. W. (Eds.). (1993). Counseling American minorities: A cross-cultural perspective (4th ed.). Madison, WI: W.C. Brown & Benchmark.

Boehnlein, J. K., Leung, P. K., & Kinzie, J. D. (1997). Cambodian American families. In E. Lee (Ed.), Working with Asian Americans: A guide for clinicians (pp. 37–45). New York: Guilford.

Brand, D. (1987, August 31). The new whiz kids: Why Asian Americans are doing so well and what it costs them. Time, 130, p. 42–46.

Chung, W. (1997). Asian American children. In E. Lee (Ed.), Working with Asian Americans: A guide for clinicians (pp. 165–174). New York: Guilford.

Educational Testing Service. (1997, March 14). Stereotyping short-changes Asian American students. Available: modelminority.com/academia/ets.html

Fisher, C. B., Wallace, S. A., & Fenton, R. E. (2000, December). Discrimination distress during adolescence. Journal of Youth and Adolescence, 29(6), 679–695.

Huang, L. N. (1997). Asian American adolescents. In E. Lee (Ed.), Working with Asian Americans: A guide for clinicians (pp. 175–195). New York: Guilford.

Kim, S. C. (1997). Korean American families. In E. Lee (Ed.), Working with Asian Americans: A guide for clinicians (pp. 125–135). New York: Guilford.

Kohatsu, E. L., Dulay, M., Lam, C., Concepcion, W., Perez, P., Lopez, C., & Euler, J. (2000, Summer). Using racial identity theory to explore racial mistrust and interracial contact among Asian Americans. Journal of Counseling & Development, 78(3), 334–342.

Lee, E. (1997). Chinese American families. In E. Lee (Ed.), Working with Asian Americans: A guide for clinicians (pp. 46–78). New York: Guilford.

Lee, E. (1996). Asian American families: An overview. In M. McGoldrick, J. Giordano, & J. K. Pearce (Eds.), Ethnicity and family therapy (2nd ed., pp. 227–248). New York: Guilford.

Lee, S. J. (1994, December). Behind the model-minority stereotype: Voices of high- and low-achieving Asian American students. Anthropology & Education Quarterly, 25(4), 413–429.

Lee, S. J. (1996). Unraveling the "model minority" stereotype: Listening to Asian American youth. New York: Teachers College Press.

Leung, P. K., Boehnlein, J. K., & Kinzie, J. D. (1997). Vietnamese American families. In E. Lee (Ed.), Working with Asian Americans: A guide for clinicians (pp. 153–162). New York: Guilford.

Lorenzo, M. K., Frost, A. K., & Reinherz, H. Z. (2000, August). Social and emotional functioning of older Asian American adolescents. Child & Adolescent Social Work Journal, 17(4), 289–304.

Moore, L. J., Keopraseuth, K.-O., Leung, P. K., & Chao, L. H. (1997). Laotian American families. In E. Lee (Ed.), Working with Asian Americans: A guide for clinicians (pp. 136–152). New York: Guilford.

Phinney, J. S., & Chavira, V. (1995). Parental ethnic socialization and adolescent coping with problems related to ethnicity. Journal of Research on Adolescence, 5(1), 31–53. (EJ 498 126)

Siu, S.-F. (1996, December). Asian American students at risk: A literature review. Report No. 8. Baltimore, MD: Johns Hopkins University, Center for Research on the Education of Students Placed At Risk. (ED 404 406)

Yeh, C. J. (2001, June). An exploratory study of school counselors' experiences with and perceptions of Asian-American students. Professional School Counseling, 4(5), 349–356.

Yin, X. H. (2000, May 7). The two sides of America's "model minority." Los Angeles Times, Part M, p. 1.

Thinking About Content

1. Kim and Yeh refer to a common stereotype of Asian Americans as the "model minority." What does this mean?
2. How can the "model minority" stereotype be harmful for many Asian-American students?

Thinking About Strategy

1. Kim and Yeh repeatedly cite research studies on Asian-American students in education throughout their essay. How does this affect your reading of the essay? Does the research help or hinder, or both? How does this use of research affect the authors' credibility?
2. Kim and Yeh begin the essay with a brief overview of statistics related to Asian immigrants to the United States. Why is this information important, and why is it placed at the beginning of the essay?

Prompts for Extended Writing Assignments

Personal Response
Have you or someone you know experienced any of the "cultural misunderstandings" Delpit describes in her essay? Write an essay describing the misunderstanding(s) and how this affected your education.

From Another's Perspective
Interview someone who has a different cultural background than your own. Write a biographical essay about this person's experiences in education and how these experiences are similar to or different than your own.

Call for Social Action
Write a letter to the superintendent of your local school district arguing for or against English-only instruction in the public schools. What are your concerns? Use evidence from the readings in this chapter as well as outside research to support your assertions.

Research Opportunity
Research one of the issues concerning language in the classroom (such as intensive English, Ebonics, or immersion) and explore connections between language and education.

What Can We Do to Make Education Better?

Education reform is often one of the most important issues in any political election. Politicians have their plans for reform; teachers have their plans for reform; parents have their plans for reform. And more often than not, all disagree about these plans and exactly what we need to do to make our educational system better. The one thing that everyone seems to agree on, however, is that we need to do something.

In this chapter on reforming education, we ask you to think about your own experiences and to read about the experiences and opinions of others, some more expert than others, and to consider what it will take to improve our educational system. What ideas do you have? How do these ideas differ from the ideas of others? Which ideas could really work? Is major social reform necessary? We ask you to consider these questions and more as you read "What Can We Do to Make Education Better?"

A New Day in American Education
THE COMMISSION ON NO CHILD LEFT BEHIND

The following essay is excerpted from a 2007 report on the No Child Left Behind Act(NCLB), a federal plan for national educational reform signed into law in January 2002. The Commission on No Child Left Behind, led by Tommy G. Thompson, secretary of the Department of Health and Human Services, and Roy E. Barnes, former governor of Georgia, was partially funded by the Bill and Melinda Gates

Foundation, and sought to report on the law's successes and failures since its implementation in 2002.

————————— ◆ —————————

America today faces a stark choice: do we take bold steps to accelerate progress in education and fulfill our promise to our nation's children? Or do we risk jeopardizing the future of our nation's children and our competitiveness in the global economy by maintaining the status quo?

Unacceptable achievement gaps pervade our schools. The National Assessment of Educational Progress (NAEP) reading assessment reveals a troubling truth—that African American 17-year-olds read at the same level as white 13-year-olds. The results for mathematics are just as disconcerting—only 13 percent of African American and 19 percent of Hispanic 4th graders scored at or above the proficient level on NAEP mathematics tests, compared to 47 percent of their white peers (NCES 2005).

The picture for students with disabilities and English language learners* is also alarming—only 6 percent of 8th graders with disabilities scored at or above proficiency on NAEP reading assessments, compared with 33 percent of students without disabilities. Only 4 percent of English language learners in the 8th grade scored at or above proficiency on NAEP reading tests (NCES 2005).

We are also failing to ensure that our children are academically prepared to compete with their international peers. Students in other nations consistently outperform even our top students on international tests. In international comparisons of 15-year-olds' performance in mathematics, American students scored significantly lower than their peers in 20 of the other 28 industrialized countries participating (Lemke et al. 2004).

Contributing to this urgent picture is the fact that many students do not even finish high school. Students drop out of school at distressing rates—7,000 students every school day (Alliance for Excellent Education 2007). Worse yet, those who do make it to graduation are often left unprepared for life in an increasingly rigorous global economy.

5

————————————————

* Although the No Child Left Behind Act refers to "limited English proficient" students, we use the term "English language learners" throughout this report to refer to students whose first language is not English and who lack English proficiency.

These are significant education challenges facing the nation today. Over the past five years, the No Child Left Behind Act (NCLB) has laid the groundwork for closing those achievement gaps and improving public schools. The law, which was passed by overwhelming majorities in the House and Senate, had strong support from Republicans and Democrats, who agreed that standards, accountability, teacher quality and options for students were vital for improving student achievement, and that collaboration among the federal government, states and school districts—based on results rather than simple compliance—could bring about those improvements.

More than any other federal education law in history, NCLB has affected families, classrooms and school districts throughout the country. Virtually every aspect of schooling—from what is taught in elementary, middle and high school classes, to how teachers are hired, to how money is allocated—has been affected by the statute. These changes appear deeply embedded. Regardless of their opinions about the law, many agree that if the law were to disappear tomorrow, American schools would remain fundamentally transformed.

While these changes are substantial, they have not been enough. The problems that NCLB was intended to address remain. Achievement gaps between white students and racial and ethnic minorities and students with disabilities are still unconscionably large. Many schools with reputations for high quality are not educating all students, in all subject areas, to high standards. Expectations for too many students are not high enough to ensure that America can succeed and remain competitive in a global economy.

All of this has spurred both strident opposition to and hardened support for the law. Numerous bills have been introduced in Congress to address difficulties in the law's implementation, as well as to make changes to its requirements and focus. NCLB, and the controversy and support it has generated, has sparked heated conversations around dinner tables, at school board meetings, in state legislatures and in courtrooms.

Fortunately, the consensus that produced the impetus to pass 10 NCLB remains—a widespread commitment to closing achievement gaps and raising the academic achievement of all students. Although the extremes in the debate—those who believe the law is nearly perfect and those who believe it is fatally flawed—attract nearly all of the attention, most Americans continue to believe that the law's principles are moving us in the right direction.

While our work has uncovered shortcomings in both implementation of the statute and some tenets of the law itself, we have concluded that this nation cannot back away from carrying on with this effort to ensure that all children achieve to high expectations. The challenge for the nation is to learn from NCLB and prior efforts and create a high-achieving education system that succeeds for every student, in every school. This system must ensure that children are academically proficient, are able to meet the demands of good citizenship and have a sense of self-worth and accomplishment that comes from a high-quality education and the opportunities it affords. We must close achievement gaps and raise achievement for all so that each child can be prepared to succeed in the future and the nation can remain preeminent in the world economy.

BUILDING A FOUNDATION

School improvement, of course, did not begin with NCLB. The law represented a logical progression in nearly two decades of reform that began with *A Nation at Risk*, the 1983 report of the National Commission on Excellence in Education. In the wake of that report, virtually every state increased graduation requirements, added tests of student achievement and stepped up qualifications for teachers. By the late 1980s, state and national officials began to recognize that the reforms that had taken place were inadequate. While student achievement had improved, it was not high enough or widespread enough to meet the demands of citizenship and an increasingly competitive global economy. In response, policymakers and educators urged states and the federal government to set challenging standards for student performance and to require all students to meet those standards. To codify this demand, new national education goals, set in the wake of a historic education summit convened by President George H.W. Bush and attended by nearly all the nation's governors in 1989, called for all students to attain proficiency in challenging subject matter by the year 2000.

The effort to set standards for student performance gained considerable momentum with the passage of the Goals 2000. Educate America Act of 1994, which provided funding for states to develop standards and related assessments, and especially with the passage later that year of the Improving America's Schools Act (LASA), the 1994 reauthorization of the Elementary and Secondary Education Act (ESEA) of 1965. IASA required states to set challenging standards for student performance, create assessments aligned with the standards and develop accountability systems that measured student performance against the standards. The law did not, however, require substantial interventions and sanctions to be applied to schools that chronically struggled to meet academic goals.

These laws were controversial. Some states objected to the federal mandates, and there was considerable opposition to a proposed panel that would approve standards and assessments. Many states moved slowly to implement these laws or even actively resisted doing so. Not surprisingly, by the end of the 1990s, results from national and international assessments suggested that student achievement had not improved rapidly enough to ensure that all students would be proficient in the core subjects of reading and mathematics, nor were American students, as a group, competitive with their peers from other countries. Most disturbingly, achievement gaps that divided white students from African Americans and Hispanics remained substantial. In fact, these gaps, which narrowed in the 1980s, widened during the 1990s. According to NAEP, African American and Hispanic 12th graders were reading at the level of white 8th graders. Bolder steps would be needed to close those gaps and accelerate improvements in student learning.

NCLB was a bold step. The law ramped up testing requirements, mandating annual assessments in reading and mathematics in grades 3 through 8 and once in high school, called for reporting test results separated by race, ethnicity and other key demographic groups of students and required schools to demonstrate "adequate yearly progress" (AYP) on state tests overall and for each group of students. If schools could not demonstrate AYP, they first faced interventions followed by increasingly severe sanctions. Further, the law allowed students in schools that did not demonstrate sufficient progress to transfer to better-performing schools or receive tutoring, required states to ensure that every teacher was "highly qualified" and mandated detailed reports to parents on school performance and teacher quality.

While these changes were substantial, they have not been enough. Unacceptable achievement levels continue to plague our schools. Our hearings around the country, our discussions and other interactions with people affected daily by NCLB and our research have shown us that this law, like others before it, is not perfect. While many problems can be attributed to implementation challenges, our work has revealed that statutory changes are also needed to improve the law itself.

15

Now is the time for another bold step, one that builds on the foundation of NCLB while addressing the shortcomings we have identified in the law and in its implementation. Having the benefit of hindsight, we can clearly view the consequences of the law, intended and unintended, that its original architects could not. We believe that the task at hand is to preserve the goals and foundational principles of this law by refining its approaches in ways that are informed by the five years of experience in classrooms, central offices and state houses since its passage.

Only with such a careful effort—to keep what works and improve what doesn't—can we fulfill the worthy promise the architects of NCLB made to America's children. By creating a high-achieving education system that closes achievement gaps and raises expectations and performance for all students, America can ensure that all children have the opportunity for a fulfilling, productive future. This report lays out a vision for such a system, the steps the nation should take to get there and the changes in the law necessary to accomplish this task.

NCLB: WHAT WE HAVE ACHIEVED, WHAT CHALLENGES REMAIN

One of the most significant effects of NCLB was to turn what many schools and districts had established as a goal—"that all children will learn"—into national policy. There has been wide agreement on this declaration of purpose among educators, parents, community members and public officials. NCLB put this goal into action by declaring that all children should reach a proficient level of academic achievement by 2014. In the words of the Koret Task Force on K–12 Education, a panel of education scholars convened by the Hoover Institute, NCLB's goal of ensuring proficiency for all students in reading and mathematics is "audacious . . . morally right . . . and attainable." The task force also characterized the law as having "the potential to improve public education more than any federal education initiative since *Brown v. Board of Education*," adding, "*Brown* set the historic precedent for equality in education; NCLB could set the precedent for quality" (Chubb 2005).

There is also broad support for holding schools accountable for reaching that ambitious goal. As one parent from Lancaster, Pennsylvania, put it at a national forum held by the Public Education Network (PEN), a national association of local education

20

funds: "Passing the buck cannot continue when it comes to our children. There should be no reason why our children are graduating without the necessary skills to be productive members of society, and far too many are" (PEN 2006).

The law has also had substantial effects on school practice. A report from the Center on Education Policy (CEP), a national advocacy organization for public education, concludes that these effects have been profound and far-reaching. The report states:

> [T]eaching and learning are changing as a result of NCLB. Administrators and teachers have made a concerted effort to align curriculum and instruction with state academic standards and assessments. Principals and teachers are also making better use of test data to adjust their teaching to address students' individual and group needs. Many districts have become more prescriptive about what and how teachers are supposed to teach. Some districts encourage teachers to follow pacing guides that outline the material to be covered by different points in the school year, while others have hired instructional coaches to observe teachers teaching, demonstrate model lessons and give teachers feedback on ways to improve (Renther et al. 2006).

Although progress has been slow, there is growing evidence that NCLB is producing some results where it counts: in improved student achievement. According to NAEP, scores in mathematics increased nationwide for 4th and 8th graders from 2003 to 2005, and average scores improved for 4th graders in 31 states. Mathematics scores for African American and Hispanic students improved significantly during that period.

In reading, the national average of 4th graders' scores improved from 2003 to 2005. The achievement gap between white and African American and Hispanic 4th graders closed slightly during that period. Although these results come from the early years of NCLB and may have also been influenced by other factors, achievement trends are moving in the right direction (NCES 2005).

State test results also show some improvement since NCLB has taken effect. A survey by CEP found that 78 percent of districts reported that scores on tests used for NCLB had risen from 2003 to 2005, and 35 states reported that scores improved in reading and 36 reported scores improved in mathematics. More than two-thirds of the states reported that in mathematics, test score gaps based on race/ethnicity, income, disability status or language background have narrowed or stayed the same (Rentner et al. 2006).

However, despite these promising signs, there are also concerns that NCLB has not been enough to ensure that all students reach proficiency in reading and mathematics. The NAEP scores, while showing progress, have moved up only slightly, and reading achievement seems to have stalled. The number of schools eligible for the federal Title I program (see sidebox) that did not make AYP has risen, from 6,094 in school year 2002–03 to 9,028 in 2004–05, which

25

Average Scale Scores and Achievement-Level Results in Reading, by Race/Ethnicity, Grade 4: Various Years, 1990–2005

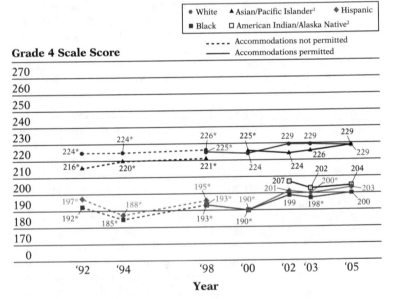

* Significantly different from 2005
[1] Sample size was insufficient to permit reliable estimates for Asian/Pacific Islander students in 1998 (accommodations-permitted sample)
[2] Sample sizes were insufficient to permit reliable estimates for American Indian/Alaska Native students in 1992, 1994, 1998 and 2000.

Source: U.S. Department of Education, Institute of Education Sciences, National Center for Education Statistics, National Assessment of Educational Progress (NAEP), various years 1992–2005 Reading Assessments.

Average Scale Scores and Achievement-Level Results in Math, by Race/Ethnicity, Grade 4: Various Years, 1990–2005

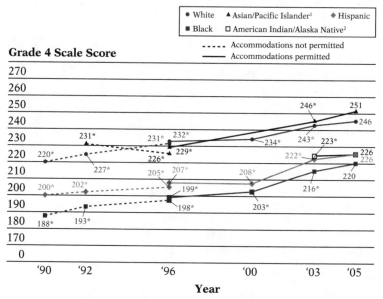

Grade 4 Scale Score

* Significantly different from 2005
[1] Sample size was insufficient to permit reliable estimates for Asian/Pacific Islander students in 1990. Special analyses raised concerns about the accuracy and precision of national grade 4 Asain/Pacific Islander results in 2000. As a result, they are omitted
[2] Sample sizes were insufficient to permit reliable estimates for American Indian/Alaska Native students in 1990, 1992, 1996 and 2000.

Source: U.S. Department of Education, Institute of Education Sciences, National Center for Education Statistics, National Assessment of Educational Progress (NAEP), various years. 1990–2005 Mathematics Assessments.

may suggest that increasing numbers of schools are struggling to bring all students to proficiency (Stullich et al. 2006). These numbers could also mean that NCLB is not adequately recognizing meaningful growth in student achievement numbers. More is needed to accelerate progress and to produce richer and more useful data on student performance.

In addition, there are concerns that NCLB is having unintended consequences that might hinder improving student achievement. One commonly cited is that the law's assessment and reporting requirements have driven educators to simply "teach to the test." Some claim that the high-stakes nature of annual assessments has forced teachers to devote instructional time to "drill-and-kill" preparation, stifling creative learning. Concerns over unintended consequences have set off heated debates and, in some cases, legal and legislative action aimed at blocking the law from taking full effect.

Some problems alleged to have been caused by NCLB have had nothing to do with the law. In one instance, in 2006, a hoax e-mail circulated falsely charging that the law required the state of Indiana to grant substandard "certificates of completion," rather than diplomas, to students who failed to pass state tests. The U.S. Department of Education (U.S. DOE) took the unusual step of refuting the charge and urging people to ignore the e-mail.

Critics have even used anecdotes to claim that NCLB is responsible for everything from a wave of principal retirements to an outbreak of head lice. (Some principals said they had been forced to let students with lice back into school earlier than they otherwise might have to ensure that students took tests required under NCLB.) While some evidence supported some of these claims, others appeared unfounded. Nevertheless, they hardened opposition to the law.

Some complaints have centered on the U.S. DOE's implementation of the law. As we document later in this report, only

> ### TITLE I SCHOOLS
>
> Title I, Part A, authorized under NCLB, provides financial assistance through states to districts and public schools with high numbers or percentages of poor children to help ensure that all children master challenging state academic content and meet student academic achievement standards.
>
> Districts target the Title I funds they receive to public schools with the highest percentages of children from low-income families. Unless a participating school is operating a schoolwide program for poor children, the school must focus Title I services on children who are failing, or most at risk of failing, to meet state academic standards. Schools enrolling at least 40 percent of students from poor families are eligible to use Title I funds for schoolwide programs that serve all children in the school.
>
> Title I reaches about 12.5 million students. Funds may be used for children from preschool age to high school, but most of the students served (65 percent) are in grades 1 through 6; another 12 percent are in preschool and kindergarten programs.

30

in the last two years has the U.S. DOE adequately focused on ensuring that NCLB's teacher quality provisions are being implemented by states. In addition, multiple, hard to access and sometimes contradictory versions of U.S. DOE guidance and regulations have made it difficult for districts and schools to comply with the law. Some have charged that this late focus on teacher quality and the confusion over some U.S. DOE guidance has hampered progress in implementing some of NCLB's key provisions.

Other concerns stem from the way the law has been implemented by states, school districts and schools. For example, states have widely disbursed funds for professional development with little regard for effectiveness or content quality, rather than targeting these funds to the schools and teachers who need them most. Some schools have reacted to the law's focus on reading and mathematics by decreasing the amount of curriculum time devoted to the arts, social studies and other subjects. The law did not require either of these actions; they are the result of state, district and school implementation decisions.

In addition, some states and districts have failed to carry out important parts of law that existed before NCLB. For instance, despite federal requirements for students with disabilities to be included in statewide assessments since 1997, some states have only recently begun to try to properly include those children in these assessments. NCLB, for its part, has provided little help to states with their continuing struggle to properly test these children despite the law's demands to hold schools accountable for their performance.

> **CONFLICTING GOALS IN UTAH**
>
> Some states are actively challenging NCLB's reach over state policy and practice. In April 2005, the Utah legislature passed a bill that ordered Utah educators to "provide first priority to meeting state goals" when those goals conflict with NCLB. The bill also required educators to minimize the amount of state money they diverted to implement federal programs. In May 2005, Utah Governor John Huntsman signed the bill into law.
>
> U.S. Secretary of Education Margaret Spellings warned in a letter to Utah Senator Orrin G. Hatch that depending on how the state were to implement the bill's provisions, the U.S. DOE might withhold $76 million of the $107 million that Utah receives in federal education money (Michigan Education Report 2005).

Community members and others have charged that districts have done little or nothing to push plans to restructure schools that have been persistently low performing. They also claim that districts have thwarted public participation in the process even though the law clearly requires districts to include parents in such decisions. Similarly, parents have complained that, in some cases, districts have struggled or outright failed in making options, such as transferring to a higher-performing school or supplemental educational services (SES or free tutoring), available to all eligible children. Effective implementation of NCLB's provisions is essential to its success. Failure to carry out parts of the law has likely significantly affected progress toward achieving its goals of the law.

Some complaints about NCLB, however, do reveal significant shortcomings in the law; others reveal a lack of clarity. As stated earlier, our work to understand the impact of NCLB revealed difficulties with the statute itself as well as the challenges of implementing the law at the federal, state or local levels. Conducting our work without bias, we discovered from our hearings and discussions with those who implement NCLB at the state and local levels, those who administer it from the U.S. DOE and those who passed this law in Congress, that problems with the law go beyond implementation.

For example, the statutory provisions requiring all classrooms to be staffed with "highly qualified" teachers are laudable but do not go far enough to accomplish NCLB's ambitious goals. There needs to be recognition of the connection between teacher effectiveness and increased student performance as well as stronger focus on ensuring teachers receive the supports and training necessary to be effective once they are in the classroom.

The requirements for AYP in student achievement have not recognized that many schools have taken action resulting in significant improvement, even if they have not achieved this standard. In addition, NCLB's requirements have identified thousands of struggling schools, but these same requirements have done little to ensure these schools have the leadership, knowledge and tools necessary to improve. Most significantly, the fact that NCLB allows states to set their own standards has led to wide and unacceptable variations in expectations across states. Many states have not set standards high enough or they have chosen to set a low bar for what constitutes proficiency.

This report will address these statutory and implementation issues as well as other challenges. Our recommendations build on the foundation of NCLB and fill in those pieces that the Commission believes are needed to address shortcomings in the law and its implementation, as well as other necessary actions to produce a true high-achieving education system for all children.

THE COMMISSION ON NO CHILD LEFT BEHIND

The Commission on No Child Left Behind was established by the foundations that have generously supported us and the Aspen Institute. Our charge was to move beyond heated and uninformed rhetoric about NCLB and examine the evidence about the law's effects in a dispassionate, nonpartisan process. The Commission has sought to determine what's working and what's not and how the law could be improved to ensure that it works for every child and every school. The Commission's co-chairs are former governors, one a Republican, one a Democrat. The Commission's remaining membership comprises 13 members who represent the full spectrum of interests in this law, including K–12 and higher education, school and school-system governance, civil rights and business.

Although the Commission members came to the table from a variety of perspectives, we were united from the outset in our firm commitment to the goals of the law: to harness the power of standards, accountability and increased student options, so that every child becomes proficient in core subjects and to eliminate the achievement gaps that have left too many students behind. We were also united in our firm commitment that our recommendations would be informed by parents, educators, community members, policymakers and researchers from across the country.

We went about our task in a bipartisan, evidence-based 40 way. We held six formal public hearings in all parts of the country—Pomona, California; Hartford, Connecticut; Atlanta, Georgia; Madison, Wisconsin; Cambridge, Massachusetts; and the District of Columbia—where we heard from 46 witnesses, including state officials, superintendents, teachers, parents and their advocates, experts and policymakers at the district and state levels. While some of the witnesses testified as individuals, many testified on behalf of hundreds, thousands and even millions of people impacted by the law in some way. These hearings were widely attended, both in person and via our Web broadcasts. We made time at each of these hearings to open the floor to anyone who wished to speak and submit a statement to the Commission. As a result, we heard from many interested citizens who do not always have a voice in these discussions. We visited schools and met with principals, teachers and students to see firsthand the effects of NCLB in the classroom and to talk in-depth with individuals who live the law every day.

In addition to the formal hearings, we held a series of roundtables during the summer to focus on topics of interest to the Commission, including views on the law from parents and their advocates, rural schools, students with disabilities, English language learners, early child-hood providers and high schools. At these roundtables, we heard from 33 witnesses and many audience members. In addition to our public events, we talked to hundreds of other individuals who affect public education in some way. We also invited members of the public to contact the Commission via our Web site and received close to 10,000 comments to date from a wide range of national, state and local leaders, interested citizens and students.

The Commission and its staff also conducted profiles of schools in cities, suburbs and rural areas throughout the country, and scoured the literature for information about the effects of NCLB. Our goal was to test the claims made by both supporters and critics to see what the data actually showed. In some cases, this research backed up claims about the law; in many others, the claims proved to be without foundation. Our staff also produced white papers that presented findings about some key issues, such as the effects of subgroup performance on schools' ability to make AYP and the use of growth models to measure school performance.

This report forms the product of all of this data gathering—and our discussions about the findings. We are submitting

---

RESEARCH REPORTS WRITTEN BY COMMISSION STAFF

- *Growth Models: An Examination Within the Context of NCLB*
- *Children with Disabilities and LEP Students: Their impact on the AYP Determinations of Schools*
- *The State of the Achievement Gap*

PROFILES CONDUCTED BY COMMISSION STAFF

- P.S. 161 Pedro Albizu Campos School, New York City? New York
- Washington Middle School, Albuquerque, New Mexico
- Yough School District, Herminie, Pennsylvania
- Belt Public Schools, Belt, Montana

this report to the U.S. House of Representatives, the U.S. Senate and the President of the United States in the hope that it will inform their deliberations about the upcoming reauthorization of NCLB. But we will not stop with simply delivering a report. We will travel across the country to gain support for our recommendations and to build a constituency for a reauthorized NCLB that we believe will accomplish its ambitious aims—to improve achievement for all students and eliminate achievement gaps.

OUR VISION: HIGH ACHIEVEMENT FOR ALL

We strongly believe that America is ready to take the next bold steps to go beyond the foundation NCLB has established. We must improve the law in order to help states, districts, schools and communities fulfill the nation's promise to our children and to ensure our continued economic competitiveness internationally.

What would an education system look like that truly leaves no child behind? First, such a system ensures that all teachers are not only highly qualified but also *effective*. They know what children need to learn and how to impart that knowledge, and they demonstrate their ability to raise student achievement through fair, credible and reliable measures of effectiveness. Those teachers who are not able to demonstrate student learning gains and do not receive positive evaluations from principals or their peers would receive additional high-quality professional development designed to address their specific needs and on-site support in developing practical strategies to improve student learning. If teachers do not improve after they receive this support, they will no longer be eligible to teach students most in need of help.

Such a system also ensures that principals are effective in their work as leaders. Like teachers, principals should demonstrate their ability to provide the leadership necessary to raise student achievement through fair, credible and reliable measures of effectiveness. As with teachers, principals should also be supported in improving their skills and knowledge through high-quality professional development.

A high-achieving system rates schools fairly and accurately. States and districts need to know which schools have the largest and most persistent achievement gaps so that they can prioritize efforts and interventions to those schools. Parents and communities need to know which schools are making

45

strides and which are chronically struggling, so that they can choose the best options for their children. To accomplish these goals, states evaluate student growth and determine whether schools are improving at a sufficiently rapid rate. To make such judgments, states have in place sophisticated data systems to track student achievement and teacher and principal effectiveness over time.

For schools identified as being "in need of improvement," states and districts in a high-achieving system have effective and proven tools to turn around those schools. States and districts have the flexibility they need to use the tools that are best suited to each school's circumstances, as well as the data and authority to make tough decisions and apply meaningful remedies. Importantly, this system ensures that states and districts have the knowledge and tools to turn around struggling schools.

A high-achieving system provides a complete picture of student progress through fair and accurate measures of achievement. It uses the best available assessments of student achievement and provides timely and informative reports about student progress to parents, teachers and members of the public. It also provides more tools to parents and teachers to help them understand student progress. Regular formative assessments of student learning throughout the year help teachers improve instruction, provide timely information about test outcomes to parents and seek to improve the likelihood of all students' success on end-of-the-year exams. In addition, a high-achieving system administers screening assessments in preschool and kindergarten that provide information needed to ensure that young children are on track to learn at high levels.

A system that leaves no child behind sets high expectations for 50 what is needed to prepare all students—including poor students, minority students, students with disabilities, English language learners and migrant students—for success in college and the workplace. It sets these expectations through high voluntary national standards, more rigorous state standards and meaningful comparisons of student achievement among states. It is a cruel hoax if students do all they are asked to do, yet find themselves ill-prepared for life after high school. If expectations reflect what students need to know and be able to do, and are realistic, students will achieve them.

A high-achieving system also prepares high school students for college and the workplace. Such a system does not tolerate the unacceptably low graduation rates that plague many of the "dropout factories"—the worst-performing high schools—in our country. Instead, the system addresses the unique challenges faced by high schools and focuses on what is necessary to ensure all children graduate on time and prepared for success in college and the workplace. Districts systemically approach problems and provide useful supports and remedies to high schools struggling to raise achievement for all student groups.

This vision of a high-achieving system is bold, yet attainable. It can be reached, in large measure, based on the principles of NCLB coupled with the policies we recommend. It will require federal and state partnerships to use existing resources in new ways and to prioritize additional investments in key areas, such as conducting research and development on school improvement, creating high-quality professional development and learning opportunities for principals and teachers and implementing data systems to track student achievement over time. The system will also require well-targeted changes to provide the information, tools and incentives states, districts and schools need to create a high-achieving system that truly leaves no child behind.

Thinking About Content

1. According to the commission, what have been some of the successes of No Child Left Behind? In what way has the law not worked well?
2. In the last section of the essay, "Our Vision: High Achievement for All," how do the authors describe their vision for improving American education?

Thinking About Strategy

1. Early on the authors of this essay explain that the No Child Left Behind Act was passed by "overwhelming majorities in the House and Senate, [and] had strong support from Republicans and Democrats." Why do you think it is important for the commission to share this information with its audience?
2. In this essay, the authors explain some of their methods for assessing the No Child Left Behind Act. Why is this an important strategy for writers?

Evaluating "No Child Left Behind"
LINDA DARLING-HAMMOND

The following essay was published in May 2007 in The Nation *as Congress began to consider reauthorizing the No Child Left Behind Act.* The Nation *asked the author of this piece, Linda Darling-Hammond, to examine the law and propose possibilities for improving it. Darling-Hammond is a leading education expert; she is an educator and former professor at Teachers College, Columbia University. She is a leading voice in issues related to education reform in the United States.*

———————— ✦ ————————

When Congress passed George W. Bush's signature education initiative, No Child Left Behind, it was widely hailed as a bipartisan breakthrough—a victory for American children, particularly those traditionally underserved by public schools. Now, five years later, the debate over the law's reauthorization has a decidedly different tone. As the House and Senate consider whether the law should be preserved—and if so, how it should be changed—high-profile Republicans are expressing their disenchantment with NCLB, while many newly elected Democrats are seeking a major overhaul as well.

What happened? Most discussions focus on the details of the more than 1,000-page law, which has provoked widespread criticism for the myriad issues it has raised. All of its flaws deserve scrutiny in the reauthorization debate, but it's also worth taking a step back to ask what the nation actually needs educationally. Lagging far behind our international peers in educational outcomes—and with one of the most unequal educational systems in the industrialized world—we need, I believe, something much more than and much different from what NCLB offers. We badly need a national policy that enables schools to meet the intellectual demands of the twenty-first century. More fundamentally, we need to pay off the educational debt to disadvantaged students that has accrued over centuries of unequal access to quality education.

NCLB'S PROMISE—AND PROBLEMS

In 2002 civil rights advocates praised NCLB for its emphasis on improving education for students of color, those living in poverty, new English learners and students with disabilities.

NCLB aims to raise achievement and close the achievement gap by setting annual test-score targets for subgroups of students, based on a goal of "100 percent proficiency" by 2014. These targets are tied to school sanctions that can lead to school reconstitutions or closures, as well as requirements for student transfers. In addition, NCLB requires schools to hire "highly qualified teachers" and states to develop plans to provide such teachers.

NCLB contains some major breakthroughs. First, by flagging differences in student performance by race and class, it shines a spotlight on longstanding inequalities and could trigger attention to the needs of students neglected in many schools. Second, by insisting that all students are entitled to qualified teachers, the law has stimulated recruitment efforts in states where low-income and "minority" students have experienced a revolving door of inexperienced, untrained teachers. While recent studies have found that teacher quality is a critical influence on student achievement, teachers are the most inequitably distributed school resource. This first-time-ever recognition of students' right to qualified teachers is historically significant.

This noble agenda, however, has been nearly lost in the law's problematic details. Dubbed No Child Left Untested, No School Board Left Standing and No Child's Behind Left, among other nicknames, the law has been protested by more than twenty states and dozens of school districts that have voted to resist specific provisions. One state and a national teachers association have brought lawsuits against the federal government based on the unfunded costs and dysfunctional side effects of the law. Critics claim that the law's focus on complicated tallies of multiple-choice-test scores has dumbed down the curriculum, fostered a "drill and kill" approach to teaching, mistakenly labeled successful schools as failing, driven teachers and middle-class students out of public schools and harmed special education students and English-language learners through inappropriate assessments and efforts to push out low-scoring students in order to boost scores. Indeed, recent analyses have found that rapid gains in education outcomes stimulated by reforms in the 1990s have stalled under NCLB, with math increases slowing and reading on the decline.

At base, the law has misdefined the problem. It assumes that what schools need is more carrots and sticks rather than fundamental changes.

A Focus on Testing Rather Than Investing.   Most centrally, the law does not address the profound educational inequalities that plague our nation. With high-spending schools outspending low-spending schools at least three to one in most states, multiplied further by inequalities across states, the United States has the most inequitable education system in the industrialized world. School funding lawsuits brought in more than twenty-five states describe apartheid schools serving low-income students of color with crumbling facilities, overcrowded classrooms, out-of-date textbooks, no science labs, no art or music courses and a revolving door of untrained teachers, while their suburban counterparts, spending twice as much for students with fewer needs, offer expansive libraries, up-to-date labs and technology, small classes, well-qualified teachers and expert specialists, in luxurious facilities.

The funding allocated by NCLB—less than 10 percent of most schools' budgets—does not meet the needs of the under-resourced schools, where many students currently struggle to learn. Nor does the law require that states demonstrate progress toward equitable and adequate funding or greater opportunities to learn. Although NCLB requires "highly qualified teachers," the lack of a federal teacher supply policy makes this a hollow promise in many communities.

At a time when the percentage of Americans living in severe poverty has reached a thirty-two-year high, NCLB seeks to improve the schools poor students attend through threats and sanctions rather than the serious investments in education and welfare such an effort truly requires. As Gloria Ladson-Billings, former president of the American Educational Research Association, has noted, the problem we face is less an "achievement gap" than an educational debt that has accumulated over centuries of denied access to education and employment, reinforced by deepening poverty and resource inequalities in schools. Until American society confronts the accumulated educational debt owed to these students and takes responsibility for the inferior resources they receive, Ladson-Billings argues, children of color and of poverty will continue to be left behind.

Disincentives for Improving Learning.   Even if NCLB funding were to increase, its framework does not allow for important structural changes—for example, a system of teacher preparation and professional development that would routinely produce high-quality teaching; curriculums and assessments that encourage critical thinking and performance skills; high-quality preschool education, libraries and learning materials; and healthcare for poor children. Instead, the law wastes scarce resources on a complicated test score game that appears to be narrowing the curriculum, uprooting successful programs and pushing low-achieving students out of many schools.

To go back to first principles, we must ask what US schools should be doing in a world where education is increasingly essential and the nature of knowledge is rapidly changing. What would we need to do to graduate all of our students with the ability to apply knowledge to complex problems, communicate and collaborate effectively and find and manage information?

We might want to be doing some of the things that higher-achieving countries have been doing over the past twenty years as they have left us further and further behind educationally. As an indicator of the growing distance, the United States ranks twenty-eighth of forty countries in mathematics, right above Latvia, and graduates only about 75 percent of students, instead of the more than 95 percent now common elsewhere. Most high-achieving countries not only provide high-quality universal preschool and healthcare for children; they also fund their schools centrally and equally, with additional funds going to the neediest schools. Furthermore, they support a better-prepared teaching force—funding competitive salaries and high-quality teacher education, mentoring and ongoing professional development for all teachers. NCLB's answer to the problem of preparing teachers for the increasingly challenging job they face has been to call for alternative routes that often reduce training for the teachers of the poor.

Finally, high-achieving nations focus their curriculums on critical thinking and problem solving, using exams that require students to conduct research and scientific investigations, solve complex real-world problems and defend their ideas orally and in writing. These assessments are not used to rank or punish schools, or to deny promotion or diplomas to students. (In fact, several countries have explicit proscriptions against such practices.) They are used to evaluate curriculum and guide investments in learning—in short, to help schools improve. Finally, by asking students to show what they know through real-world applications of knowledge, these other nations' assessment systems encourage serious intellectual activities that are being driven out of many US schools by the tests promoted by NCLB.

Narrowing the Curriculum. No Child Left Behind has actually made it harder for states to improve the quality of teaching. At the core of these problems is an accountability system borrowed from Texas and administered by an Education Department with a narrow view of what constitutes learning. This system requires testing every student in math, reading and, soon, science and issuing sanctions to schools that do not show sufficient progress for each subpopulation of students toward an abstract goal of "100 percent proficiency" on state tests—with benchmarks—that vary from state to state.

Ironically, states that set high standards risk having the most   15 schools labeled "failing" under NCLB. Thus Minnesota, where eighth graders are first in the nation in mathematics and on a par with the top countries in the world, had 80 percent of schools on track to be labeled failing according to the federal rules. In addition, states that earlier created forward-looking performance assessment systems like those used abroad have begun to abandon them for antiquated, machine-scored tests that more easily satisfy the law. As emphasis on drilling for multiple-choice tests has increased, the amount of research, project work and scientific inquiry has declined, and twelfth grade reading scores have dropped nationwide.

The Education Department has discouraged states from using more instructionally useful forms of assessment that involve teachers in scoring tasks requiring extensive writing and analysis. Connecticut, Maine, Rhode Island, Nebraska and Vermont, among others, had to wrestle with the department to maintain their sophisticated performance-based assessment systems, which resemble those used in high-scoring nations around the world. Connecticut, which assesses students with open-ended tasks like designing, conducting and analyzing a science experiment (and not coincidentally ranks first in the nation in academic performance), sued the federal government for the funds needed to maintain its assessments on an "every child, every year" basis. The Education Secretary suggested the state drop these tasks for multiple-choice tests. Thus the administration of the law is driving the US curriculum in the opposite direction from what a twenty-first-century economy requires.

Distracting Schools from Productive Reforms. Other dysfunctional consequences derive from the law's complicated accountability scheme, which analysts project will label between

85 and 99 percent of the nation's public schools "failing" within the next few years, even when they are high-performing, improving in achievement and closing the gap. This will happen as states raise their proficiency levels to a national benchmark set far above grade level, and as schools must hit targets for test scores and participation rates for each racial/ethnic, language, income and disability group on several tests—often more than thirty in all. Missing any one of these—for example, having 94 percent of low-income students take the test instead of 95 percent—causes the school to fail to "make AYP" (adequate yearly progress).

Worse still, there is a Catch-22 for those serving English-language learners and special-needs students. In *Alice in Wonderland* fashion, the law assigns these students to special subgroups because they do not meet the proficiency standard, and they are removed from the subgroup as they catch up, so it is impossible for the subgroups ever to be 100 percent proficient. Schools serving a significant share of these learners will inevitably be labeled failing, even if all their students consistently make strong learning gains. Those who warned that the law was a conservative scheme to undermine public schools and establish vouchers were reinforced in their view when the Bush Administration's recent reauthorization plan recommended that students in schools that do not achieve their annual test benchmarks be offered vouchers at public expense.

As a result of these tortuous rules, more than 40 percent of the nation's public schools have been placed on intervention status at some point in the past four years, including some of the highest-achieving schools in the nation and many that are narrowing the achievement gap. These schools have sometimes been forced to dismantle successful programs in favor of dubious interventions pushed by the Education Department—including specific reading programs under the Reading First plan, which, the inspector general found, was managed in such a way as to line the pockets of favored publishers while forcing districts to abandon other, more successful reading programs. Although some of these schools are truly failing and require major help to improve, it is impossible to separate them from schools caught in the statistical mousetrap.

Punishing the Neediest Schools and Students. At least some 20 of the schools identified as "needing improvement" are surely dismal places where little learning occurs, or are complacent schools that have not attended to the needs of their less advantaged students. It is fair to suggest that students in such schools deserve other choices if the schools cannot change. However, there is growing evidence that the law's strategy for improving schools may, paradoxically, reduce access to education for the most vulnerable students.

NCLB's practice of labeling schools as failures makes it even harder for them to attract and keep qualified teachers. As one Florida principal asked, "Is anybody going to want to dedicate their life to a school that has already been labeled a failure?" What's more, schools that have been identified as not meeting AYP standards must use their federal funds to support choice and "supplemental services," such as privately provided after-school tutoring, leaving them with even fewer resources for their core educational programs. Unfortunately, many of the private supplemental service providers have proved ineffective and unaccountable, and transfers to better schools have been impossible in communities where such schools are unavailable or uninterested in serving students with low achievement, poor attendance and other problems that might bring their own average test scores down. Thus, rather than expanding educational opportunities for low-income students and students of color, the law in many communities further reduces the quality of education available in the schools they must attend.

Perhaps the most adverse unintended consequence of NCLB is that it creates incentives for schools to rid themselves of students who are not doing well, producing higher scores at the expense of vulnerable students' education. Studies have found that sanctioning schools based on average student scores leads schools to retain students in grade so that grade-level scores will look better (although these students ultimately do less well and drop out at higher rates), exclude low-scoring students from admissions and encourage such students to transfer or drop out.

Recent studies in Massachusetts, New York and Texas show how schools have raised test scores while "losing" large numbers of low-scoring students. In a large Texas city, for example, scores soared while tens of thousands of students—mostly African-American and Latino—disappeared from school. Educators reported that exclusionary policies were used to hold back, suspend, expel or counsel out students in order to boost test scores. Overall, fewer than 40 percent of African-American and Latino students graduated. Paradoxically, NCLB's requirement for disaggregating data by race creates incentives for eliminating those at the bottom of each subgroup, especially where schools have little capacity to improve the quality of services such students receive. As a consequence of high-stakes testing, graduation rates for African-American and Latino students have declined in a number of states. In the NCLB paradigm, there is no solution to this problem, as two-way accountability does not exist: The child and the school are accountable to the state for test performance, but the state is not held accountable to the child or his school for providing adequate educational resources.

HOW TO (REALLY) LEAVE NO CHILD BEHIND

There are hundreds of proposals for tweaking NCLB, but a substantial paradigm shift is required if our education system is to support powerful learning for all students. The Forum on Educational Accountability, a group of more than 100 education and civil rights organizations—including the National Urban League, the NAACP and the League of United Latin American Citizens, as well as the associations representing teachers, administrators and school boards—has argued that "the law's emphasis needs to shift from applying sanctions for failing to raise test scores to holding states and localities accountable for making the systemic changes that improve student achievement."

How might this be done? A new paradigm for national educa-   25
tion policy should be guided by dual commitments to support meaningful learning on the part of students, teachers and schools; and to pay off the educational debt, making it possible for all students to benefit from more productive schools.

A new Elementary and Secondary Education Act (ESEA) should start by helping states develop world-class standards, curriculums and assessments and to use them for improving teaching. Returning to the more productive approach of President Clinton's Goals 2000 initiative, the federal government should assist states in developing systems for evaluating student progress that are performance based—including assessments like essays, research papers and science experiments that are embedded in the curriculum and scored by teachers using common criteria—leveraging intellectually ambitious learning and providing information that continuously improves teaching.

School progress should also be measured in a more comprehensive manner—including such factors as student progress and continuation, graduation and classroom performance on tasks beyond multiple-choice tests—and gains should be assessed by how individual students improve over time. To eliminate the statistical gantlet that penalizes schools serving the most diverse populations, the AYP system should be replaced with a continuous improvement model. While continuing to report test scores by race and class, schools should be judged on whether students make progress on multiple measures of achievement, including those that assess higher-order thinking and understanding, and insure appropriate assessment for special-education students and English-language learners. And "opportunity to learn" standards specifying the provision of adequate materials, facilities and teachers should accompany assessments of student learning, creating benchmarks for the pursuit of equity.

The new ESEA must finally address the deep and tenacious educational debt that holds our nation's future in hock and insure that every child has access to adequate school resources, facilities and quality teachers. Federal education funding to states should be tied to each state's movement toward equitable access to education resources. Furthermore, the obvious truth—that schools alone are not responsible for student achievement—should propel attention to programs that will provide adequate healthcare and nutrition, safe and secure housing, and healthy communities for children.

Major investments must be made in the ability of schools to hire and support well-prepared teachers and leaders. While NCLB sets an expectation for hiring qualified teachers, it does not include supports to make this possible. Federal leadership in developing an adequate supply of well-qualified teachers is needed. Just as it has helped provide an adequate supply of physicians for more than forty years, it can provide training for those who prepare in specialties for which there is a shortage and agree to locate in underserved areas.

A Marshall Plan for Teaching could insure that all students   30 are taught by well-qualified teachers within the next five years through a federal policy that (1) recruits new teachers using service scholarships that underwrite their preparation for high-need fields and locations and adds incentives for expert veteran teachers to teach in high-need schools; (2) strengthens teachers' preparation through support for professional development schools, like teaching hospitals, which offer top-quality urban teacher residencies to candidates who will stay in high-need districts; and

(3) improves teacher retention and effectiveness by insuring that novices have mentoring support during their early years, when 30 percent of them drop out.

For an annual cost of $3 billion, or less than one week in Iraq, the nation could underwrite the high-quality preparation of 40,000 teachers annually—enough to fill all the vacancies taken by unprepared teachers each year; seed 100 top-quality urban-teacher-education programs and improve the capacity of all programs to prepare teachers who can teach diverse learners well; insure mentors for every new teacher hired each year; and provide incentives to bring expert teachers into high-need schools by improving salaries and working conditions.

Students will not learn at higher levels without the benefit of good teaching, a strong curriculum and adequate resources. Merely adopting tests and punishments will not create genuine accountability. In fact, adopting punitive sanctions without investments increases the likelihood that the most vulnerable students will be more severely victimized by a system not organized to support their learning. A policy agenda that leverages equitable resources and invests strategically in high-quality teaching would support real accountability—that is, accountability to children and parents for providing the conditions under which students can be expected to acquire the skills they need to succeed.

Thinking About Content

1. According to Darling-Hammond, what "major breakthroughs" does No Child Left Behind offer? What are its "problematic details"?
2. What does Darling-Hammond offer as a better way to improve education in America?

Thinking About Strategy

1. What effect does it have when the author lists some of the derogatory nick-names for No Child Left Behind? Why do you think she would include those in this article?
2. Darling-Hammond goes beyond criticism of No Child Left Behind and offers some solutions to the problems the law fails to address. How does this work as a strategy for the author? Explain whether or not you find it effective.

A Strategic Vision for Higher Education

MARGARET SPELLINGS

Margaret Spellings was confirmed by Congress in 2005 as the eighth secretary of the department of education. Before serving as secretary of education, Spellings served George W. Bush as assistant to the president for domestic policy, where she helped put together educational policies like the No Child Left Behind Act. The following article is adapted from a speech she gave in February 2005, at the American Council on Education's 87th annual meeting.

---------------- ✦ ----------------

It's been noted that I am the first mother of school-age children to become U.S. Secretary of Education. Less well known is that one of my children will be going to college next year. That's right. I have just gone through the college application and selection process with my daughter. That may make me either your dream candidate for secretary or your worst nightmare—take your pick.

My experiences are not unique. Every year, millions of parents and students face the same choices and challenges. My own window into the process has taught me a few things you won't find in any manual. And that's the problem.

A STRATEGIC VISION

Where is the manual on American higher education in the 21st century? There is none. It is up to us to write it—to provide a strategic vision for higher education.

Webster's defines *vision* two ways: first, "unusual discernment, foresight, or imagination." And second, "the act or power of seeing." We must be adept at both. We must have the vision to see where higher education can take us in a future where both freedom and competition are on the move. At the same time, we must clearly see—with 20/20 sight and without rose-colored glasses—the conditions that lead to a well-educated citizenry. And we must hold ourselves accountable for providing them.

If we do those two things, we will fulfill the social compact   5
developed over generations and passed down to ours. And we will
help the next generation realize the long-held promise of higher
education—a stake in the American experiment and a shot at the
American dream. It is a major step toward what the president
calls the "Ownership Society" and the "security, dignity, and inde-
pendence" it would bring.

ROLES IN THE COMPACT

So let's talk specifics. In this compact, what does the federal government owe parents, students, and the community? What
should you, as higher education leaders, expect from us in government? And what should we expect of you?

What We Owe Parents and Students

Of course, we all owe it to parents and students to make college as
affordable as possible. President Bush has said, "Higher education
is the best investment one can make to succeed in life." But the
newspaper headlines read, "Is college getting out of reach?"

The president believes a person's financial state should not be a
barrier to access. So, while tuition continues to increase at rates
well above inflation, so does student aid. Grants are up by 6 percent
and federal loans are up by 13 percent over last year. Funding for
Pell Grants has increased by nearly 50 percent over five years.

We're continuing our commitment. President Bush's proposed 2006 budget would provide an additional $19 billion over
10 years for Pell Grants, to fund more than 5 million recipients
next year alone. It uses savings and efficiencies from student aid
programs to increase the maximum award by $100 for each of the
next five years, to a total of $4,550 annually. This is a significant
change. The budget also would retire the $4.3 billion funding
shortfall, which was an impediment in the past to raising the
award. And grants would be made available year-round, so that
students could learn on their own timetable, not someone else's.

This is truly a reform budget when it comes to student loans.   10
It would direct a greater proportion of benefits toward students
enrolled in school, and a smaller one toward borrowers no longer
enrolled. It would increase loan limits for qualified students,
which have remained essentially flat since the mid-1970s, even as
costs have tripled. And a variable interest rate would be adopted
for all student loans, with flexible extended repayment plans for

borrowers. This will help students benefit from historically low interest rates. All in all, once Congress passes the president's 2006 budget, aid for postsecondary students and institutions will have risen by 38 percent on our watch, from $48 billion to $78 billion.

Just as important as financial aid is information. President Teddy Roosevelt knew this when he called on the federal government to provide citizens with "the fullest, most accurate, and ... most helpful information" about the nation's best education systems.

A century later, how are we doing? As students search for the right college and parents navigate through the application process, are they getting information that's clear, accurate, timely, and relevant?

Well, we do not suffer from a lack of data. In fact, we at the Department of Education collect about 4,000 pieces of data about each education institution. They're logged into a database with the bureaucratic-sounding name of Integrated Postsecondary Education Data System, or IPEDS. IPEDS does some things well and some things not as well. For instance, we can tell you almost anything you want to know about first-time, full-time degree-seeking students who have never transferred. The trouble is, that's less than half of today's total student population.

We also can tell you what the tuition rates are at each institution. But we cannot pinpoint as easily the actual costs after student aid is considered. This is a problem because, as many college presidents know, families often overestimate costs. A 1999 survey found nearly half of all 11th- and 12th-graders with college plans had not obtained accurate cost information, nor had their parents. There's no telling how many are discouraged from applying for aid—or admission.

Some good news is the Free Application for Federal Student   15
Aid, or FAFSA, on our web site. It's eight pages and more than 100 questions long, not counting the six-page FAFSA "pre-application worksheet." There's a shortened form for low-income families called EZ-FAFSA. Unfortunately, fewer than 20 states accept it. I hope you'll work with us to bring the others on board.

While these systems are an improvement over the past, we are definitely working to make them more user-friendly. One of our biggest challenges is a lack of compatible and comprehensive measurements—the kind of information parents have come to expect from K–12 schools. Parents see a mosaic of fine higher education institutions, each with wonderful qualities, but find it difficult to piece the puzzle together. How do credit hours compare? Is the coursework aligned with the state's K–12 system? Are there work-study programs? How long does it take, on average, to graduate, and does that differ by major course of study? What if the student is African-American or Hispanic—what are their prospects? Is a student better off attending a less expensive state school over a five- or six-year period, or a more expensive private school that they may finish in four?

Publications like *U.S. News & World Report's* annual rankings are useful, but they do not tell the whole story. We need to encourage states and institutions to adopt common languages and metrics. That way, both traditional and nontraditional education consumers can make smart choices, based on information, not anecdote. Developing a compatible, connected, data-based system would offer a way to publicize your school's most attractive qualities.

I emphasize information because it has worked so well for us in improving K-12 education. Even though we federally fund less than one-tenth of it—compared to about one-third for higher education—we've leveraged our investment through the No Child Left Behind Act. In just three years, we've managed to put a real dent in the achievement gap. The vast majority of states credit No Child Left Behind with improving academic performance. And I believe states and postsecondary institutions should view it as a model as you work to close your own achievement gap.

What We Owe Colleges and Universities

Which brings me to the next part of the compact. What does the federal government owe colleges and universities?

I believe the single best thing we can do is to send you students who are ready and able to learn from day one. Preparing students for success in college does not begin with freshman orientation week. It begins much earlier. And we are a long way from where we need to be.

A study by the Manhattan Institute found that only 32 percent of students who exit high school are prepared for college. I use the word "exit" because not all high school diplomas are created equal. Though there are many, many fine public high schools, your skyrocketing remedial education costs attest to the fact that many need help. The equation is as simple as it is brutal: While about 80 percent of the fastest-growing jobs will require at least two years of college, only 26 out of 100 of today's entering ninth-graders will still be in college their sophomore year. For Hispanic and African-American students, the rate is about half that. That's simply unacceptable. This is not a future—or an America—we should be satisfied with.

As ACE President David Ward has said, higher education must pay more attention to K–12 schools and not just wait for schools to provide them with appropriate students. President Bush agrees. And he has taken up the charge.

His budget expands the promise and principles of the No Child Left Behind Act to our high schools. Under the president's high school initiative, student performance in reading/language arts and math would be measured in at least two more high school grades than it is currently, so teachers can identify those at risk of falling behind or dropping out.

His budget also contains $1.24 billion for high school intervention. This is for highly targeted instruction—individual performance plans, dropout prevention efforts, demanding vocational and technical courses, college awareness, and more. The goal is to ensure that a high school diploma is a ticket to success, whether a graduate chooses higher education or the workforce.

Research shows that rigorous coursework is a great predictor 25
of success in higher education and the workplace—on par with or better than GPA or SAT and ACT scores. Currently, however, 40 percent of high schools offer no Advanced Placement courses; fewer than half the states require at least three years of math or science to graduate.

I believe we've done a better job of selling students on the dream of a college degree than on ensuring they have the skills to attain it. This is especially true—and hurtful—when it comes to aspiring first-generation college graduates.

We must encourage a realistic vision of success. The president's budget provides $52 million—a $22 million increase—to expand AP and International Baccalaureate programs in schools with large numbers of disadvantaged students. The funds would help defray costs such as exam fees and also would train teachers to instruct those courses. And the budget creates a new Presidential Math-Science Scholars Program, a public-private partnership to award up to $5,000 each to low-income students engaged in those vital studies. The budget also offers $12 million to increase the number of states participating in the State Scholars program, which seeks a rigorous, college-ready curriculum in every high school. Complementing that is $33 million for Enhanced Pell Grants for State Scholars, which accompany those students as they enter college. This would add up to an additional $1000 for the first two years of study.

I assure you that programs showing real results will be supported by states and schools, and will survive and thrive.

Finally, let me discuss community colleges. For many Americans, they're the bridge between a diploma and a degree; for others, they're a means to refresh their skills for a changing economy. The president's budget establishes a new Community College Access Grants Fund to support dual-enrollment credit transfers for high school students taking college-level courses. Dual enrollment plays an important role in encouraging students, particularly those with disadvantages, to go on to college. We'll encourage states and colleges to develop more transparent and flexible credit transfer systems.

And the president's budget contains $250 million for Community-   30
Based Job Training Grants to help community colleges train 100,000 new workers for the skilled, high-growth jobs in demand by local employers—the "community" in community college.

WHERE DO WE GO FROM HERE?

All of this depends on qualified teachers. We will set up a $500 million Teacher Incentive Fund to reward teachers who make outstanding progress in high-need areas. And we will increase loan forgiveness for highly qualified math and science teachers serving low-income communities. The ceiling, which has risen from $5,000 to $17,500, will be made permanent.

I hope you'll make the quality of teacher preparation programs one of your highest priorities.

Remember, you produce the teachers who produce the students who make up your freshman classes.

We're at a crossroads. We still have the finest system of higher education in the world. But the world is catching up. China graduates six times as many engineering majors as the United States; South Korea and Japan graduate four times as many. In 2001, India graduated nearly 1 million more students from college than the United States, including 100,000 more in the sciences.

Meanwhile, our young students lose ground as they age. Our   35
fourth-and eighth-graders score above the international average in math and science, but our 15-year-olds lag below it.

In the 21st century, change is the only constant—changing technology, changing competition, a changing workforce. It happens whether we're ready for it or not. The president has said, "This changed world can be a time of great opportunity for all Americans"—but only if they gain the skills to adapt.

Americans deserve more than improved communication from us. They deserve improved performance. They deserve better information to make better decisions, students prepared to learn from day one, and the skills to succeed in a fast-changing century.

Together, we can show Americans a future in which knowledge powers our economy and empowers our citizenry. If we can see it, we can achieve it—together.

Thinking About Content

1. Spellings cites increases in President Bush's proposed 2006 budget for Pell Grants and funding for community college dual-enrollment programs. Go online to research what really happened in 2006 for education spending—was funding for Pell Grants increased, and did Congress fund a dual-enrollment program?
2. According to Spellings, what can the federal government do to improve higher education? What can colleges and universities do? What other things would you like to add to her list?

Thinking About Strategy

1. Spellings begins her speech by describing herself as the first mother of school-age children to become the secretary of education. She then adds that her daughter has just completed the college application and selection process. Why do you think Spellings would begin her speech by sharing this information?
2. As secretary of education, Spellings is a political figure. How do you see her political position affecting the content of this essay?

Beyond Markets and Individuals: A Focus on Educational Goals

HOWARD GARDNER

Howard Gardner is Hobbs Professor of Cognition and Education at the Harvard Graduate School of Education. He is the author of Changing Minds: The Art and Science of Changing Our Own and Other People's Minds *and coauthor of* Good Work: When Excellence and Ethics Meet. *The following essay appeared in the 2005 book,*

Declining by Degrees: Higher Education at Risk, *edited by Richard H. Hersh and John Merrow, which explores serious problems of higher education.*

———————— ✦ ————————

When an institution determines to do something in order to get money, it must lose its soul.

—Robert Maynard Hutchins

CROSS-EYED COLLEGES

If a person familiar with the college scene in the 1950s were to alight on a campus in 2005, much would seem familiar. To be sure, structures scattered around the periphery might seem overly modern; but the red-brick buildings near the center, the grassy campus, and the athletic fields would look unchanged. Peering into the classroom, he would see a great deal of lecturing, punctuated by occasional seminars. Nor would the calendar, the catalog, the departmental organization shock the visitor. He might be told that the conservative pace of change is a virtue. After all, colleges and universities (hereafter, colleges) have lasted for many hundreds of years, far longer than entities (such as totalitarian regimes) that might have predicted their disappearance.

Beneath the surface, however, higher education has changed dramatically in two ways. First of all, colleges (like most of the rest of the society) have been influenced by the model of the market and now think of themselves primarily in terms of competition, supply and demand, profitability, and other features of classical economics. Second, the needs, interests, and "person" of the students have come to dominate the thinking of those responsible for the college—the senior management, admissions officers, development officers, and much of the faculty. Unfortunately, the twin foci are in many ways incompatible.

I see the vast majority of American colleges as cross-eyed creatures. One eye is focused on the financial status of the college, the other on the desires of the student. This dual focus has caused harm and requires a correction in course. To the extent that colleges become indistinguishable from other commercial entities, they lose their reason for existence. When Harvard.edu morphs into Harvard.com, it should lose its tax-free status and be classified with Disney and Wal-Mart, rather than with the Sorbonne in Paris or Xinhua in Beijing.

Every profession must confirm the reason for its origin and the rationale for its continued existence (or its eventual demise). In terms of my metaphor, colleges need to focus with both eyes on their principal educational mission. Stripped to its essentials, postsecondary education—and, specifically, the traditional form of education termed liberal arts—exists to convey to students the most important intellectual knowledge and skills that have been developed to the present moment; to develop in students deep disciplinary knowledge in at least one area; to foster critical thinking, analysis, and expression across a range of topics; to contemplate the relation between accumulated knowledge and skills, on one hand, and the issues facing contemporary society, on the other; to prepare students—in a broad rather than narrow sense—for civic life and productive work. A tall order! Over the years other religious, civic, personal, and societal goals have been pursued but I consider these optional rather than required considerations in a focused academy of the twenty-first century.

Evidently, the two features that dominate conceptions of   5
college today and that threaten to overwhelm its educational mission are not wholly independent. When one thinks of an institution in market terms, one naturally thinks in terms of one's customers—in this case, students and their paying parents. Similarly, the more that one knows the needs and desires of the students, the more one can fashion an institution that directly addresses these demands. Yet, on analytic grounds, these are separable factors. One could know a great deal about students without making that knowledge the basis of market thinking. For example, one could try to meet students' needs even when it was not economically feasible to do so. By the same token, one could market an institution on grounds that do not take undue consideration of one particular client. Military academies could stress the importance of defending the nation; technology schools could emphasize the infrastructural needs of the society.

In what follows, I consider factors that gave rise to the current cross-eyed foci on markets and individual students. I then note two vital considerations that have diminished over the years: (1) a set of alternative models of how societies can work, and (2) a sense of confidence about what colleges have to offer, arrived at independently of market or student considerations. I outline what colleges should properly do, if they felt relieved of pressures of the market and ignorant of the "demands" of students. Using data obtained from an ongoing research project, I suggest some ways in which it might be possible to highlight the supply side of the market equation, thereby confirming the fundamental importance of higher education viewed in its own terms.

THE TRIUMPH OF THE MARKET AND THE INDIVIDUAL, AMERICAN STYLE

Markets have always been with us, of course. Except in the most totalitarian environments, institutions vie for support, customers, longevity—and, at least in a loose Darwinian sense, the fittest survive. In the late nineteenth century, for example, hundreds of institutions purported to train physicians. In the wake of the epochal Flexner Report on Medical Education, issued in 1910, the number of degree-granting medical schools was radically reduced.

Over the last fifty years, market considerations have become the dominant consideration in nearly every sphere of American life. The model of the corporation—with its hierarchical and centralized organizational structure, profit-and-loss ledgers, venture capital, dividends to shareholders, and the like—has influenced professions ranging from law and medicine to education and the arts.

Perhaps even more dramatically, the ways in which Americans evaluate individuals whom they know from a distance and even those whom they know personally occur increasingly in market terms. The salary an individual makes, her disposable income, her potential for moving up in an organization loom ever larger in how such a person is judged. Just think of how we monitor the salaries of movie stars, CEOs, athletes, and, yes, even college presidents and faculty. My own observations suggest that many, if not most, younger Americans are unable to think of the occupational realm *except* in market terms. It is as if the market model has become the triumphant meme, the dominant metaphor, of our time.

In comparison to most other societies—and particularly ones in East Asia—America has always had a focus on the individual—his background, his strengths, his desires. It took nerve to leave the homeland voluntarily; it took courage to explore unknown territories; accordingly, the "lone cowboy," the "frontier wife," and the "pioneer family" deserved any rewards that they accumulated. In the last fifty years, this focus has been exacerbated by two factors. On one hand, the majority of Americans have seen a steady improvement in their standard of living, and this economic jag has allowed them greater choice about where to live, whom to live with, what to purchase or exchange. On the other hand, factors that counter an individual focus—communal, family, and religious ties—have been on the wane. In the phrase of political scientist Robert Putnam, more of us are "bowling alone." To be sure, a great many Americans describe themselves as religious and exhibit the proper accouterments of piety. Yet this religious description in no way detracts from a focus on the individual: Indeed, residents of the so-called red states put equal emphasis on both—even as individuals who are less overtly religious (in the United States as well as Scandinavia) often prove more sympathetic to communitarian or socialistic forms.

To be sure, these foci have yielded some positive dividends. Colleges should compete not merely on reputation or prestige but also on the "good" and the "goods" that they actually can demonstrate. By the same token, the "person" of each student is important. Indeed, as architect of the idea of "multiple intelligences," I sympathize with the notion that students think and learn differently from one another; they are best served when these differences are taken into account in curriculum, instruction, and assessment. But I am concerned that the two foci have become so dominant that distinctly educational goals often are marginalized.

THE IMPORTANCE OF COUNTERMESSAGES

In my view collegiate educators—whether permanent or transient faculty—should be deeply knowledgeable about their subject matter and continue to bone up as needed; know how to teach their subject to novices and journeymen; relate that subject to issues of the time; be mindful of the postcollege trajectories of their students; and value the generic features of a liberal arts education (as sketched above). Teaching art or engineering in a college becomes a different matter from teaching art in an arts academy or engineering at a polytech. Both administrators and trustees ought to have as a primary goal the creation and maintenance of an institution that facilitates the achievement of these educational goals.

Why foreground these educational goals? Three reasons stand out. First of all, human knowledge is among our most precious possessions; we owe it to our predecessors and successors to privilege this human creation. Second, education is the sphere designated by society as the guardian, transmitter, and accumulator of that knowledge; if colleges do not carry out this mission, no other body can step into the breach. Third and often forgotten, the greatest gifts that we can provide to our students are the appreciation of such knowledge, the capacity to think with and about it, and the potential to add to that knowledge in whichever sphere they eventually enter. All the rest is incidental.

The central dilemma facing "cross-eyed" educators rises sharply with respect to teaching of classical Greek or Sanskrit. The utility of these subjects in the contemporary world or in post-college education is limited, and few students arrive on the scene with a burning desire to pursue either. From a strictly market perspective, both should be dropped immediately. From an individual-centered perspective, these courses should be maintained only if, for some idealistic or eccentric reason, a significant number of students have a desire to pursue them. The major justifications for offering these subjects (and for hiring specialists in them), then, have to do with the values of educators and their conception of what it means to be an educated person. Citing the three reasons just introduced, I could mount arguments here, with the case for classical Greek being different from, but not in any absolute sense stronger than, the case for Sanskrit. But it is the principle that is important—we should not decide on course offerings simply on the basis of their cash value. After all, we are dealing here with bodies of knowledge and not with species competing for survival on a tiny landmass.

Here is where countermessages or alternative conceptions are urgently needed. It is possible—and desirable—to think of colleges in ways far different from the market model, with its emphasis on profit and its reflexive assumption that "more is better." One can think of them, for example, in terms of places that preserve and extend that knowledge which has made the most difference in human history, either for the better or the worse. Or as sites that develop individuals who will challenge the orthodoxy. Or as institutions that adopt a monastic rather than a market orientation. By the same token, it is possible to direct the lenses in directions quite different from that of student wants and needs. For example, one can ask what the chief needs of the society are today and how can they be met; or the chief needs of society in the future; or the populations that most need to be served; or the skills that students should acquire so that they can bring about a better world, without reference to the campuswear of the month.

Note that these nonmarket foci might well end up having market appeal. For example, some students might be attracted to a school like St. John's, which emphasizes the great written works of the past. Other students might be attracted to a place that shuns creature comforts in favor of transmitting knowledge and skills to those in poverty. But these would be by-products—externalities, in the terms of economists. Colleges would make these decisions on the basis of principles and not in a Machiavellian or Rube Goldbergian effort to increase market share. And to the extent that market thinking intruded, it would be limited to the need for *survival* and not for accumulating the biggest possible endowment or paying the highest possible salaries to faculty, staff, or managers of the investment portfolio.

THE CURRENT SCENE: A NEED FOR "GOOD WORK"

Evidence for the increasing marketization of the college scene is ubiquitous and indisputable. Responding to the ever-rising costs of an education and the never-ending desire for expansion, the development offices of both private and public colleges have increased dramatically in size and budget. Mirroring this growth, far greater efforts are expended in attracting prospective students to learn more about the school, recruiting them to apply, furnish pleasurable visits to the college before and after admission, providing ample rewards for those—athletes, artists, academic stars—whose attendance promises to reflect glory on the institution. Colleges devote vast efforts to conforming to the requirements for a high ranking in the annual *U.S. News & World Report* sweepstakes and other tabulations, and more than a few are thought to massage their statistics in ways that add to their lure. Marketing surveys are ubiquitous and unchallenged. Colleges seek to build up those departments and attract those faculty that are newsworthy; they are proud to see news coverage of their successes, even as these same successes sometimes can prove embarrassing for departments or faculty that are not so garlanded. Finally, there are the most obvious signs of marketing: dorms, eating rooms, computers, iPods, and campus stores that promise a pleasurable, resortlike existence at the school, along with the predictable sweatshirts, caps, banners, and decals.

While I have been deeply involved with college and university life for over four decades, my own familiarity with the current scene has been enhanced by my involvement with the GoodWork Project.[1] This ambitious research project, carried out in conjunction with psychologists Mihaly Csikszentmihalyi and William Damon, and our research colleagues at four institutions, is an empirical examination of professional life in America today. We define "good work" as work that is excellent in quality and ethically responsible—work that any society should desire and honor across the professional landscape.

The question undergirding our research program can be crisply stated: How do individuals and institutions that seek to carry out good work succeed or fail at a time when conditions are changing very rapidly, market forces are extraordinarily powerful, and few if any forces can compete with these market pressures? We carry out extensive, indepth interviews with leaders of various professions; these interviews are then subjected to careful qualitative and, when appropriate, quantitative analyses. So far we have interviewed over a thousand individuals; our findings are reported in several books and many articles, described at goodworkproject.org. In the last few years, we have been studying "Good Work in Higher Education."[2] In what follows, I draw on the testimony of the approximately one hundred individuals whose protocols have been analyzed so far.

What most surprised me, as it would have surprised the mythical campus visitor introduced earlier, is the extent to which the most admired individuals in contemporary colleges focus on the needs of students. Across a wide variety of undergraduate institutions, these informants stressed how important it was to know their students well. At least four-fifths of those interviewed explicitly described the need to know the backgrounds, limitations, and aspirations of their students. Equally, they emphasized the importance of students knowing themselves—their own strengths, needs, goals. Indeed, among the ten institutions, it was only at the University of Phoenix—an unusual noncampus institution that admits only those students who are age twenty-three and older—that the focus on knowing the students was absent.

An analogous portrait emerges when one examines the missions of the schools. Of course, missions vary across and even within schools. But across these exemplary campuses one repeatedly encounters the theme of interpersonal and intra-personal growth. Informants speak about the importance of satisfying the needs of each individual and of students' learning how to interact with others, engage in dialogue, and develop a more open mind, particularly with reference to those of a different background. Indeed, our analysis confirms that the goal of learning to interact with others is as important as the development of knowledge and skills; and the majority of nominated good workers saw their own personal mission as oriented more toward the development of the human being than the transmission of any kind of canon or, indeed, anticanon. Although this trend was discernible across campuses, it was especially pronounced at the less academically oriented institutions.

Let me underscore that I do not object to a deeper understanding of students, nor to missions that include personal growth. I consider it a positive development that educators are incorporating the human dimension into their thinking and articulating their aspirations for themselves and their students. Moreover, I understand why such a focus is appropriate, at a time when the student body is growing ever more diverse, and many students arrive at school with personal or academic challenges. Nor do I believe that the focus on students necessarily represents pandering, or marketing—though I do not exclude those factors. Indeed, with reference to my own four children, an interest in each student has represented a plus in the selection of a college for matriculation.

But note the dramatic shift in the prevailing "mental model." One hundred years ago, attendance at college was restricted to a tiny elite. Schools saw themselves as institutions with a religious mission and a limited canon of offerings. The intimacy of the school was exemplified by a practice where the president of the college taught a culminating course for seniors. Students with means had a good time, but it was up to them to determine how they spent their hours and their money. Fifty years ago, in the wake of the GI Bill, colleges expanded dramatically in their size, the wealth of their offerings, the diversity of their student bodies—particularly in terms of age and geographical dispersion. Electives had become more common. It was assumed that students attended college for a range of purpose. But student affairs and activity offices were small, where they existed at all; selection of college was largely by convenience and reputation rather than by market competition; and at least some consensus obtained on what subjects should be taught and how they should be taught.

Today most colleges have given up a religious orientation as well as any notion of a rigorous core. To be sure, few colleges have gone so far as Brown University or Wesleyan University in the 1970s, where students could create a curriculum virtually from scratch; but equally few have dared to specify the courses to be taken, in what order, and with what specified curriculum and mandated form of assessment. Rather, even as students confront a large number of choices in the school dining halls, so, too, can they put together an intellectual meal that is personally satisfying, with little need to attend to disciplinary restrictions or priorities in their intellectual diet.

We are left with a disquieting situation. The looming image of the market pervades the thinking of the architects of higher education today, even as it may well represent the only model of society known to students. Those most respected within the university place overwhelming importance on knowing their students well and on seeking to anticipate their expressed and inferred needs. This emphasis on personal knowledge is well motivated and provides a needed counterbalance in institutions that were once rather cocky and authoritarian; but less happily, this emphasis is not balanced by an equivalent preoccupation with the kind of education that students need today (and tomorrow) and the kind of society that educators hope will emerge tomorrow (if not today). Countermessages are absent, or at least muted.

25

LESSONS FROM THE GOODWORK PROJECT

Good work—work that is both excellent in quality and ethically meritorious—is never easy to carry out; it proves especially challenging in times like these, when conditions are rapidly changing and market forces are powerful and largely unchecked. Higher education finds itself in just such a situation today. Across the various professions that we have examined, we have identified several conditions that encourage good work—and these lessons can inform those entrusted with the governance of our colleges.

Good work is most readily carried out when all of the interest groups connected to a profession want the same thing from that profession. We observed this condition of *alignment* in genetics at the end of the twentieth century. Scientists, the bodies that supported their research, and the general public all wanted the same thing from these researchers: findings that lead to better health and a longer life. In contrast, journalism emerged as a profession that was very poorly aligned. Journalists wanted to research important stories in depth and present them fairly; but they felt pressured, on one hand, by readers and viewers who want their news quickly and sensationally; and, on the other, by publishers and shareholders who sought ever greater profits from this once-quiet corner of the business world. Under such conditions it is difficult to carry out good work; risks abound for compromised work—as documented in recent scandals at the *New York Times, USA Today*, and other news outlets.

A second factor affecting good work concerns the duties and responsibilities of the individual worker. To use a convenient metaphor, it is easier to carry out good work if you only have to wear one professional hat. The doctor who tends to his patient's needs, the lawyer who seeks to serve his client well, the scientist who observes the canons of research scrupulously—all these workers have their proper marching orders. But nowadays, only the extremely fortunate professional experiences no pressure to don multiple hats. Most physicians belong to large health maintenance organizations that impose limits on the type of patient interaction and permissible prescriptions; most lawyers are part of huge firms or multinational corporations with multiple missions, including relentless bottom-line pressures; scientists enjoy somewhat more flexibility, but particularly in the biological sciences, many succumb to the lure of major positions in profitable biotech companies. They find themselves in the odd position of wearing the hat of an National Institute of Health–supported scientist in the morning and the hat of a venture capital–supported executive or adviser in the afternoon. All too often, compromised work results when professionals are uncertain about which hat they are wearing at what time.

At a more microscopic level, we have identified three factors that increase the likelihood of excellent and ethical work on the part of the individual worker. *Vertical support* features examples and guidance from older, more knowledgeable individuals: initially one's parents and teachers, later one's first supervisors, ultimately, the wise "trustees" of a profession. *Horizontal support* comes from one's peers at work or in the wider profession. *Periodic inoculations and booster shots* come from experiences that either confirm the value of good work or document the risks of compromised or frankly bad work. To some extent, these are factors that one cannot control; one cannot choose one's parents, and one has limited choice in terms of supervisors and peers. Still, it is misleading to think that one's associates and experiences are totally a matter of chance. Mentors and mentees are both involved in a selection process; and employees have the option of confronting objectionable peers or supervisors and, in the ultimate case, leaving a flawed institution.

Now consider the complexity of achieving good work in higher education. On alignment: Those who want to study or   30 teach classical languages clash with those whose eyes fix on the enrollment in such classes. And on "hats": It is difficult to focus on the preservation and refinement of knowledge while at the same time catering to students' desires for comfort and fun. Various kinds of support are desirable but cannot be assumed; many educators have had little exposure to exemplars of "good work," and the many individuals who want to achieve good work cannot assume that their peers, or their institution as a whole, are similarly disposed. And even when all of these enabling conditions are present, the issue of what constitutes good work can itself be contentious.

TOWARD BETTER WORK IN HIGHER EDUCATION

A thought experiment: Let us say one were planning a college from scratch, with unlimited endowment, no knowledge of student desires, but a commitment to good work; how might one proceed?

To begin with, an educational institution must be concerned first and foremost with what it means to be an educated person at the present time. The institution should be explicit about this central mission, and those who represent the institution on a regular basis must be in sympathy with it—just as a physician must honor the Hippocratic Oath and a journalist must embrace his or her organization's code of ethics. The institution should also be specific about its educational goals. For a liberal arts college, those should include the capacity to appreciate and to engage the major disciplinary ways of thinking—scientific, mathematical, historical, humanistic, and artistic. The content by which these ways of thinking is conveyed can reflect choice; but the contents should always be determined by considerations of quality, and not by expedience, conveniences, or political correctness. Interdisciplinary courses and majors should be reserved for those who have demonstrated disciplinary mastery, before or during college. Postcollege work life and preprofessional training must never be allowed to dominate. Other benefits of college—civic engagement, self-knowledge, familiarity with other cultures, ability to get along with others—should be acknowledged but considered externalities or benefits secondary to the scholarly goals. That is because, unlike the scholarly goals, each could be achieved without attendance at college.

Such a focus will necessarily foreground ways of conceiving the world that extend beyond a market view. The pursuit of knowledge for its own sake, for the sake of curiosity, or for broadening one's own perspective is different from the pursuit of knowledge for primarily pragmatic or instrumental ends. Moreover and crucially, as one assumes a humanistic, artistic, or historical perspective across time and space, one comes to appreciate that markets are but one way of construing experience. Societies have existed, and have thrived, when the principal considerations have been religious, spiritual, ideological, communal, pacific, egalitarian—as well as considerations that are less benign, such as thought control, militarism, or imperialism. Individuals have been judged in terms of their morality, their trustworthiness, their humility, their generosity, their spirituality, their beauty, and not simply in terms of their salary or exchange value. And institutions have endured on the basis of charity or communal support or sheer faith even when they have failed the most obvious dictates of the bottom line. Awareness of these alternatives should encourage debate: not that market models are necessarily worse than others, but rather that there are "competing" models, each with its own assets and liabilities. And faculty should be prepared to articulate these alternative visions, and especially so when students seem never to have considered life under any other model than that of the United States of America, circa 2005.

So far my focus may seem to fall on the excellent aspect of good work. However, there are clear ethical implications in this formulation. First of all, to the extent that educators take seriously their mission, they are realizing that sense of calling that constitutes the ethical core of any profession. Second, in being excellent teachers and advisors, educators should model care both for the curricular materials with which they are working and for the students whom they are seeking to educate. Finally, by exposing students to various ways of thinking, and to bodies of thought that embody diverse historical and cultural traditions, educators are conveying the most important lesson of all: One cannot be an incisive thinker unless one has grappled with various perspectives, appreciated their strengths and weaknesses, and reached one's own tentative conclusions about which formulations make the most sense—at least for now. Indeed, in today's atmosphere, I would consider an education a success if it helped students to question both the hegemony of market thinking and the assumption that colleges exist to serve the students' own (perhaps unreflected-upon) desires.

A focus on educational ends need not overwhelm a consideration of the backgrounds, needs, and desires of students. But the proper assumption—which should be made explicit—is that *the educational ends must come first*. They are what distinguish college from other institutions. Interest in the students does not arise in a vacuum: rather, it is germane because—indeed *just because*—such knowledge can help the institution to achieve its educational goals. In other words, we need to know students' needs and backgrounds primarily so that we can more effectively educate them in our lights, not because we want to sculpt an education to serve their aspirations, legitimate or not. Study after study documents that more students are studying business and other applied fields, while fewer enroll in core disciplinary tracks; indeed fewer than 10 percent of high school students and their families express any desire to study the humanities. A market- or student-oriented model would suggest that humanistic study be eliminated or severely curtailed. Such a decision would undercut the essence of higher education. We need to understand the resistances and hesitations of students and families so that we can better help them appreciate *why* humanistic studies are more important than ever—that, indeed, students will become neither good workers not good citizens unless they can bring to bear in thoughtful ways the value considerations that suffuse the humanities.

Although I cannot detail a program that will enable colleges to correct course, a promising starting point emerges from our Good-Work Project. Individuals and institutions should ponder four considerations—all (as it happens) beginning with the letter "m":

1. *Mission.* It is essential to define, and periodically to revisit, the core notions of what it means to be an institution of higher education and a college educator. Such a consideration must go well beyond the by-now mandated formulation of a mission statement. It must feature a perennial grappling with what is most important to this particular calling and why.

2. *Model.* It is most helpful to bear in mind positive models, ones that come closest to what one hopes to achieve. In education, these models may come from the past—Plato's fabled Academy, Mark Hopkins on one end of the log and the student on the other—or from institutions (like the ones that we have studied, or others, such as Alverno College in Milwaukee or Berea College in Kentucky) that merit our respect today. By the same token, individual educators should strive to identify teachers and mentors who epitomize the beliefs and actions that they most admire. It is sometimes salutary to bear in mind "anti-mentors" or "tormentors"—the educational

equivalents of Enron or the Internet gossip sheet, the Drudge Report—institutions or individuals that undercut the core identity of a profession. When few positive models come to mind, this situation should serve as a wake-up call.

3. *Mirror Test, Personal Version*. With regularity, all of us, as individuals and as members of institutions should pose the following questions: If we look at ourselves clearly and transparently, are we doing the best job that we can? If our efforts were fully described on the first page of the *New York Times*, would we be touched with pride or wracked with regret? And if we are not satisfied with the current portrait, what can we do to improve it and how can we judge whether we have succeeded?

4. *Mirror Test, Profession-wide*. When you begin professional work, it is hard enough to satisfy your own standards. As you gain in expertise and maturity, however, it is appropriate to consider what is happening in your profession. Even if you are personally meeting the standards of an excellent and ethical higher education, what are the implications if other institutions are falling short? Do you have a wider responsibility? Following the French playwright Jean-Baptiste Molière, you should heed the aphorism "You are responsible not only for what you do but for what you fail to do."

Higher education remains one of the most respected institutions in our society, and not without reason. One consideration is that in the past strong leaders have been willing to invoke the considerations just described and, when necessary, to correct course. They may not have been oblivious to market considerations or to the interests of their student-clients, but they did not allow these factors to overwhelm their own individual and collective aspirations. University of Chicago president Robert Maynard Hutchins and publisher John Dewey may have differed deeply on their vision of the educated person in the first half of the twentieth century; but neither would have looked to the college's ledgers when articulating their respective positions. Given the strength of current market forces, it is more important than ever that the counterforces be recognized and, as appropriate, activated. The survival of a civil society depends on a pursuit of work that is both excellent in quality and ethical in its orientation. Because of its location at the juncture of youth and work, higher education should recognize its pivotal role in determining whether graduates are proceeding along the path toward good work.

Notes

For comments on earlier versions of this draft, I thank James Freedman, Richard Hersh, John Merrow, Jeanne Nakamura, Henry Rubin, and Ellen Winner. The GoodWork Project study of Higher Education has been generously supported by the Hewlett Foundation, the Atlantic Philanthropies, The Ford Foundation, and Carnegie Corporation of New York.

1. At the start, we conducted an extensive nomination procedure that identified ten institutions that are widely and justifiably admired for their excellence: Carleton College (MN), DeAnza Community College (CA), Indiana University, LaGuardia Community College (NY), Morehouse College (GA), Mount Saint Mary's (CA), the University of Phoenix (various locations), Princeton University (NJ), Swarthmore University (PA), and Xavier University (OH). Then, within each nominated institution, we carried out an additional nominating procedure designed to identify individuals who best exemplified the excellence of the institution.
2. For information on the GoodWork Project, see H. Gardner, M. Csikszentmihalyi, and W. Damon, *Good Work: When Excellence and Ethics Meet* (New York: Basic Books, 2001). See also www.goodworkproject.org.

Thinking About Content

1. Gardner explains that the market model is a model that does not necessarily lead to "good work" in higher education. How is this so? What are some of the issues Gardner explains?
2. What does Gardner say we can do to have more "good work" in higher education?

Thinking About Strategy

1. Gardner opens his essay with a profile of an imaginary visitor to a 2005 college campus who was familiar with college life in the 1950s. What purpose does this opening serve? Did you think it was effective?
2. Gardner uses the GoodWork Project as the basis for his research and assertions. Visit the website www.goodworkproject.org to see more about this issue for yourself.

Prompts for Extended Writing Assignments

Personal Response
Thinking about the gap that exists between high school and college that Spellings mentions in "A Strategic Vision for Higher Education," write a narrative essay in which you explore any gaps you, or others you know, experienced upon making the transition from high school to college.

From Another's Perspective
Interview a teacher or several teachers to find out what they would do to make our educational system better. Then compare these ideas with the ideas presented in the essays of this chapter. What differences or similarities, or both, do you find? Summarize your findings in a formal essay.

Call for Social Action
How can we make education better? Working in groups, you will develop a system for delivering and receiving a "good" education. Use the essays from this chapter to support your ideas. Present your findings to your class, school, or perhaps even at your next local school board meeting.

Research Opportunity
Research the history of educational reform in the twentieth century. Write an essay exploring the major movements, concerns, and ideas for reform. How do past concerns and ideas for reform compare to those of today? What conclusions can you come to about our educational history?

Semester- or Quarter-Long Writing Projects

1. For this writing assignment, you will assume the identity of another. You will be given the age, gender, class, and literacy level of your assigned person. Your writing options will include: writing an educational autobiography for your assigned identity; writing about the importance of education from the point of view of your assigned persona; and joining with writing partners to design a system in which everyone in your group can receive an equal education.

2. What significant issues influence our educational system? Which ones are the most important to you? Teacher pay? Class size? Social class? Ethnic background? Use the readings from this book as well as your own research to support your assertions.

3. How can we serve others in education? Working as a class and in conjunction with outside resources, create and publish a zine that captures the best of your class writings.

4. Design your own syllabus for receiving a good education in a college writing class. Then write an essay explaining how and why you made the decisions you made about what went into your syllabus.

5. Redesign high school or college (choose one) to meet the needs of the next generation of learners and/or workers. What would your ideal high school or college be like? Write an essay explaining the specifics of your ideal high school or college.

Sherman Alexie. "Indian Education." *The Lone Ranger and Tonto Fist Fight in Heaven.* New York: Grove/Atlantic, 2005. 171–80.

American Associate of University Women. "¡Sí Puede! Yes, We Can: Latinas in School." AAUW Press Release. 2000. <www.aauw.org/research/latina.cfm>

Kenneth J. Bernstein. "What Does It Mean to Be a Teacher?" Daily Kos. Online Posting. 20 March 2005.<www.dailykos.com/story/2005/3/20/133411/748>

Katherine C. Boles and Vivian Troen. "America's New Teachers: How Good, and for How Long?" *Education Week.* 19 (2000): 39.

Commission on No Child Left Behind. Beyond NCLB: Fulfilling the Promise to Our Nation's Children. "A New Day in American Education." The Aspen Institute, Washington, D.C. 2007.

Linda Darling-Hammond. "Evaluating 'No Child Left Behind.'" *The Nation* 21 May 2007.www.thenation.com

Lisa Delpit. "Education in a Multicultural Society: Our Future's Greatest Challenge." *Other People's Children.* New York: The New Press, 1995. 167–83.

T. S. Eliot. Excerpt from "Little Gidding" in *Four Quartets*, copyright 1942 by T.S. Eliot and renewed 1970 by Esme Valerie Eliot, reprinted by permission of Harcourt, Inc. Canadian permission granted by Faber and Faber, Ltd.

Howard Gardner. "Beyond Markets and Individuals: A Focus on Educational Goals." *Declining by Degrees: Higher Education at Risk.* Ed. Richard H. Hersh and John Merrow. Hampshire: Palgrave Macmillan, 2005. 97–112. Reproduced with permission of Palgrave Macmillan.

Robert Haveman and Timothy Smeeding. "The Role of Higher Education in Social Mobility." From *The Future of Children,* a publication of The Woodrow Wilson School of Public and International Affairs at Princeton University and the Brookings Institution. 16.2 (2006) www.thefutureofchildren.org

Ann Hulbert. "Boy Problems." First published in *The New York Times Magazine,* April 2005. © 2005 by Ann Hulbert, Permission of The Wylie Agency.

Angela Kim and Christine J. Yeh. "Stereotypes of Asian American Students." *ERIC Digests.* 2002. www.ericdigests.org

Lynette Lamb. "Are All Girls Schools Best?" Reprinted, with permission, from New Moon® Network: For Adults Who Care About Girls; copyright New Moon® Publishing, Duluth, MN. <www.newmoon.org>

Sara Mead. "The Truth about Boys and Girls." *Education Sector.* 27 June 2006. www.educationsector.org

Daniel Moulthrop, Ninive Clements, and Dave Eggers. "Look Dad, My Biology Teacher Is Selling Stereos at Circuit City." *Teachers Have It Easy.* New York: The New Press, 2005. 49–60.

Anna Quindlen. "The Wages of Teaching." *Newsweek* 28 November 2005: 100.

Peter Sacks. "Do No Harm: Stopping the damage to American School." *Standardized Minds.* Cambridge: Perseus, 1999. 153–66.

Myra and David Sadker. "Higher Education: Colder by Degrees." *Failing at Fairness: How Our Schools Cheat Girls.* New York: Simon & Schuster, 1994. 168-73.

Peter Schmidt. "What Color Is an A?" *The Chronicle of Higher Education.* 53.39 (2007) 1 June 2007. www.chronicle.com/weekly/v53/i39/39a02401.htm

Margaret Spellings. "A Strategic Vision for Higher Education." *The Presidency.* Spring 2005: 23-26. © American Council on Education.

Michelle M. Tokarczyk. Reprinted from Michelle M. Tokarczyk: "Promises to Keep: Working Class Students and Higher Education" from *What's Class Got to Do With It?* American Society in the Twenty-first Century, edited by Michael Zweig. Copyright © 2004 by Cornell University. Used by permission of the publisher, Cornell University Press.

The Washington Post. "Sex Bias Cited in Vocational Ed." *The Washington Post* 6 June 2002, A8.